T3-AJK-136

Translated Texts for Historians

300–800 AD is the time of late antiquity and the early middle ages: the transformation of the classical world, the beginnings of Europe and of Islam, and the evolution of Byzantium. TTH makes available sources translated from Greek, Latin, Syriac, Coptic, Arabic, Georgian, Gothic and Armenian. Each volume provides an expert scholarly translation, with an introduction setting texts and authors in context, and with notes on content, interpretation and debates.

Editorial Committee
Phil Booth, Trinity College, Oxford
Sebastian Brock, Oriental Institute, University of Oxford
Averil Cameron, Keble College, Oxford
Marios Costambeys, University of Liverpool
Carlotta Dionisotti, King's College, London
Jill Harries, St Andrews
Peter Heather, King's College, London
Robert Hoyland, Institute for Study of the Ancient World,
        New York University
William E. Klingshirn, The Catholic University of America
Michael Lapidge, Clare College, Cambridge
Neil McLynn, Corpus Christi College, Oxford
Richard Price, Heythrop College, University of London
Claudia Rapp, Institut für Byzantinistik und Neogräzistik,
        Universität Wien
Judith Ryder, University of Oxford
Raymond Van Dam, University of Michigan
Michael Whitby, University of Birmingham
Ian Wood, University of Leeds

General Editors
Gillian Clark, University of Bristol
Mark Humphries, Swansea University
Mary Whitby, University of Oxford

A full list of published titles in the **Translated Texts for Historians** series is available on request. The most recently published are shown below.

Bede: On the Nature of Things and On Times
Translated with introduction and notes by CALVIN B. KENDALL and FAITH WALLIS
Volume 56: 371pp., 2010, ISBN 978-1-84631-495-7

Theophilus of Edessa's Chronicle
Translated with introduction and notes by ROBERT G. HOYLAND
Volume 57: 368pp., 2011, ISBN 978-1-84631-697-5 cased, 978-1-84631-698-2 limp

Bede: Commentary on Revelation
Translated with introduction and notes by FAITH WALLIS
Volume 58: 343pp., 2013, ISBN 978-1-84631-844-3 cased, 978-1-84631-845-0 limp

Two Early Lives of Severos, Patriarch of Antioch
Translated with an introduction and notes by SEBASTIAN BROCK and BRIAN FITZGERALD
Volume 59, 175pp., 2013, ISBN 978-1-84631-882-5 cased, 978-1-84631-883-2 limp

The Funerary Speech for John Chrysostom
Translated with an introduction and notes by TIMOTHY D. BARNES and GEORGE BEVAN
Volume 60, 193pp., ISBN 978-1-84631-887-0 cased, 978-1-84631-888-7 limp

The Acts of the Lateran Synod of 649
Translated with notes by RICHARD PRICE, with contributions by PHIL BOOTH and CATHERINE CUBITT
Volume 61, 476pp., ISBN 978-1-78138-039-0 cased

Macarius, *Apocriticus*
Translated with introduction and commentary by JEREMY M. SCHOTT and MARK J. EDWARDS
Volume 62, 476pp., ISBN 978 1 78138 129 8 cased, ISBN 978 1 78138 130 4 limp

Khalifa ibn Khayyat's *History* on the Umayyad Dynasty (660–750)
Translated with introduction and commentary by CARL WURTZEL
and prepared for publication by ROBERT G. HOYLAND
Volume 63, 332pp., ISBN 978 1 78138 174 8 cased, 978 1 78138 175 5 limp

Between City and School: Selected Orations of Libanius
RAFFAELLA CRIBIORE
Volume 65, 272pp, ISBN 978 1 78138 252 3 cased, 978 1 78138 253 0 limp

Isidore of Seville *On the Nature of Things*
Translated with introduction, notes, and commentary by
CALVIN B. KENDALL and FAITH WALLIS
Volume 66, 328pp., ISBN 978 1 78138 293 6 cased, ISBN 978 1 78138 294 3 limp

For full details of **Translated Texts for Historians**, including prices and ordering information, please write to the following: **All countries, except the USA and Canada:** Liverpool University Press, 4 Cambridge Street, Liverpool, L69 7ZU, UK (*Tel* +44-[0]151-794 2233, *Fax* +44-[0]151-794 2235, Email janmar@liv.ac.uk, http://www.liverpooluniversitypress.co.uk). **USA and Canada:** Turpin Distribution, www.turpin-distribution.com.

Translated Texts for Historians
Volume 67

Imperial Invectives against Constantius II

Athanasius of Alexandria, *History of the Arians*, **Hilary of Poitiers,** *Against Constantius* **and Lucifer of Cagliari,** *The Necessity of Dying for the Son of God*

Translated with introduction and commentary

by RICHARD FLOWER

Liverpool
University
Press

DG
316.7
.I47
2016

First published 2016
Liverpool University Press
4 Cambridge Street
Liverpool, L69 7ZU

Copyright © 2016 Richard Flower

The right of Richard Flower to be identified as the author of this book has been asserted by him in accordance with the Copyright, Designs and Patents Act 1988.

All rights reserved. No part of this book may be reproduced stored in a retrieval system, or transmitted, in any form or by any means, electronic, mechanical, photocopying, recording, or otherwise, without the prior written permission of the publisher.

British Library Cataloguing-in-Publication Data
A British Library CIP Record is available.

ISBN 978 1 78138 327 8 cased
ISBN 978 1 78138 328 5 limp

Typeset by Carnegie Book Production, Lancaster
Printed and bound in Poland by BooksFactory.co.uk

For my mother, Margaret Flower,
who was most unlike any of these men

CONTENTS

PREFACE

After the death of his brother Constans in 350, Constantius II was the last surviving son of Constantine the Great and the only 'legitimate' Augustus of the Roman empire. Over the following decade he became progressively more involved in attempts to define Christian orthodoxy and so aroused the ire of the three bishops whose works appear in this volume. Perhaps appropriately, I have also spent a decade producing these translations of their bitter invectives against that emperor. I originally submitted the proposal for this volume in 2005, when I was still a doctoral student at Clare College, Cambridge. My research focused on the ways in which Athanasius, Hilary and Lucifer engaged with tropes of political and religious discourse in order to create sharply contrasting images of both themselves and their 'Arian' opponents, with the latter being led by the impious tyrant Constantius. A revised and expanded version of this thesis became my first monograph, entitled *Emperors and Bishops in Late Roman Invective*, which was published by Cambridge University Press in 2013. This Translated Texts for Historians volume should, therefore, be seen as a counterpart to it, providing annotated English translations of the most important texts discussed in that book and so, I hope, bringing the subject of late-antique invective to a wider audience.

Many individuals and organisations contributed towards the creation of this volume. It was made possible by the A. G. Leventis Foundation, whose generous award of the Leventis Scholarship in Hellenic Studies funded my doctoral studies, as well as the Master and Fellows of Clare College, Cambridge, the Faculty of Classics and the Worshipful Company of Fishmongers of the City of London, who all provided financial support during this time; by Sidney Sussex College, Cambridge, who kindly awarded me a Junior Research Fellowship; and by the Arts and Humanities Research Council, whose grant of an Early Career Fellowship gave me the research leave during which I made the final amendments to this book. I would like to thank my doctoral supervisor, Christopher Kelly, who has provided immeasurable support at every stage of this project; Barrie

Fleet, who helped with the preparation of the original proposal; Rosamond McKitterick and Mark Humphries, who were extremely genial examiners of my doctoral thesis; Richard Price, who was a very helpful and attentive reader of my translation of Athanasius; Mary Whitby, who has guided me through the last decade as an exceptional editor, as well as also taking the time to improve my translations of Hilary and Lucifer; Gillian Clark and Mark Humphries (again), who, together with Mary Whitby, Richard Price and Jenny Barry, provided expert advice for the preparation of the introduction and glossary; my student intern, Friederike Ach, who checked my references and footnotes meticulously; Michael Whitby and Mark Edwards, who gave permission for the map to be based on the one in *Constantine and Christendom* (Liverpool University Press, 2003), which is, in turn, based on the map drawn by David Taylor in *The Ecclesiastical History of Evagrius Scholasticus* (Liverpool University Press, 2000); Mark Humphries (yet again) for drawing the cover image; and my colleagues at Sidney Sussex College and the Universities of Sheffield and Exeter, who have created a succession of extremely pleasant environments in which to carry out this work. Finally, my thanks, as always, go to my friends and family, who have for many years tolerated my fascination with angry bishops.

ABBREVIATIONS

Barrington Atlas	R. J. A. Talbert (ed.) (2000) *Barrington Atlas of the Greek and Roman World*, Princeton.
CCSL	*Corpus Christianorum, Series Latina*, Turnhout, 1967– .
CSEL	*Corpus Scriptorum Ecclesiasticorum Latinorum*, Vienna, 1866– .
GCS	*Die griechischen christlichen Schriftsteller der ersten Jahrhunderte*, Leipzig and Berlin,1897– .
Lampe	G. W. H. Lampe (ed.) (1961) *A Patristic Greek Lexicon*, Oxford.
Lewis & Short	C. T. Lewis and C. Short (1879) *A Latin Dictionary, founded on Andrews' Edition of Freund's Latin Dictionary*, Oxford.
OLD	P. G. W. Glare (ed.) (1982) *Oxford Latin Dictionary*, Oxford.
PCBE	*Prosopographie chrétienne du Bas-empire*, Paris and Rome, 1982– .
PG	J.-P. Migne (1857–1866) *Patrologia Graeca*, Paris.
PL	J.-P. Migne (1844–1865) *Patrologia Latina*, Paris.
PLRE I	A. H. M. Jones, J. R. Martindale and J. Morris (edd.) (1971) *The Prosopography of the Later Roman Empire I: A.D. 260–395*, Cambridge.
RE	A. Pauly et al. (edd.) (1894–1980) *Real-Encyclopädie der classischen Altertumswissenschaft*, Stuttgart.
Souter	A. Souter (1949) *A Glossary of Later Latin to 600 A.D.*, Oxford

INTRODUCTION:
SCREEDS, COUNCILS AND CONTROVERSIES

The three texts translated in this volume were all written in the febrile environment of the late 350s, when a rapid sequence of ecclesiastical councils was held and a number of statements of faith were written in an attempt to find a theological settlement that would be acceptable to most bishops in the Roman empire. The impetus for this policy is often identified as having come from the emperor Constantius II, who was famously described by the historian Ammianus Marcellinus as having disturbed Christianity with his constant meddling and thus hamstrung the empire's system of post-horses because of the number of bishops who were using it to get to his various councils.[1] This sarcastic remark is, in fact, relatively mild by the standards of the time. It is vital to note that the ancient accounts of these events range from markedly partial to vehemently polemical, with the three invectives translated here falling firmly into the latter category. Owing to the nature of the material and the number of different councils and meetings that took place, the reconstruction of the chronology of these events poses a number of difficulties for modern historians. This introduction seeks to provide as neutral an account as possible both of the context within which Athanasius, Hilary and Lucifer wrote their works and of the roles that they played in the major events and debates of the period. It also gives a guide to the themes of their texts and the tendentious narratives that they created, presenting Nicene Christians as the persecuted faithful while demonising their theological opponents, chief of whom was Constantius himself.

The first section of the introduction consists of a brief survey of the convoluted doctrinal arguments of the period from the start of the 'Arian controversy' in 318 to the death of Constantius in 361, as well as the many councils and creeds that sought to bring a resolution to the ongoing disunity among the empire's bishops. This provides the historical context

---

1 Amm. 21.16.18.

for the careers of Athanasius, Hilary and Lucifer, which are discussed in the next part of this chapter, as are the dating and characteristics of the text that are translated in the main body of this volume. A final section of the introduction covers the nature of their invective and the rhetorical methods involved in the construction of their portraits of the main figures of the period, most notably themselves.[2]

ECCLESIASTICAL AND THEOLOGICAL POLITICS, 318–361

Around 318, a few years after the end of the 'Great Persecution' of the Christians, Alexander, bishop of Alexandria in Egypt, addressed his clergy on a matter of theology, specifically the unity of the Holy Trinity. One of his presbyters, a clever character by the name of Arius, was concerned that Alexander's teachings did not distinguish sufficiently between the Father, the Son and the Holy Spirit and thus resembled the unorthodox views of the third-century theologian Sabellius.[3] Arius' response was to challenge his bishop, declaring, 'If the Father begat the Son, then the begotten has a beginning of coming into existence. So from this it is clear that there was a time when the Son was not, and it follows necessarily that he got his subsistence from nothing.'[4] This account comes from the opening chapters of the *Ecclesiastical History* of Socrates, written in the middle of the fifth century. Like all surviving accounts of the life and opinions of Arius, it cannot be taken at face value, particularly with regard to the

---

2 I have, as far as possible, sought to direct the reader towards commonly available English works on this subject, at least in the first instance, in order to make the material as accessible as possible for a broad audience. It has, however, been necessary to refer to a number of more specialised pieces of scholarship for certain specific issues.

3 Sabellius was a presbyter at Rome who described the three persons of the Trinity (the Father, the Son and the Holy Spirit) as being 'modes' of the Godhead, rather than differentiating between them as much as other theologians did. For this reason, the accusation of 'Sabellianism' was sometimes used by fourth-century Christians as a way of attacking positions which they regarded as not articulating the relationship between the Father and the Son (or of the Trinity as a whole) with sufficient distinctions. On Sabellius, see Epiphanius, *Panarion* 62; Simonetti (1980); Bienert (1993).

4 Soc. *HE* 1.5.1–2, quoting 1.5.2. The Greek term for 'subsistence' used here is *hypostasis*. This word does not figure as prominently as *ousia* in the debates of this period, although it was to come to prominence later, especially in the creed agreed at the Council of Constantinople in 381. On these terms, see the Glossary.

theological statements that Socrates attributes to the presbyter. As the Christological controversies of this period wore on, and even after they had been largely resolved, Arius was progressively vilified in polemical Christian literature, being transformed into the archetypal heretic: he was portrayed as following in the footsteps of Jews and other earlier enemies of Christ, as well as spawning a host of newer depraved doctrines that continued to assail the orthodox in the succeeding decades.[5] As Rowan Williams has remarked, Arianism came to be

> irrevocably cast as the Other in relation to Catholic (and civilized) religion. Arius himself came more and more to be regarded as a kind of Antichrist among heretics, a man whose superficial austerity and spirituality cloaked a diabolical menace, a deliberate enmity to revealed faith [...] No other heretic has been through so thoroughgoing a process of 'demonization'.[6]

Attempts to reconstruct the origins of this controversy and the authentic theology of Arius are therefore faced with significant challenges.[7] It would appear, however, that he took a 'subordinationist' position that the Son was inferior to the Father, as well as not being co-eternal with him. This introduction will be concerned less with the historical Arius and his own 'Arianism' than with the theological developments and ecclesiastical disputes that followed and which are often associated with him under the title of 'the Arian controversy'. Even though Arius was widely disavowed by participants in these events, his name was frequently invoked, since any association with him gradually came to be regarded as poisonous. As the texts translated in this volume make abundantly clear, the term 'Arian' developed into a damaging label to attach to one's enemies, placing them clearly outside the boundaries of acceptable Christian orthodoxy. For example, Hilary of Poitiers described his opponents as denying that the Son was truly God or properly the Son of the Father, while Lucifer of Cagliari accused the 'Arians' of saying that the Son had been created from nothing.[8] It should also be recognised that, although ecclesiastical historians and polemicists were keen to present Arius as the originator of these disputes,

---

5 For this phenomenon, especially in the works of Athanasius, see Lyman (1993); Brakke (2001) 467–75; Ayres (2004) 105–17; Gwynn (2007) 169–244; Flower (2013) 189–90.

6 Williams (2001) 1.

7 On the theology of Arius and the difficulties involved in its reconstruction, see Simonetti (1975) 46–55; Kelly (1977) 226–31; Hanson (1988) 5–18; Williams (2001) 95–116; Ayres (2004) 54–7; Gwynn (2007) 186–202.

8 Hilary, *In Const.* 5, 9, 22; Lucifer, *Moriundum* 3.

their roots lay in earlier theological speculation, rather than being produced by the presbyter *ex nihilo*. Nonetheless, since it features so prominently in contemporary narratives, the confrontation between Arius and his bishop acts as a useful starting point for this introduction to the historical context of the translated texts.[9]

Although Arius was swiftly rebuked by Alexander for challenging both his theology and his authority, the argument was far from settled. Both men looked for support from other figures in the church, not only within Egypt but also further afield, and Arius soon found supporters who were sympathetic to his concerns, including Eusebius, bishop of Nicomedia.[10] When the emperor Constantine defeated his colleague Licinius in 324 and took control of the eastern part of the empire he intervened in the situation, much as he had previously done (with little success) in the Donatist schism in North Africa. In his biography of the emperor, Eusebius of Caesarea preserves a letter sent by Constantine to Alexander and Arius in which the emperor exhorted them to agree to disagree on these minor matters and to focus their attention on the beliefs that they shared, which were more important to the Christian faith.[11] This move failed, however, as did other attempts to resolve the issue through letters or small synods. Constantine, therefore, gave his support to the summoning of an ecclesiastical council to settle the issue, as well as to consider other matters of dispute between the churches, most notably over the date of Easter. Approximately 250–300 bishops gathered at Nicaea in 325, under the presidency of Ossius, bishop of Cordoba in Spain, with Constantine and a number of his court officials in attendance.[12] The council rejected Arius' view that the Son was not

9 This introduction is focused on the 340s and 350s, since these decades are most relevant to the texts in this volume. The best and clearest reconstruction of the events of this period is to be found in Barnes (1993). Galvão-Sobrinho (2013) represents an attempt to understand the early years of the Arian controversy, while Gwynn (2007) focuses on the reign of Constantius II, particularly the presentation of 'Arianism' by Athanasius. Hanson (1988) and Ayres (2004) provide detailed guides to the theological developments of this period, although the former is rather dated in places, especially in the use of the term 'Arian', while there is also much useful information in Kelly (1972) 205–95 and (1977) 223–51. The councils and creeds are also covered in depth in Simonetti (1975) 153–249, 313–49, and Brennecke (1984) and (1988) 5–56.

10 On this early stage of the controversy, see Barnes (1993) 14–16; Ayres (2004) 11–17; Galvão-Sobrinho (2013) 35–77 (although caution should be exercised over his characterisation of Alexander).

11 Eus. *VC* 2.64–72.

12 On the Council of Nicaea and its Creed, see, for example, Kelly (1972) 205–54; Hanson (1998) 152–72; Barnes (1993) 16–18; Ayres (2004) 85–100; Galvão-Sobrinho (2013) 84–91.

co-eternal with the Father, leading to the presbyter being exiled by imperial authority. In addition, the bishops also agreed the text of a creed which excluded 'Arian' beliefs and defined the Son as being *homoousios* ('of the same essence') with the Father. Even though some participants were not pleased with the wording of this statement of faith, all those present, with the exception of two bishops from Libya, assented to the creed. Despite signing this document, Eusebius of Nicomedia and Theognis of Nicaea would not, however, agree to the condemnation of Arius and so were also exiled a few months later.[13]

The Council of Nicaea and the Nicene Creed have come to occupy a pivotal position in the history of the Christian Church. It should be borne in mind, however, that this canonical status is primarily a product of the afterlife of this event, rather than a reflection of its perceived significance at the time. It was the largest Christian council ever convened up to that point, as well as being attended by the emperor himself, which led to it being assigned a prominent position in the biography of Constantine written by Eusebius of Caesarea over a decade later.[14] Nevertheless, even for its supporters, Nicaea's designation as the first 'ecumenical' council and a touchstone of orthodoxy emerged only decades later, particularly in the 350s, when the writings of Athanasius of Alexandria played a key role in promoting an image of the divinely inspired nature of the council's discussions and the unassailable supremacy of its creed.[15] In 325, however, it represented an attempt to define a statement that would defend against and exclude 'Arian' beliefs, rather than an ambitious project to create a foundational document for imperial orthodoxy. The events of the following decades demonstrate that many theologians felt comfortable with creating other creeds without having to explain or excuse their departure from the profession of faith agreed at Nicaea.

Within a few years the apparent settlement of 325 had started to unravel. Eusebius of Nicomedia and Theognis of Nicaea were formally restored to the church and soon came into conflict with Athanasius, who had succeeded Alexander as bishop of Alexandria in 328 and continued his predecessor's policy of refusing to readmit Arius and his followers into communion. Athanasius was accused of violent behaviour towards clergy

13 Hanson (1988) 173; Barnes (1993) 17.
14 Eus. *VC* 3.4–22.
15 On this issue, see Lienhard (1999) 30–3; Gwynn (2007) especially 169–70, 224–44, and (2012) 76–90. For the vital role played by Athanasius in promoting the Council of Nicaea as important and 'ecumenical', see Chadwick (1972).

from the Egyptian schismatic group known as the Melitians, leading to him being deposed from his see at a Council held in Tyre in 335 and then exiled to Gaul soon afterwards in rather unclear circumstances.[16] In the next year there was an attempt to persuade Alexander, bishop of Constantinople, to readmit Arius to communion, but the presbyter expired suddenly, providing an opportunity for Athanasius to write up his death as a grisly example of divine punishment.[17] Around the same time, Marcellus, bishop of Ancyra and a fierce opponent of 'Arian' theology, was also deposed from his see at a Council in Constantinople and went into exile. Moreover, Eusebius of Nicomedia came back into imperial favour and baptised Constantine when the emperor was on his deathbed in 337.

After a brief period of uncertainty and a massacre of other potential rivals within the imperial family, Constantine's three sons – Constantine II, Constantius II and Constans – shared the empire between themselves.[18] They decreed that exiled bishops could return to their homelands, which led to both Athanasius and Marcellus taking control of their respective sees. The two bishops were, however, soon deposed once more, when a council was held in Antioch in 338/9; the participants included Eusebius of Nicomedia, who had recently moved to become bishop of Constantinople. Athanasius and Marcellus travelled to the West, where they gained the support of Julius, bishop of Rome. The political situation also changed in 340, when Constans became sole ruler of the West after the death of his brother Constantine II during a civil war.[19] Soon after this came the first significant occasion since Nicaea when a large ecclesiastical council drafted a statement of faith: the so-called 'Dedication Council' of Antioch

16 For more detail on these events, and Athanasius' career more generally, see pp. 21–4 below. The Melitians were a set of rigorist schismatics in Egypt who rejected the authority of the bishop of Alexandria after a dispute about the readmission of lapsed Christians during the Great Persecution. They were involved in some of the accusations against Athanasius in the 330s and are mentioned by him at *Hist. Ar.* 3.2, 78.1–79.2. See also Epiphanius, *Panarion* 68; Martin (1974) and (1996) 217–319; Barnes (1993) 20–28.

17 See Ath. *De morte Arii*, especially 3.3, where Arius' death is narrated using the same phrase that appears at *Acts* 1.18 to describe Judas' demise. The development of the story of Arius' gruesome death is explored in Muehlberger (2015). This is the traditional date of Arius' death, although it has been suggested that he was readmitted to communion in the late 320s and then died shortly afterwards: see Brennecke et al. (2007) xxxvi–xxxviii. Barnes (2009) is a forceful response to this proposal and reasserts the standard chronology, while Brennecke (2010) is a rejoinder to Barnes.

18 On this dynastic massacre, see n. 252 to Ath. *Hist. Ar.* 69.1 on p. 98 below, as well as Burgess (2008).

19 See Hunt (1998) 5.

in 341, which took its name from the fact that the bishops were dedicating a grand new church in the city, with Constantius II in attendance.[20] Four different creedal statements have been transmitted by Athanasius as being associated with this gathering, possibly in an attempt to portray its participants as vacillating and indecisive, but only the 'Second Creed' was actually formally agreed during the council and then circulated as part of its letter to other bishops in the eastern part of the empire.[21] This text does not use the term *homoousios* that appears in the Nicene Creed, but does state that the Son is 'the exact image of the *ousia* of the Father', while also challenging the 'Monarchian' heresy of Sabellianism by distinguishing between the members of the Trinity in terms of *hypostasis* ('subsistence'), echoing the words of the third-century theologian Origen.[22] J. N. D. Kelly regards the creed as rejecting the views of Marcellus of Ancyra for being too close to Sabellianism, as well as being an attempt to create a fairly moderate and widely acceptable definition: 'The synod was working with a theology which, while by no means sympathetic to Arianism, was subordinationist and pre-Nicene [...] Their real object was to steer a middle course between Arianism and the Sabellianism they dreaded.'[23] Also of note is the 'Fourth Creed' of Antioch, which actually appears to have been written separately a few months after the council, and which avoids any use of *ousia* ('essence') language, while also condemning Arius' ideas forcefully. This text was brought to the western emperor Constans in 342 by an eastern delegation and may have been intended as another attempt at compromise.[24]

Julius of Rome remained unhappy with the actions of the eastern councils, particularly their refusal to repeal their depositions of Athanasius

---

20 On this council, see Simonetti (1975) 153–60; Brennecke (1984) 5–16; Barnes (1993) 57–9; Martin (1996) 419–22.

21 Ath. *De synodis* 22–5. The 'First Creed' was a statement made by the council, but apparently not intended as a formal creed; the 'Second' was officially ratified by the council; the 'Third Creed' was merely a formulation put forward by a single bishop, Theophronius of Tyana; the 'Fourth Creed' was a separate statement of faith written after the council by a group of eastern bishops and sent to Constans. On all these creeds, see Kelly (1972) 263–74; Hanson (1988) 284–92; Ayres (2004) 117–22. The 'Second Creed' is preserved at Hilary, *De synodis* 29–30 and Ath. *De synodis* 23.

22 The term 'Monarchian' is used to refer to theological views which stress that God is a single 'person' or 'principle': see (1977) 115–23; Ayres (2004) 68 (with remarks on Marcellus' relationship to this tradition). For more on these other theological terms, see the Glossary.

23 Kelly (1972) 271.

24 See Ath. *De synodis* 25; Kelly (1972) 272–3; Hanson (1988) 291–2; Ayres (2004) 121–2.

and Marcellus, and made his views known in a forceful letter.[25] The bishop of Rome also played a key role in helping the exiled eastern bishops, who also included Paul of Constantinople, who had recently been expelled from his see, so that they could gain the support of Constans.[26] The western emperor communicated with his surviving brother Constantius II, who controlled the eastern part of the empire, and arranged for an ecclesiastical council to take place at Serdica in 343.[27] The western delegation included Ossius of Cordoba and exiles from the East, most notably Athanasius and Paul, but the eastern bishops were not willing to join them in a general council. The divisions were irreconcilable, so the two groups of prelates never actually met for a joint session, but instead acted independently and both claimed that their own gathering constituted the council. The eastern delegates wrote a letter to bishops elsewhere in the empire strongly criticising the behaviour of the exiled bishops, especially Athanasius and Marcellus, as well as accusing the latter of heresy, before deposing Julius, Ossius and their associates.[28] They also attached a statement of faith consisting of the 'Fourth Creed' of Antioch together with some extra anathemas which condemned Marcellus and his supposedly 'Sabellian' teachings, as well as defending themselves against any accusations of regarding the Trinity as consisting of three separate gods.[29] The western bishops also wrote a number of missives, including an encyclical letter which defended many of the exiles of the charges against them and accused a number of eastern bishops of being violent persecutors and 'Ariomaniacs'.[30] Included among the supposed ringleaders

25 See Ath. *Apol. c. Ar.* 21.1–35.8; Barnes (1993) 58–61.

26 Paul had become bishop of Constantinople early in the reign of Constantius II, but had been deposed and replaced with Eusebius of Nicomedia. When Eusebius died in 341, Paul had attempted to regain the episcopal throne, but was unsuccessful and sought the help of Constans for his cause. For a reconstruction of the career of Paul, including the problems with identifying his date of election, see Barnes (1993) 35–6, 68, 212–17.

27 On this council, see Kelly (1972) 274–9; Hanson (1988) 293–306; Barnes (1993) 71–86; Martin (1996) 422–36; Ayres (2004) 122–6; Parvis (2006) 210–45; Maraval (2013) 251–3. See also the version of events given by Athanasius in *Apol. c. Ar.* 36–50 (with relevant documents) and *Hist. Ar.* 15–19. A number of documents relating to this council are preserved in Hilary's *Against Valens and Ursacius*, which is translated by Lionel Wickham in TTH volume 25.

28 See Hilary, *Adu. Val. et Ursac.* A.IV.1.

29 See Hilary, *Adu. Val. et Ursac.* A.IV.2; Kelly (1972) 275–6; Hanson (1988) 298–9; Barnes (1993) 75.

30 See Hilary, *Adu. Val. et Ursac.* B.II.1 and Ath. *Apol. c. Ar.* 44–50 for versions of this letter in Latin and Greek respectively. Barnes (1993) 77 notes that the letter does

of the heretics were two Illyrican bishops, Ursacius of Singidunum and Valens of Mursa, who were to feature frequently in 'anti-Arian' polemic for the next two decades.[31] Theodoret of Cyrrhus also preserves a version of this letter that concludes with a creedal formula that is absent from the text transmitted by both Athanasius and Hilary.[32] This includes a forceful rejection of the recent 'eastern' theological statements, most notably by stating that there was a single *hypostasis* ('subsistence') for the Trinity.[33]

After the divided council broke up, relations between the various individuals and groups continued to be fractious. A subsequent council at Antioch in 344 was particularly notable for a failed attempt by the local bishop, Stephen, to discredit a western delegate, the aged bishop Euphrates of Agrippina, by sending a prostitute into his bedroom while he was asleep.[34] The following year, however, Constantius was pressured by his brother Constans into agreeing to allow Paul and Athanasius to return.[35] This was followed by a period of relative calm lasting a few years, during which Ursacius and Valens attended a council at Rome in 347, where they declared that their accusations against Athanasius had been false.[36] This all

not discuss the case of Paul of Constantinople explicitly, but argues that this should not be taken to indicate that the western bishops did not seek to restore him to his see. The term 'Ariomaniacs', or 'Arian madmen', is a polemical label that was particularly favoured by Athanasius: see n. 144 to *Hist. Ar.* 39.2 on p. 72 below.

31 These two bishops, who are nearly always mentioned together, are referred to as 'the Rosencrantz and Guildenstern of the Arian controversy' at Parvis (2006) 125. Hanson (1988) 591 compares them to Laurel and Hardy.

32 Theod. *HE* 2.8.1–52.

33 Kelly (1972) 277–9; Hanson (1988) 300–305; Barnes (1993) 76–7; Ayres (2004) 124–5. This creed is widely regarded as a poor attempt to define the faith and is described as 'rambling' by both Kelly (1972) 277 and Barnes (1993) 76.

34 For this episode, see Ath. *Hist. Ar.* 20.2.–5 in this volume. Agrippina is modern Cologne. This council also wrote the so-called Macrostich or 'Long Creed', which expanded on the 'Fourth Creed' and rejected the use of *ousia* terminology: see Ath. *De synodis* 26; Kelly (1972) 279–80; Hanson (1988) 309–12; Ayres (2004) 127–9.

35 See Barnes (1993) 89–91 on the form of this pressure, which also included a threat of civil war if his demands were not met, at least according to the letter quoted by Socrates: Soc. *HE* 2.22.4–5. Maraval (2013) 254–5 regards Constans' threat as unlikely to have been serious. Barnes (1993) 92–3 notes that support for Marcellus had ebbed and that Constans did not lobby his brother on his behalf.

36 Ath. *Hist. Ar.* 26; Ath. *Apol. c. Ar.* 58; Hilary, *Adv. Val. et Ursac.* B.II.6–8. Barnes (1993) 97–100 reconstructs the events of this period, including the condemnation of Paul of Constantinople at a council, possibly in early 349, and the calling of another synod at Antioch to depose Athanasius. Barnes argues for dating this council to 349, as opposed to 351, or even 352, which appears in some other modern accounts, including Hanson (1988) 325.

changed, however, with the death of Constans in 350 during the usurpation of the Gallic military commander Magnentius, leaving Constantius II as the sole surviving son of Constantine I. In 351 Constantius marched westwards and inflicted a defeat on his new rival at the Battle of Mursa, which took place in late September.[37] In the same year Constantius was also present in Sirmium for a council at which the local bishop Photinus was condemned, as were his beliefs and those of his former teacher, Marcellus of Ancyra.[38] The bishops also followed the established practice of deposing Athanasius, as well as issuing a letter incorporating a statement of faith that consisted of the 'Fourth Creed' of Antioch. To this were added twenty-six anathemas, which included condemnations of many beliefs associated with Marcellus and Photinus, as well as a growing sense of hostility towards the language of *ousia* employed at Nicaea in 325.

The next two years saw victories for Constantius in the ongoing civil war, with Italy falling under his control in 352 and the usurpation finally coming to an end in the summer of 353, with the suicide of Magnentius after the defeat of his troops in Gaul.[39] Constantius was the sole Augustus of the Roman empire and, having gained control over the western provinces for the first time in his reign, he now had an unprecedented opportunity to bring about an ecclesiastical consensus across his dominion. At this point, Ursacius of Singidunum and Valens of Mursa also become more prominent in the accounts of ecclesiastical affairs, especially in the works of Hilary and Athanasius, with the latter presenting them as being the leading 'Arians' who were involved in forcing western bishops to agree to Constantius' demands.[40] In 353/4 a council at Arles condemned Marcellus, Photinus and Athanasius, with Paulinus of Trier being exiled after refusing to reject the bishop of Alexandria.[41] There has been speculation concerning whether the bishops at this council were also asked to subscribe to a theological formula, and Timothy Barnes has suggested plausibly that the

37 Hunt (1998) 17–20.
38 On this council, its decisions and its creed, see Kelly (1972) 281–2; Hanson (1988) 325–9; Barnes (1993) 109–10; Ayres (2004) 134–5. Ayres presents the council as taking place while Constantius was on his way to the West, and Hunt (1998) 17 also suggests that it took place in early 351, before the Battle of Mursa. Hanson and Barnes date the council to late in the year, when Constantius had returned to spend the winter in Sirmium before resuming the campaign in the following year.
39 Hunt (1998), 21–2.
40 See, for example, Ath. *Hist. Ar.* 31.4; Hilary, *In Const.* 2.
41 Sulpicius Severus, *Chronicle* 2.37.4, 39.2; Hilary, *Liber I ad Constantium* 8.1. On the career of Paulinus of Trier, see PCBE IV.2 1443–4 (Paulinus 1).

epistola which Paulinus refused to sign was the letter issued by the Council of Sirmium in 351.[42] This did not, however, settle matters in the West. In 354 Liberius, bishop of Rome, wrote to the emperor to complain about the state of affairs and to ask for the calling of another council.[43] This letter is also notable for the bishop's reference to the faith of Nicaea, explicitly described as confirmed in the presence of Constantius' father, as a statement that ought to be defended and reaffirmed.[44] When the proposed council met at Milan in 355 a similar stance appears to have been taken by some of the bishops present there.[45] According to Hilary of Poitiers, when Eusebius, bishop of Vercelli, was asked to condemn Athanasius at this synod, he produced a copy of the Nicene Creed and declared that, before this could happen, the faith of those present ought to be tested.[46] Dionysius of Milan started to sign the document, but Valens of Mursa angrily snatched the pen and paper away from him and a great commotion ensued.[47] Regardless of whether this dramatic event actually took place or not, a small number of bishops certainly refused to agree to the council's decisions.[48] Dionysius of Milan, Eusebius of Vercelli and Lucifer of Cagliari were exiled, while imperial envoys pressured other bishops to agree to the same matters, including the condemnation of Athanasius.[49] Liberius himself was also

---

42 Barnes (1993) 115. Hanson (1988) 329–31 discusses the evidence for bishops being instructed to sign up to a theological formula at Arles, as well as the Council of Milan in 355, and concludes that this is likely to have occurred. The *epistola* is referred to at Sulpicius Severus, *Chronicle* 2.37.4.

43 The letter is preserved at Hilary, *Adu. Val. et Ursac.* A.VII. See Hanson (1988) 338–40 for a discussion of it. Liberius had succeeded Julius as bishop of Rome in 352.

44 Hilary, *Adu. Val. et Ursac.* A.VII.6.

45 On this council, see Kelly (1972) 284–5; Hanson (1988) 332–4; Barnes (1993) 117–18; Ayres (2004) 136–7; Maraval (2013) 266–8. These events, together with the exile of Lucifer of Cagliari, are also discussed further on pp. 31–2 below.

46 Hilary, *Liber I ad Constantium* 8.1–2. On Eusebius, see PCBE II.1 692–7 (Eusebius 1).

47 On Dionysius of Milan, see PCBE II.1 563–5 (Dionysius 1).

48 Barnes (1993) 117–18 argues that this event is plausible, against suggestions to the contrary.

49 A particularly colourful account of all these events can be found in Ath. *Hist. Ar.* 31–4. There is no evidence to suggest that new bishops were appointed to take the places of Eusebius and Lucifer, who were both able to return to their sees after their exile came to an end with the death of Constantius and the general amnesty proclaimed by Julian. Dionysius died in exile, but had already been replaced by the 'Homoian' bishop Auxentius, who maintained control of the see of Milan until his death in the 370s, despite a number of attempts to dislodge him, including one by Hilary in the 360s: see pp. 18–19 below. At *Hist. Ar.* 75.1, Athanasius complains about the fact that Auxentius was not a local candidate for the position, but had been sent by Constantius from Cappadocia and did not even know Latin.

exiled later that year, although he eventually relented and subscribed to the condemnation of Athanasius in 357, at which point he was allowed to return to his see.[50]

In early 356 imperial officials used troops to drive Athanasius from Alexandria and into exile for the next six years, installing George 'the Cappadocian' in his place.[51] Ossius of Cordoba, now very advanced in age, was also summoned to Sirmium and kept there for a year until, according to Athanasius, he agreed to enter communion with Ursacius and Valens, although he still refused to condemn the Alexandrian bishop.[52] In addition, Ossius was also persuaded to put his name to a new theological statement, which has come to be known by the name assigned to it by Hilary of Poitiers: the 'Blasphemy of Sirmium'.[53] This document, probably heavily influenced (and quite possibly written) by Ursacius and Valens, should be regarded not as a formally adopted creed but rather as an attempt to shape the debate.[54] It is notable not only for its unambiguously subordinationist position regarding the relationship of the Son to the Father but also for its

50 Ath. *Hist. Ar.* 35–41 covers these events, arguing also at 41.3–4 that Liberius' eventual capitulation was far from an expression of his actual beliefs. Another bishop, Felix, was consecrated in his place, as is described highly tendentiously at Ath. *Hist. Ar.* 75.3. On Felix, who left Rome after Liberius' return, see Jerome, *De uiris illustr.* 98; PCBE II.1 770–71 (Felix 7); Barnes (1993) 118. He retained some support within the city, which contributed to the factional violence between the supporters of Damasus and Ursinus in the disputed episcopal election of 366 after the death of Liberius, as is famously described in Amm. 27.3.12–13.

51 On these events, see Ath. *Hist. Ar.* 47–63, 81 and p. 24 below. The bishop George, who was appointed to replace Athanasius by a council at Antioch in 349, is often called 'George the Cappadocian' because he was from this part of Asia Minor. Athanasius used the fact that George was from so far away, as well as his former role as an imperial official, as a way of criticising his rival as being an imperial stooge rather than a legitimate bishop: see *Hist. Ar.* 75.1. Even after Athanasius was driven from the city George himself did not arrive until the next year, before being driven out himself by rioting in 358. He finally returned in late 361, but, soon afterwards, following the death of Constantius II, he was killed by an angry crowd: see Barnes (1993) 119, 155.

52 Ath. *Hist. Ar.* 42–5, esp. 45.4–5 for the 'fall' of Ossius. In this section, Athanasius also transmits what he claims is a very bold and forthright letter sent to Constantius by Ossius.

53 Hilary, *De synodis* 10, with the text of the statement following at 11. Hilary refers to it as 'the nonsense of Ossius' at *In Const.* 23. This document is also preserved at Ath. *De synodis* 28. On this theological formulation, also sometimes referred to as the 'Second Creed of Sirmium', see Kelly (1972) 285–8; Simonetti (1975) 229–33; Brennecke (1984) 312–25, esp. 323–4; Hanson (1988) 343–7; Barnes (1993) 138–9; Ayres (2004) 137–9.

54 Barnes (1993), 139 refers to it as a 'manifesto' or 'trial balloon'.

rejection of all *ousia* language in theology, including *homoousios*, which is to be shunned because it does not appear in Scripture. This represented a direct challenge to the Nicene Creed and demonstrates the growing criticism of the term as unbiblical during this period, which led Athanasius to defend it in his *De decretis* (*On the Decisions of the Nicene Council*).[55] As part of their proscription of definitions involving *ousia*, the transmitted versions of the 'Blasphemy' also condemn the notion of referring to the Son as *homoiousios* ('of like essence') with the Father, perhaps reflecting the recent appearance of this term in theological discourse.[56]

While the statement from Sirmium caused some consternation, especially in the West, concerns also started to be raised about the theologian Aetius and his pupil Eunomius. Aetius was probably born early in the fourth century, most probably at Antioch, while Eunomius, who acted as his secretary, was born in Cappadocia around the middle of the 320s, and both men placed great emphasis on the ingenerate (i.e., not having been generated from anyone or anything else) nature of God in their theological statements, which made prominent use of formal logical arguments and syllogisms.[57] They are sometimes referred to as 'Anomoians', from their supposed belief that the Son was *anomoios* ('unlike') the Father, although, as is sometimes noted, this is a hostile description by their opponents and they actually rejected such terminology.[58] Lewis Ayres has described their theology as 'Heterousian' ('of different essence'), since it stressed that, while there were a number of ways in which the Father and

---

55 This is stated explicitly at *De decretis* 1.1. Most suggestions for the date of this work fall in the range 350–356: see Kopecek (1979) I 116–17; Kannengiesser (1982) 988; Barnes (1993) 110–12, 198–9; Gwynn (2007) 29–33 (2012) 11; Ayres (2004) 140, although Hanson (1988) 419 dates it to 356–7 and Brennecke (1984) 11 n. 41 places it later in Athanasius' third exile.

56 Hanson (1988) 346 notes that this statement is the first documented appearance of *homoiousios*. Barnes (1993) 281 n. 26, 282 n. 32 suggests that this term was not coined until later and that it was not present in the original version of the 'Blasphemy', but Ayres (2004) 138 accepts the transmitted text.

57 On these two men and their beliefs, see Kopecek (1979); Hanson (1988) 598–636; Vaggione (2000); Ayres (2004) 144–9. For the date and place of Aetius' birth, see Kopecek (1979) I 61 (suggesting a date c. 313). On Eunomius' origins, see Vaggione (2000) 2. The text of the *Syntagmation*, the only surviving work by Aetius, can be found at Epiphanius, *Panarion* 76.11.1–12.37. For a critical edition and translation of Eunomius' writings, see Vaggione (1987).

58 Kelly (1972) 283 and (1977) 249 repeats the claim that they promoted *anomoios* theology. Hanson (1988) 598 and Ayres (2004) 145 both reject the label 'Anomoian' as polemical and inaccurate.

Son were similar, they were fundamentally different in their *ousiai*.[59] In addition, after the death of Leontius of Antioch in late 357, Eudoxius of Germanicia managed to become bishop of the nearby see of Antioch and started espousing ideas associated with Aetius.[60] Opposition to the views of these men was soon expressed at a council convened in Ancyra in 358 by Basil, bishop of the city.[61] A letter written from the council by Basil rejected the views of the 'Heterousians' and asserted that the Son was *homoios kat' ousian* ('like according to essence') the Father, leading to the common modern designation of this position as 'Homoiousian'.[62] They also anathematised the use of the terms *homoousios* ('of the same essence') or *tautoousios* ('of identical essence').[63] The council then sent delegates, including Basil, to Constantius to apprise him of their decisions.[64] The emperor approved of what they said and sent a letter to Antioch in which he condemned the views of Aetius and Eudoxius, as well as affirming that he had for a long time supported the Homoiousian formula that the Son was *kat' ousian homoios* ('like according to essence') the Father.[65] According to Philostorgius, who demonstrated hostility to Basil of Ancyra in his *Ecclesiastical History*, Aetius, Eunomius and Eudoxius were then all exiled, as were a number of others who shared their beliefs.[66] Sozomen also reports that a council was held in Sirmium at this time and that it approved a statement that the Son is *kata' ousian kai kata panta homoios* ('like according to essence and in all respects) the Father, and that Liberius of Rome agreed to this formulation.[67] Around the same time Hilary also sought to create a theological rapprochement between 'Nicene' and 'Homoiousian' Christians through his *De synodis* (*On the Councils*), which

59 Ayres (2004) 144–9. Kopecek (1979) refers to them as 'Neo-Arians' and is followed by Hanson (1988) 598. Barnes (1993) 137 rejects this label as inappropriate. The term *anomoiousios* ('of unlike essence') is employed by Hilary at *In Const.* 12.

60 Hanson (1988) 348; Barnes (1993) 139.

61 On this council and its immediate aftermath, as well as Basil's letter from it, see Kelly (1972) 287–8; Hanson (1988) 349–57; Barnes (1993) 139–40; Ayres (2004) 149–53.

62 This letter is preserved at Epiphanius, *Panarion* 73.2–11. Hilary uses the term *homoiousios* in his *In Constantium* to define the theological position of Basil of Ancyra and others.

63 Epiphanius, *Panarion* 73.11.10.

64 Soz. *HE* 4.13.4–6.

65 Soz. *HE* 4.13.6–14.7.

66 Philostorgius, *HE* 4.8.

67 Soz. *HE* 4.15. This document, which is not extant, is sometimes referred to as the 'Third Creed of Sirmium': see Kelly (1972) 288; Hanson (1988), 357–8.

defended the term *homoousios* against a number of potential criticisms, including its absence from Scripture and its association with the third-century 'heretic' Paul of Samosata, but also affirmed that *homoiousios* was acceptable and should be regarded as carrying the same meaning as *homoousios*.[68]

Constantius also agreed to hold another council at Nicomedia, but after the city was hit by a massive earthquake in 358 it was agreed that this gathering would be split into two, with the western delegates assembling at Ariminum (modern Rimini) in Italy and the eastern group at Seleucia in Isauria.[69] In preparation for these events a small group of bishops, including Mark of Arethusa, Ursacius, Valens and Basil of Ancyra, produced a statement of faith at Sirmium. The preface to this text states that it was produced on 22 May 359 and so it has become known as the 'Dated Creed'.[70] It not only avoided the language of *ousia* in its theological definition but also stated that any such discussion of the 'essence' of the Father and Son should not take place, as this term was not found in Scripture and was not recognised by the laity. Even though *homoiousios* had seemed to be on the ascendancy, it was now rejected, as was *homoousios* once again. This new creed then closed by defining the Son as *homoios* ('like') the Father *kata panta* ('in all respects'), picking up part of the statement also written at Sirmium in the previous year. To this was also appended the phrase 'as the Holy Scriptures both say and teach', emphasising the difference between this definition and the 'non-Scriptural' use of *ousia*. Because of the use of the key term *homoios* this theological position is often referred to as 'Homoian'.[71]

68 Hilary, *De synodis* esp. 64–91. Paul of Samosata was a bishop of Antioch who was deposed from his see at a council in that city in 268, possibly for stating that Christ possessed a human soul and body and that 'the Son' did not exist before the Incarnation, although it is hard to reconstruct his theology from the polemical representations of his opponents: see Eus. *HE* 7.27.1–30.19; Epiphanius, *Panarion* 65; Hanson (1988) 70–72; Burrus (1989); Lang (2000); Ayres (2004) 76. The council that condemned him had also condemned the term *homoousios*, which made the Nicene position vulnerable to criticism: see Ayres (2004) 94.

69 On these councils and the surrounding events, see Kelly (1972) 288–93; Kopecek (1979) I 199–215; Hanson (1988) 362–80; Brennecke (1988) 16–53; Barnes (1993) 140–41, 144–8; Ayres (2004) 157–64; Maraval (2013) 272–6.

70 The text is given at Ath. *De synodis* 8.3–7. At *De synodis* 3 Athanasius mocks the idea of creating the Catholic faith on a particular day.

71 On the broader history of Homoian theology and its proponents in the fourth-century Roman empire, see Brennecke (1988).

This document was presented to the bishops at Ariminum, who were said to be more than 400 in number, making it the largest church council ever held up to that time, although it was clearly divided sharply from an early stage.[72] A majority of those present were unwilling to accept the 'Dated Creed' and, instead, produced a statement which explicitly endorsed the Council of Nicaea, as well as defending the use of *ousia* terminology as 'nothing new', but rather as something that 'was introduced into our minds by many Holy Scriptures'.[73] In a document dated to 21 July 359 this group of bishops also condemned Ursacius, Valens, Germinius of Sirmium and another bishop called Gaius, whose see is unknown.[74] In addition, they sent a ten-man delegation to Constantius with a letter in which they repeated their accusations against these four bishops and affirmed their view that no change ought to be made to the decisions of Nicaea, which were here described as being agreed in Constantine's presence and adhered to by him at the time of his baptism and death in 337.[75] At the same time the minority group at the council, which included Ursacius and Valens, also sent its own delegation of ten to Constantius and wrote him a letter in which they once again condemned *ousia* and *homoousios*, calling them 'words unknown to the Church of God'.[76] Constantius refused to receive the majority delegation and had them moved to Niké in Thrace, where, on 10 October, and under the leadership of Restitutus of Carthage, they eventually relented, rescinded their condemnation of their opponents and agreed to endorse a statement that was very similar to the 'Dated Creed', although omitting the term *kata panta* ('in all respects').[77] According to Sulpicius Severus, the rest of the bishops were then not allowed to leave

72 See Ath. *De synodis* 8.1; Soz. *HE* 4.17.2.

73 The text of this statement is preserved at Hilary, *Adu. Val. et Ursac.* A.XI.1. The term *ousia* is here rendered into Latin as *substantia*.

74 Hilary, *Adu. Val. et Ursac.* A.XI.2–3. A Greek version appears at Ath. *De synodis* 11. This group of four bishops also appears at Hilary, *Contra Auxentium* 5, where they are associated with both Auxentius of Milan and Arius himself. The trio of Valens, Ursacius and Gaius were also condemned, along with some other bishops, at a council held in Paris shortly after Hilary had returned from the East – see *Adu. Val. et Ursac.* A.I.4.2.

75 Hilary, *Adu. Val. et Ursac.* A.V.1. This letter is also preserved in a Greek translation at Ath. *De synodis* 10.

76 Rival delegations: Hilary, *Adu. Val. et Ursac.* A.V.2. Letter: Hilary, *Adu. Val. et Ursac.* A.VI.

77 Theod. *HE* 2.21.1–2. This event is also referred to by Hilary at *In Const.* 26 and *Contra Auxentium* 8, while the text of the capitulation is preserved at Hilary, *Adu. Val. et Ursac.* A.V.3. On Restitutus of Carthage, whose name is given as Restutus in Hilary's text, see PCBE I 968–9 (Restitutus 1). The text of the creed is given at Theod. *HE* 2.21.3–7. As well as

Ariminum until they assented to this decision, which the vast majority eventually agreed to do.[78]

The Council of Seleucia met in late September, with about 160 bishops attending, including Hilary of Poitiers.[79] Most of them appear to have been happy with a 'Homoiousian' Christology, but a minority group, headed by Acacius, bishop of Caesarea, and also including Eudoxius of Antioch, was keen to approve a new statement.[80] After some debate the majority reaffirmed the 'Second Creed' from Antioch in 341, but then Acacius presented a new theological statement for consideration. This accepted the 'Second Creed' as orthodox, but rejected *anomoios*, as well as *homoousios* and *homoiousios*, which were deemed unscriptural, and instead affirmed that the Son was *homoios* the Father, 'according to the Apostle', before quoting *Colossians* 1.15.[81] The bishops could not, however, reach agreement and, like their colleagues at Ariminum, the two groups engaged in mutual condemnations and sent separate delegations to the emperor. When they reached the court, Constantius showed himself more receptive to the 'Homoian' approach and pressured the majority delegation from Seleucia to accept the same theological statement that those from Ariminum had already signed.[82] They eventually did so on

rejecting *ousia*, this creed also proscribed the use of *hypostasis* ('subsistence') in Trinitarian theology.

78 Sulpicius Severus, *Chronicle* 2.41, 2.43–4. The complaint about the confining of western bishops at Hilary, *In Const.* 7 probably also refers to these events.

79 Ath. *De synodis* 12.1. Hilary describes his experience of the council in tendentious terms at *In Const.* 12–15. On the circumstances of his attendance, see p. 27 below.

80 Hilary states at *In Const.* 12 that most bishops present originally supported *homoiousios*. Ath. *De synodis* 12.4 does not mention this term, but instead states that the majority were happy to accept the Nicene Creed, with the exception of the term *homoousios*. See Ayres (2004) 163 on the problems with accepting Athanasius' claim. Acacius had been bishop of Caesarea since he succeeded Eusebius, the ecclesiastical historian and biographer of Constantine, early in the reign of Constantius. He had aroused the ire of Nicene Christians early in his episcopate and was among the list of bishops deposed by the 'western' delegation at Serdica in 343 (Ath. *Apol. c. Ar.* 47.3; Hilary, *Adu. Val. et Ursac.* B.II.1.8), but he rose to particular prominence in 359. On Eudoxius, who had previously been bishop of Germanicia, see p. 14 above.

81 For this creed, which is extremely similar to the 'Dated Creed', see Ath. *De synodis* 29.2–8. There is also a version with a longer preamble preserved at Soc. *HE* 2.40.8–17 and at Epiphanius, *Panarion* 73.25.1–26.8 (with a list of signatories). Hilary discusses the use of the quotation from *Colossians*, which describes the Son as 'the image of God invisible', at *In Const.* 21.

82 Soc. *HE* 2.41.2–4; Soz. *HE* 4.23.

the final day of 359.[83] Another council was then held in Constantinople in January 360 to confirm these decisions, with Acacius taking a leading role.[84] This gathering issued a final 'Homoian' creed, which was extremely similar to the one agreed to at Niké the previous year.[85] It once again condemned the use of *ousia* theological language, as well as prohibiting the employment of the term *hypostasis* ('subsistence') for discussing the Trinity. Like the formula approved at Niké, it affirmed that the Son was *homoios* ('like') the Father 'as the Holy Scriptures both say and teach', rather than saying *homoios kata panta* ('like in all respects') as had been the case in the 'Dated Creed'. The council also deposed a number of its opponents, including Basil of Ancyra, Macedonius of Constantinople and Cyril of Jerusalem. Eudoxius was rehabilitated and became bishop of Constantinople, while Eunomius was elevated to the see of Cyzicus.

After this sequence of councils the 'Homoian' creed could be regarded as having been agreed by more bishops than any earlier statement of faith, and therefore gained widespread legitimacy. There were, of course, a number of bishops who still opposed it vehemently, including Athanasius, Hilary and Lucifer. The situation in the West was also soon altered by the usurpation of Constantius' cousin and *caesar*, Julian, in February 360, allowing Hilary and other Gallic bishops a freer hand to promote the Nicene Creed instead, since Constantius could no longer enforce his decisions in that area.[86] Nonetheless, the creed of Constantinople, which was often described as 'Arian' by its opponents, enjoyed continued legitimacy after the death of Constantius II in late 361. The eastern emperor Valens upheld it as orthodox, while his western colleague, his brother Valentinian I, although he may have held Nicene beliefs himself, did not remove 'Homoian' bishops from their sees.[87] In the middle of the 360s, when Hilary of Poitiers challenged the orthodoxy of Auxentius of Milan, the bishop confidently responded by informing the emperors that he stood by the faith agreed at Ariminum and Niké, which

---

83 Soz. *HE* 4.23.8.

84 On the Council of Constantinople and its creed, see Kelly (1972) 293–5; Hanson (1988) 380–82; Brennecke (1988) 54–6; Barnes (1993) 148–9; Ayres (2004) 164–5; Maraval (2013) 276–8.

85 For the text of this creed, see Ath. *De synodis* 30.2–10, as well as Soc. *HE* 2.41.8–16.

86 On the uncertain details of Hilary's return to Gaul from the East, see p. 28 below.

87 Lenski (2002) 238–42 discusses both the religious policies of Valentinian and the difficult question of the emperor's own confessional position. On the 'Homoian Church' during the reign of Valens, see Brennecke (1988) 181–242.

led to him retaining his see while Hilary was expelled from Milan as a troublemaker.[88] It was not until the Council of Constantinople in 381 that 'Nicene' theology could be said to have reached the ascendancy again, since it then received imperial support from the new eastern emperor Theodosius I, although the creed promulgated in 381 (and often referred to as the 'Nicene Creed' in the present day) was not identical to the one written at Nicaea in 325.[89] Even after that the 'Homoian' position was soon to receive a new lease of life as the standard of faith supported by a number of the 'barbarian' groups who went on to establish kingdoms on the territory of the western empire in the fifth century.

The traditional picture of Constantius that emerges from these events is of an overbearing autocrat whose desire to impose his theological views on all his Christian subjects led him to use force and coercion to a degree that could be termed persecution. This image is, however, largely a product of the negative rhetoric of his opponents, among whom Athanasius, Hilary and Lucifer were major figures, as well as of the works of later authors who used and embellished their accounts, including the heresiologist Epiphanius of Salamis and the ecclesiastical historians Socrates, Sozomen and Sulpicius Severus. An alternative, more positive version of Constantius' actions can, however, occasionally be glimpsed in a small number of texts, such as the fragmentary work of the fifth-century author Philostorgius.[90] Nonetheless, it would be wrong to accept these as a clear corrective to the dominant, 'Nicene' strand of condemnatory literature, just as it would be an error to take that literature at face value. Instead, it is necessary to acknowledge the inherent difficulties present in the interpretation of these events, where polemic pervades the vast majority of the contemporary material. This is particularly evident in the use of labels such as 'Arian' or 'Sabellian', with which individuals or groups sought to destroy the reputations of their enemies by denying them the name of 'Christian', associating them with known 'heretics' and thus situating them outside the boundaries of acceptable religious belief.

The preceding section has sought to give a reasonably uncontentious insight into the key events and concerns of this period, as well as the roles

---

88 Hilary, *Contra Auxentium* 8, 15. On these events and this text, see Flower (2013) 207–17, 252–60.

89 For the creed from Constantinople, sometimes called the 'Nicene-Constantinopolitan Creed', and the differences between it and the original Nicene Creed, see Kelly (1972) 296–331; Hanson (1988) 815–20; Ayres (2004) 255–8.

90 On this issue, see Flower (2013) 95–6, 107–8.

played by notable figures, as far as is possible under the circumstances. Moreover, while it can be hard to reconstruct actions, the identification of motives is even more challenging. For example, not only is it uncertain whether the initiative for certain policies came from Constantius or from particular bishops, but also a historian of this period is faced with diametrically opposed presentations of the emperor's wishes: was he driven by a pure and pious desire for Christian unity or a tyrannical, diabolical urge to enforce his wicked will? The answer is almost certainly neither, but any conclusions about such matters must remain highly speculative. It is, instead, more fruitful to examine the representations of these events as representations, to understand the ways in which their authors shaped particular narratives of history and created literary personas for their major characters, including themselves. Although some of their details can appear extreme or even ridiculous, such as when Athanasius calls his opponents 'Ariomaniacs' or presents them as saying 'If we run away, we can protect the heresy somehow', these texts must be understood as attempts to sway opinion through the language of invective, which relied on these seemingly exaggerated caricatures, just as late-antique panegyric employed hyperbolic praise.[91] The disputes of this period were conducted at least as much through rhetorical presentation as through rigorous theological argument, and the three texts translated in this volume are prime examples of this phenomenon. Moreover, as was noted at the start of this introduction, it should be recognised that such polemical labelling and language was extremely successful, with many of these authors' opponents going down in history as 'Arian heretics'. The following sections will discuss the lives of Athanasius, Hilary and Lucifer, as well as exploring the ways in which they crafted their polemical works to persuade others to accept their particular versions of reality.

---

91 For this quotation, see Ath. *Hist. Ar.* 15.5.

AUTHORS AND TEXTS

Athanasius of Alexandria and the *Historia Arianorum*

Athanasius was probably born late in the third century and was a deacon in the church of Alexandria under Bishop Alexander.[92] Despite his very extensive literary output, his level of education is a subject of debate, although it is clear that he had some acquaintance with the techniques of oratory that were current in fourth-century political discourse.[93] After attending the Council of Nicaea in 325, he assumed the episcopate as Alexander's successor in 328, after an election that was disputed on the grounds that he was not yet old enough to be a bishop.[94] During the following years he was involved in a number of controversies within Egypt, including the accusation that he had acted violently towards the schismatic Melitians, who refused to accept Athanasius' authority as bishop.[95] Attempts were made to remove him from his office and a number of accusations were made against him: on one occasion, he was alleged to have ordered an attack on a priest called Ischyras in which a chalice was smashed, while he also faced the charge of having masterminded the murder of Arsenius, bishop of Hypsele in Egypt.[96] Although he was able to disprove the latter accusation by producing the bishop alive and well, the Council of Tyre in 335 sent a commission to the area of the Mareotis near Alexandria to investigate the claims concerning the chalice and, after receiving its report, declared him to be deposed from his see.[97] He fled from this meeting to Constantinople, where he managed to persuade Constantine that he was being treated

---

92 Barnes (1993) 10 (suggesting a date of 299 for his birth); Gwynn (2012) 1 (suggesting a birthdate sometime in the 290s). For introductions to Athanasius' life and works in English, see more generally Barnes (1993); Gwynn (2012) esp. 1–17.

93 For a similar view, see Louth (2004) 275, suggesting that Athanasius may not have progressed as far as undertaking formal study with a *rhetor*. Barnes (1993) 11–12, 126 and Gwynn (2012) 3–4 both argue that Athanasius does not show the same knowledge of rhetoric and 'classical' literature as some more highly educated bishops of the period. In contrast, Stead (1976) sees more influence of traditional education in his works.

94 Barnes (1993) 14, 18–20; Martin (1996) 321–9; Gwynn (2012) 5–6.

95 On these Egyptian rigorists, see n. 16 above.

96 One these alleged events and the ensuing controversies, including the Council of Tyre in 335, see Ath. *Apol. c. Ar.* 59–89 (which includes various relevant documents); Barnes (1993) 20–33; Martin (1996) 348–57. They are also alluded to at *Hist. Ar.* 3.2.

97 On this council, see Barnes (1993) 22–3; Martin (1996) 357–87.

unfairly, as is evident from the letter that Constantine dispatched to the bishops at Tyre.[98] During the ensuing discussions, however, an argument arose between emperor and bishop, which Athanasius later attributed to a false accusation that he had threatened to withhold the grain supply from Alexandria to Constantinople.[99] Constantine therefore exiled him to Gaul.[100]

The death of the emperor in 337 was followed by an amnesty for exiled bishops, issued by his three sons, who now shared the empire between them. Athanasius preserves the text of the letter from Constantine II to the city of Alexandria allowing him to return to his see.[101] His stay in the city was, however, to be short-lived, as attempts were soon made to remove him again.[102] At a council held in Antioch in 338/9 he was once against condemned for his behaviour towards Ischyras, as well as being accused of inciting violence after he had returned to Alexandria in 337, and was replaced as bishop by a man called Gregory, often referred to as 'the Cappadocian'.[103] In the spring of 339 Gregory arrived in the city with the help of the prefect of Egypt, Philagrius, as well as armed supporters, leading to Athanasius' departure into exile in the West for the second time.[104] He travelled to Rome, where he gained the support of Bishop Julius, who wrote to eastern bishops requesting that they come to a council

98 For the text of this letter, see Ath. *Apol. c. Ar.* 86.2–12. It is worth noting, however, that, although Constantine's support for Athanasius would mean that the decision of council could not be enforced, as is noted at Barnes (1993), 24, the condemnation at Tyre was never formally rescinded, which proved useful to his enemies in later years: see, for example, the remarks in the letter of the 'eastern' bishops from Serdica in 343, preserved at Hilary, *Adu. Val. et Ursac.* A.IV.1.7–8.

99 Ath. *Apol. c. Ar.* 9. The letter from the 'eastern' bishops at Serdica in 343 simply states that Athanasius was questioned by Constantine, who recognised the bishop's crimes and so sent him into exile: see Hilary, *Adu. Val. et Ursac.* A.IV.1.7.

100 In *Hist. Ar.* 50.2 Athanasius presents a more positive version of these events, with the emperor protecting Athanasius from his enemies through this action, as does the letter of Constantine II preserved at Ath. *Apol. c. Ar.* 87.4–7.

101 Ath. *Apol. c. Ar.* 87.4–7. See also *Hist. Ar.* 8.

102 Ath. *Apol. c. Ar.* 3–19 contains a letter from a council held at Alexandria in 338 to defend Athanasius against the charges made against him.

103 Barnes (1993) 45–6. Gregory, who died in 345 before Athanasius' return from his second exile, is not to be confused with George 'the Cappadocian', who was another rival bishop of Alexandria later in Athanasius' episcopacy: on George, see n. 51 above and p. 24 below.

104 A very colourful account of these events is given by Athanasius in his *Epistula Encyclica* (*Encyclical Epistle*), as well as being discussed briefly at *Hist. Ar.* 9–10. On Philagrius, see n. 30 to Ath. *Hist. Ar.* 7.5 on p. 45 below. On the *Epistula Encyclica*, see Barnes (1993) 47–50; Gwynn (2007) 51–7; Flower (2013) 118–20, 196–7.

at Rome.[105] Julius' envoys attended the 'Dedication Council' of Antioch in 341, but were rebuffed.[106] Julius nonetheless held his own council and wrote a letter to complain to the bishops who had refused to attend.[107] As described above, the emperor Constans now became involved in the ongoing ecclesiastical discord, leading first to the unsuccessful Council of Serdica in 343 and then to Constantius II consenting to Athanasius's return to Alexandria.[108] Although this was agreed in 345, Athanasius did not arrive home until the autumn of 346, and he was keen to trumpet the fact that Constantius had written to him three times requesting that he do so.[109] His account of his own arrival back into the city of Alexandria is filled with self-praise and depicts the popular celebrations as extraordinary, evoking panegyrical accounts of the imperial ceremony of *aduentus*, in which the emperor entered a city in a vast procession.[110]

Athanasius was to remain in possession of his see for the next decade, but this period was far from free of dispute and controversy.[111] He was already facing challenges to his position before the death of his erstwhile champion Constans in 350 destabilised the situation further.[112] Athanasius was now placed in a precarious position, especially as he was accused of having been in contact with the western usurper Magnentius, and he was condemned at the Council of Sirmium in 351.[113] After Constantius

---

105 See Barnes (1993) 50–52 for the suggestion that Athanasius also sought the help of the emperors Constans and Constantine II at this time. On Athanasius' time in the West, see also Martin (1996) 410–19.

106 Ath. *Hist. Ar.* 11.

107 Ath. *Hist. Ar.* 15.1. See *Apol. c. Ar.* 20–35 for the text of this letter. For a survey of the events of this period, including Julius' involvement, see Barnes (1993) 56–62.

108 See Ath. *Apol. Const.* 2–5 for Athanasius' later rejection of the charge that he turned Constans against his brother Constantius.

109 Barnes (1993) 90–92; Martin (1996) 442–7. For these letters and other relevant documents, see Ath. *Apol. c. Ar.* 51–6, as well as Athanasius' account of these events in *Hist. Ar.* 21–4.

110 Ath. *Hist. Ar.* 25. For discussion of this passage and its relationship to *aduentus*, as well as the reuse of this image in Gregory of Nazianzus' speech celebrating the life of Athanasius, see Flower (2013) 121–3.

111 See Barnes (1993) 94–120 for a succinct account of these years.

112 Barnes (1993) 99 suggests that Athanasius' *Apologia contra Arianos* (*Defence against the Arians*) was compiled into its current form to defend him against charges at a council in Antioch in 349. Gwynn (2007) 16–19 does not agree with this conclusion, but dates the work to around the same time.

113 For Athanasius' defence against this charge, see *Apol. Const.* 6–13. The events of the years preceding Athanasius' expulsion from Alexandria in 356 are also covered in *Hist. Ar.* 28–47.

became sole Augustus of the Roman world in 353 and then set about trying to create ecclesiastical agreement through the councils at Arles and Milan he finally attempted to remove Athanasius from Alexandria, firstly in 355 and then again in early 356.[114] On the latter occasion the military commander Syrianus led an assault on a church in the early hours of 9 February, which caused Athanasius to flee the city and start what is usually referred to as his third exile.[115] This was followed by other acts of violence against those who sided with Athanasius, but, despite these actions, the man appointed to replace him, George 'the Cappadocian', was never able to take possession of his see for any sustained period of time.[116] Athanasius' sojourn away from his see lasted until 362, and the bishop spent this period in hiding in various places around Egypt. He finally returned openly to Alexandria under the amnesty proclaimed by the pagan emperor Julian, a few months after George had been killed by an angry mob shortly after the people of the city learned the news of Constantius' death.[117] He was, however, soon exiled again by Julian, only to return after the emperor had met his end on campaign in Persia in 363. He was then to suffer his fifth and final period of exile – or, rather, of concealing himself from the imperial authorities – under the 'Homoian' emperor Valens during a short time in 365–6, before enjoying a period of relative peace until his death in 373 after almost half a century as bishop of Alexandria.[118]

For much of our knowledge of the events of this period, and particularly of Athanasius' involvement in them, we are heavily reliant on the bishop's own writings, with the *Historia Arianorum*, or *History of the Arians*, playing an important part, especially for reconstructing the ecclesiastical history of the 350s. It was probably written relatively early during his third exile and consists mostly of a polemical and tendentious account of events from the last years of the reign of Constantine I to the time of

---

114 See Ath. *Apol. Const.* 19–24, including the bishop's attempt to explain why he had not responded to an earlier imperial letter instructing him to go to Italy.

115 *Hist. Ar.* 48.2–3 (narrative), 81 (description of these events in a petition by Athanasius' supporters). See also *Apol. Const.* 25–7; Hilary, *In Const.* 11; Lucifer, *Moriundum* 2, 8; Barnes (1993) 118–19; Martin (1996) 474–8. Athanasius presented a defence of his actions in his *De fuga*.

116 For this ongoing violence, see *Hist. Ar.* 48–63, as well as *Apol. Const.* 28. For the repeated attempts to secure George's position, see Barnes (1993) 119. On George and his designation as 'the Cappadocian', see n. 51 above.

117 Barnes (1993) 155.

118 Barnes (1993) 162–4; Martin (1996) 590–96; Gwynn (2012) 16–17.

composition.[119] The greatest part of this narrative concerns events since the death of Constans in 350, with particular emphasis on the Councils of Arles in 353/4 and Milan in 355, the confrontations between Constantius and the bishops Liberius of Rome and Ossius of Cordoba, and also the violence in Alexandria and Egypt that surrounded Athanasius' expulsion from the city in early 356. Compared with other more guarded or deferential works, such as the *Apologia ad Constantium* (*Defence to Constantius*), it is notable for the force of the invective directed against Constantius himself, particularly in its later chapters, where he is said to resemble Saul, Ahab and Pilate, and to be preparing the way for the coming of the Antichrist, or even to be the Antichrist himself.[120] Athanasius also consistently refers to his ecclesiastical opponents as 'the Arians' or 'the Eusebians' (after the presbyter Arius and the bishop Eusebius of Nicomedia, respectively) and presents them as being like wild animals, especially snakes, or as worse than earlier enemies of Christianity, especially Jews.[121] His polemical language also involves other little quips and puns designed to undermine the positions of his enemies, including accusing some of the hostile 'bishops' of actually being imperial 'spies' by making use of the similarity between the Greek words ἐπίσκοπος ('bishop') and κατάσκοπος ('spy').[122] It is uncertain exactly what audience it was written for, although it has often been believed that it was circulated among pro-Athanasian monks. This assumption is, however, largely based on the fact that it is preceded in manuscripts by the *Epistula ad monachos* (*Letter to the Monks*), which mentions an associated text that the recipients are instructed not to share with others.[123] There is now widespread agreement that the *History of the Arians* is not the work referred to in this letter, meaning that there is no definitive evidence for its intended audience or the means and breadth of its distribution.[124] Timothy Barnes argues that the text 'was addressed, if indeed it had a definite audience, to monks sympathetic to the author', but David Gwynn does not agree with this suggestion, proposing instead that it had 'a wider

119 For the suggested dating of the work to late 357, see Barnes (1993) 126; Gwynn (2012) 13 and n. 19 to *Hist. Ar.* 4.2 on p. 42 below.

120 See *Hist. Ar.* 67–80.

121 See, for example, *Hist. Ar.* 45.3, 61.4 and 66.1–5.

122 *Hist. Ar.* 3.4, 48.3, 75.3.

123 There is also a comment at the end of the text in the manuscript tradition of the *Historia Arianorum* that claims that it was addressed 'to the monks everywhere': see *Hist. Ar.* 80.4.

124 See the first note to the edition of the *Epistula ad monachos* at Opitz (1935–41) 181, as well as Barnes (1993) 278 n. 23 and Gwynn (2007) 41.

but still Egyptian audience'.[125] Whatever the immediate readership was, it is clear that this was an inflammatory text designed to persuade anyone who encountered it that Constantius was a heretical persecutor. It would therefore be sensible to assume that it came into the possession of a larger number of people only once Constantius was safely dead.

Hilary of Poitiers and the *In Constantium*

Compared with the large amount of information surviving about the life and episcopate of Athanasius, relatively little is known about the pre-exile activities of Hilary, with even the date of his election as bishop of the Gallic city of Poitiers being uncertain.[126] From the style of his work he is generally believed by modern scholars to have had a reasonable level of literary and rhetorical education.[127] Along with bishop Rhodanius of Toulouse he was exiled at, or soon after, a council held in the Gallic city of Béziers (Bitterae), probably in 356.[128] At *In Constantium* 2 Hilary claims that he had suggested that a hearing be held to expose the heresy of certain 'false apostles', but that they had refused to listen to him and so he had been in exile ever since. Similarly, in his more deferential letter to Constantius, known as the *Ad Constantium* (*Address to Constantius*), which was probably written shortly before the *In Constantium*, he argued that, despite being an exile, he was still 'a bishop in communion with all the churches and bishops of the Gauls' and that he had been exiled 'not by an accusation, but by a faction and false messages from the synod to you, pious emperor'.[129] Hilary was keen to claim that he remained bishop of Poitiers and had not been formally condemned and deposed from his see, although it is unclear whether this was the case. Certainly, the causes and circumstances of his exile have been the subject of much debate, with the main issue of contention being whether Hilary was condemned for theological reasons, such as standing up for the Nicene Creed and refusing to accept an alternative statement of faith,

125 Barnes (1993) 126; Gwynn (2007) 41.

126 For a good, brief introduction to Hilary's life and the ancient references to him, see PCBE IV.1 989–997 (Hilarius 1).

127 See Borchardt (1966) 6–8; Wickham (1997) xii; Rocher (1987) 9–10.

128 Hilary, *In Const.* 2, 11; Sulpicius Severus, *Chronicle* 2.39. Wickham (1997) 18 also sees a reference to these events at Hilary, *Adu. Val. et Ursac.* B.I.5 by accepting the proposed emendation of the text from *in terris* to *Bitteris*. On this suggestion, see Smulders (1995) 89–91. See also Jerome, *De uiris illustr.* 100.1. On the relatively minor figure of Rhodanius, see PCBE IV.2 (1610) (Rhodanius 1).

129 Hilary, *Ad Const.* 2. On this text, see n. 133 below.

or because of political motives, possibly related to the usurpation of the military commander Silvanus in Gaul in 355.[130] As well as being opposed to Ursacius of Singidunum and Valens of Mursa, as Athanasius was, he also singles out Saturninus of Arles for criticism in his work, and it may be that his disagreement with this bishop contributed to his being sent into exile.[131]

As has already been seen, Hilary stated that he had not been formally deposed as a bishop and it is clear that he enjoyed relative freedom of movement and even the opportunity to attend ecclesiastical councils during his time in exile. He went to Phrygia and seems to have become more involved in the theological debates of the time, since he then wrote his *De synodis* (*On the Councils*) to some of his western colleagues to attack the 'Blasphemy of Sirmium' and to argue that the term *homoiousios* could be acceptable to those who defended the Nicene concept of *homoousios*. He also attended the Council of Seleucia in 359, which he describes in vivid terms at *In Constantium* 12–15, and travelled on from there to Constantinople.[132] Early in 360 he composed his *Ad Constantium*, which

---

130 The various questions concerning the root cause of Hilary's exile are raised at Wickham (1997) xiii and there is a good survey of the debate at Beckwith (2005) 21–4. Beckwith's own view in this article is that, while Hilary did exaggerate his experiences at Béziers to some extent, his account can largely be accepted. Other 'conservative' descriptions of Hilary's life up to and including his exile can be found at Borchardt (1966) 1–39, 165–77; Doignon (1971); Hanson (1988) 459–64. The suggestion of mostly 'political' motives is favoured by Brennecke (1984) 223–43 and Williams (1991), although the two scholars disagree on certain points. Barnes (1992) and Burns (1994) see theological matters as of primary importance in this matter. Smulders (1995) 126–31 argues that the main accusation concerned Hilary's refusal to be in communion with Saturninus and others and that he was not condemned at the council, but was instead exiled by Constantius after a report of the proceedings was sent to him by Julian. See also Barry (2016), which does look at this issue (at 159–60), but moves away from attempts to reconstruct the precise cause of Hilary's exile and focuses instead on his literary construction of it.

131 Hilary states at *In Const.* 2 that he, 'together with the Gallic bishops', withdrew from communion with Ursacius, Valens and Saturninus after the condemnations at the Councils of Arles in 353/4 and Milan in 355, and then places this action at the head of a chain of events that led to Béziers and his own exile. These three bishops are also mentioned together by Hilary at *Adu. Val. et Ursac.* B.II.5.3, while the letter of the synod held in Paris after Hilary's return from exile also mentions Saturninus' excommunication: see Hilary, *Adu. Val. et Ursac.* A.I.4.4. Saturninus is similarly singled out for criticism by Hilary at *De synodis* 3. On the career of this bishop, see PCBE IV,2 1714–16 (Saturninus 1).

132 See Sulpicius Severus, *Chronicle* 2.42, 2.45.2, where it is stated, amongst other things, that imperial officials enforced Hilary's attendance at the council. As Barnes (1993) 287 n. 48 rightly remarks, Sulpicius clearly exaggerates the level of involvement that Hilary had in the discussions at Seleucia.

praises the emperor Constantius, but he was frustrated in his attempts to gain an imperial audience.[133] In this work he describes the emperor in the panegyrical terms that were common to imperial rhetoric, including calling him 'most pious emperor' and 'best and most religious emperor', although he was soon to invert these virtues to create expressions of Constantius' extreme vice for his *In Constantium*.[134] At some point Hilary then returned home under circumstances that are far from clear, especially as Sulpicius Severus' claim that Constantius now sent him back to Gaul to stop him disrupting the East seems, once again, to exaggerate the bishop's importance in the theological and ecclesiastical controversies of the day.[135] Moreover, in another of his works Sulpicius offers another explanation for Hilary's return, this time attributing it to Constantius' repentance.[136] Neither explanation is satisfactory. It seems likely that he either gained permission from the emperor to return to Gaul or was simply able to do so without Constantius' consent.[137] A brief mention in a text known as the

133 Barnes (1993) 287 n. 50 argues convincingly for dating this text to 360, since at 5.2 it refers to the 'Dated Creed' of 359 as 'the creed of last year' (*proximi anni fides*). Since Hilary also refers to Julian as Constantius' *caesar* at 2.1, the news of his usurpation at Paris in February 360 cannot have reached Constantinople at the time of composition. An English translation can be found at Wickham (1997) 104–9. This text is also sometimes referred to as the *Liber II Ad Constantium* in order to distinguish it from the so-called *Liber I Ad Constantium*. The latter is not an address by Hilary, but rather the text of a letter to Constantius from the 'western' delegation at Serdica in 343, followed by some later commentary by Hilary and remarks on the Council of Arles in 353/4 and Milan in 355. Discussion of these passages can be found at Wickham (1997) xxiii–xxiv, 6, with a translation at 65–9.

134 Hilary, *Ad Const.* 1.1, 4.1. On the laudatory forms of address to Constantius in this text, as well as similar terms in Athanasius' *Apologia ad Constantium*, see Flower (2013) 99–102. The same sort of deferential rhetoric also appears in Eusebius of Vercelli's letter to Constantius concerning the Council of Milan in 355, with the emperor referred to as 'most merciful' and 'most glorious' – Eus. Verc. *Ep.* 1. For a translation of this text with introduction, see Flower (2013) 242. On Hilary's presentation of his relationship with Constantius in both the *Ad Constantium* and the *In Constantium*, see also Barry (2016).

135 Sulpicius Severus, *Chronicle* 2.45.2. As discussed above, Sulpicius Severus both accepted and inflated Hilary's own self-presentation as a key figure in the battle against the 'Arian heresy'. On the issue of his return from exile, see Duval (1970) esp. 253–66; Brennecke (1984) 352–61; Williams (1992) 10–12; Barnes (1993) 150–51; Pelland (1997) 249–50; Wickham (1997) xiv; Barry (2016) 160.

136 Sulpicius Severus, *Vita Martini* 6.7. The two different versions put forward by Sulpicius are discussed at Duval (1970) 261–6.

137 Modern views are split on this subject: see, for example, Hanson (1988) 464 favouring the former explanation and Barnes (1993) 153 opting for the latter. If he did receive imperial permission for his return, Sulpicius' different versions could have been attempts to ensure that Hilary retained his image as a fearless opponent of orthodoxy, just as Athanasius put a

Altercatio Heracliani cum Germinio (*The Dispute between Heraclianus and Germinius*) suggests that Hilary made his way through Sirmium on his westward journey, but he was soon back in Gaul, which had now passed out of Constantius' control after the usurpation of Julian.[138] He attended a council held in Paris in 360 or 361 and a letter from this synod, preserved by Hilary himself, mentions him repeatedly as the bearer of information and greetings from the East.[139] Among the bishops excommunicated by this gathering are not only the usual suspects Ursacius of Singidunum and Valens of Mursa but also Auxentius of Milan, who was to become another target for Hilary later in the 360s, as has been described above.[140] He also probably brought his *Aduersus Valentem et Ursacius* (*Against Valens and Ursacius*), which is now fragmentary but nonetheless preserves many useful documents, into its final form shortly before his death in 367/8.[141]

The *In Constantium*, or *Against Constantius*, can be dated to the very end of Hilary's exile or shortly thereafter. Perhaps because of the highly polemical tone of the work, Jerome claimed that it was not written until after Constantius' death, but this suggestion has been largely rejected by modern scholars.[142] In chapter 2 Hilary states that he and the bishops of Gaul withdrew from communion with Saturninus, Ursacius and Valens *quinto abhinc anno*, after the exile of Paulinus, Eusebius, Lucifer and Dionysius.[143] Since these bishops were condemned at the Councils of Arles in 353/4 and Milan in 355, this suggests that the work was composed in 359 or 360.[144]

---

positive spin on his exile under Constantine at *Hist. Ar.* 50.2. It should not be assumed that Hilary's dramatic switch from effusive panegyric in the *Ad Constantium* to fierce invective in the *In Constantium* was the result of disappointment in his attempt to gain an audience with the emperor. Rather than treating one text or the other (or both) as representing Hilary's 'sincere' views, these works should be seen as examples of the malleability of imperial rhetoric, which could be directed to different audiences for different purposes.

138 *Altercatio Heracliani* 345 (Hamman).

139 Hilary, *Adu. Val. et Ursac.* A.I. On this council, see Barnes (1993) 153–4.

140 Hilary, *Adu. Val. et Ursac.* A.I.4.2. On Hilary's unsuccessful attempt to unseat Auxentius, see p. 18 above.

141 Wickham (1997) xxvi. His *Against Ursacius and Valens* was a polemical account of ecclesiastical affairs that presented the Church as under threat from 'Arian' heretics, chief amongst whom were Valens of Mursa and Ursacius of Singidunum. The surviving fragments cover the period from 343 to 366: see Smulders (1995); Wickham (1997) xxii–xxvi.

142 Jerome, *De uiris illustr.* 100.3. Wickham (1997) ix is unusual in accepting this dating.

143 I have translated this phrase as 'more than four years ago'. Rocher (1987) 171 renders it as 'plus de quatre ans que'.

144 Hilary could be giving a rounded figure here, but it nonetheless suggests an approximate date which can then be compared with the other evidence.

The text also contains a reference to the capitulation of the delegation of bishops who had come to Constantius from the Council of Seleucia.[145] As this event took place on the last day of 359, it seems reasonable to date the work to 360. André Rocher, in the introduction to his edition and French translation of the text, suggested a two-stage process of composition, with the first version being distributed to bishops in Gaul after Hilary's return, but before the death of Constantius, but the revised version being completed only after Constantius had died in 361.[146] This seems, however, to be unnecessarily convoluted in its attempt to incorporate the testimony of Jerome, and Timothy Barnes has presented an excellent argument for dating the whole work to 360.[147]

The *In Constantium* provides a tendentious account of the religious policies of Constantius in the final part of Hilary's exile in the East. It opens with a defence of Hilary's policy of remaining quiet about Constantius' impious and persecuting behaviour up to this point, but this is combined with a justification for his decision to speak out finally, all supported with biblical quotations and allusions. The first six chapters address the anonymous readers, but from chapter 7 onwards Hilary speaks to the emperor himself in the second person, employing a range of abusive terms and accusations, including calling him a persecutor, a wolf in sheep's clothing, the son of the Devil and the Antichrist, as well as criticising his repeated involvement in the drafting of theological statements. Apart from the brief interlude on the Council of Seleucia and its aftermath in chapters 12–15, this direct address to the emperor is maintained for the rest of the work, thereby giving it the rhetorical form of an invective, even though it will never have been delivered to Constantius himself. After the opening criticism of the emperor, chapters 12–22 feature a detailed discussion of some of the theological issues involved in the discussions at Seleucia in 359 and Constantinople in 360, with Hilary analysing a number of biblical passages in order to criticise the 'Homoian' concept of 'likeness' (here rendered into Latin using the term *similitudo*). Towards the end of the work he also accuses Constantius of inconstancy, since the emperor repeatedly changes his mind about the definition of orthodoxy, as well as forcing bishops to condemn their earlier statements of faith. Hilary then concludes by stating that Constantius should be regarded as a rebel against

145 *In Const.* 15.
146 Rocher (1987) 29–38.
147 Barnes (1988) 610. Brennecke (1984) 361 supports this dating and also suggests that Hilary wrote the work after he had arrived back in Gaul.

his father, Constantine I, because he has chosen to reject the creed adopted at the Council of Nicaea in 325. The immediate audience for the work is uncertain, but it is likely to have been primarily intended for Christians who were sympathetic to Hilary's cause, particularly those in other parts of the West.[148]

Lucifer of Cagliari and the *Moriundum esse pro dei filio*

The final author translated in this volume, Lucifer, bishop of the Sardinian metropolitan see of Cagliari, first appears in the historical record in the middle of the 350s.[149] There is little information about his early life and education, although his writings display some knowledge of classical literature, including echoes of Virgil and Cicero, who were standard authors in the late-antique Latin schoolroom.[150] Lucifer, along with a presbyter named Pancratius and a deacon called Hilarius, acted as a delegation to Constantius from Liberius of Rome after the Council of Arles in 353/4.[151] They then proceeded to participate in the Council of Milan in 355 and wrote an extant letter to Eusebius of Vercelli, encouraging him to attend.[152] As discussed earlier, Lucifer refused to agree to the decisions of the council and was exiled, along with his associates Pancratius and Hilary and the bishops Eusebius of Vercelli and Dionysius of Milan.[153]

---

148 Rocher (1987) 41–2 suggests an audience of Gallic bishops. Despite the issues with Rocher's reconstruction of the process of composition, his hypothesis here remains reasonable, although Hilary could also have been addressing some people outside Gaul, as he did in the preface to his *De synodis*.

149 For a brief survey of Lucifer's life and the ancient evidence, see PCBE II.2 1324–8 (Lucifer 1). A collection of ancient testimonia to the life of Lucifer is also provided at Ugenti (1980) xvii–xxxv.

150 Laconi (2004) 119 makes the plausible suggestion that Lucifer had some degree of literary education. His quotations from, and allusions to, other authors are tabulated at Diercks (1978) 363–4 and Laconi (1998) 437–8.

151 The letter concerning their role is preserved at Hilary, *Adu. Val. et Ursac.* A.VII. See also Jerome, *De uiris illustr.* 95.1. The evidence for Lucifer's life, up to the Council of Milan, is surveyed at Diercks (1978) vii–x. On Lucifer's two companions in the delegation, see PCBE II.2 1581–2 (Pancratius 1); PCBE II.1 985–6 (Hilarius 1).

152 The text of this letter can be found at Diercks (1978) 319 and is translated in Flower (2013) 240–41.

153 The narrative of events presented by Athanasius at *Hist. Ar.* 41.1 gives the impression that the exile of the presbyter and deacon occurred shortly after that of the bishops. A letter from Liberius to Eusebius, Dionysius and Lucifer, probably sent soon after these events took place, is preserved by Hilary at *Adu. Val. et Ursac.* B.VII.1–2. On Lucifer at the Council

His case was obviously quite well known, since, unlike Hilary, he came to the attention of Athanasius, who mentions him several times.[154] He was sent to the eastern part of the empire, first to Germanicia, a city to the north of Antioch and the see of Eudoxius, then to Palestine and finally to the Thebaid in Egypt.[155] After the death of Constantius, Lucifer, like Athanasius, was able to leave his exile through the amnesty issued by the emperor Julian.[156] While his fellow exile Eusebius of Vercelli joined Athanasius at a council in Alexandria, Lucifer travelled to Antioch, where he intervened in the existing dispute among the city's Christians in a manner that was not necessarily particularly helpful: although there were already two rival bishops – Euzious and Meletius – Lucifer exacerbated the situation by consecrating a pro-Nicene character called Paulinus as bishop, thereby creating a three-way contest for the episcopal see.[157] After this he returned to the West and died in Sardinia in around 370 or 371. A group of rigorist Nicene Christians known as Luciferians sprang up as his followers and were criticised by Jerome in his *Altercatio Luciferiani et orthodoxi* (*Dispute between a Luciferian and an Orthodox Person*).[158]

A number of polemical works by Lucifer are extant. All appear to have been composed during the bishop's exile and it is widely believed that the *Moriundum esse pro dei filio*, or *The Necessity of Dying for*

of Milan, as well as the references given above, see also Diercks (1978) x–xiii; Brennecke (1984) 164–95, esp. 182–92; Hanson (1988) 332–4; Corti (2004) 63–85; Laconi (2004) 38–9. As is mentioned in n. 49 above, there is no evidence of a replacement for Lucifer being appointed to the see of Cagliari at this time, but that does not mean that he was not formally deposed from this office by the council.

154 Lucifer appears, always discussed alongside Paulinus of Trier, Dionysius of Milan and Eusebius of Vercelli, at *Hist. Ar.* 33.6, 41.1, 46.3, 76.3. Hilary also mentions the four bishops together at *In Const.* 2.

155 The evidence for Lucifer's exile, including the succession of places that he was sent to, is discussed clearly at Diercks (1978) xiii–xviii. See also Meloni (2001); Corti (2004) 136–47. On Eudoxius, who was successively the bishop of Germanicia, Antioch and Constantinople, see pp. 14, 17–18 above.

156 Ammianus Marcellinus attributed Julian's policy for exiled bishops to the emperor's view that most Christians were worse than wild beasts in their ferocity towards each other, meaning that his amnesty would sow factional dissent among them: see Amm. 22.5.4. It is not clear whether this represents Julian's actual intention or merely Ammianus' reconstruction of it, but Lucifer's rhetoric and behaviour might be seen as an extreme example of this intra-Christian hostility.

157 Hanson (1988) 509; Barnes (1993) 155–6.

158 On the later years of Lucifer's life and the subsequent schism, see Diercks (1978) xxvii–xxxiv. The Luciferians also feature at Augustine, *De haeresibus* 81.

the Son of God, was the last of his major works to be written.[159] In chapter 11 Lucifer mentions the establishment of Eudoxius as bishop of Constantinople, which means that the work must postdate the council held in that city in January 360, and so it is likely to have been composed very close to the time that Hilary was writing the *In Constantium*. Lucifer's prose style is quite opaque, with very long sentences and convoluted word order and syntax combined with some rhetorical flourishes, including a fondness for asyndeton.[160] The overriding theme of the text is Lucifer's own presentation of his 'persecution' by Constantius and his profession of his willingness to undergo martyrdom for the sake of his Nicene faith. As Hilary does in his own diatribe, Lucifer addresses the emperor directly in the second person throughout the work. There is less 'serious' historical and theological discussion in the *Moriundum* compared with the polemics of Athanasius and Hilary, but the work is impressive for the sustained and vitriolic nature of the invective hurled at Constantius, particularly in the characterisation of him throughout the text as a violent persecutor.[161] Amongst other things, the emperor is described as the precursor to the Antichrist, an imitator of Judas, a 'worm of Arius' and resembling an ulcer, as well as being an inhuman monster, a rabid dog, a devourer of innocents and 'an egregious idiot'.[162] Lucifer also makes sarcastic references to Constantius' supposed imperial virtues, such as prudence and piety, in order to demonstrate their absence, as well as inverting the forms of praise found in panegyrics by addressing him as the possessor of superlative vices, using phrases such as 'most brutal emperor', 'most cruel', 'most ignorant' or 'most unjust'.[163] The emperor's current power and happiness is repeatedly described as temporary and insignificant,

---

159 On Lucifer's writings and their chronology, see Diercks (1978) xviii–xxv.

160 I have tried to retain these characteristics in the translation as far as is possible, but have, through necessity, broken up some sentences and rearranged their structure. Modern editions do not provide any paragraph breaks in the text beyond dividing it into fifteen chapters, but I have split these up into paragraphs to make it easier to read.

161 There is, however, some mention of recent events, including the violence in Alexandria, as well as criticism of 'Arians' for denying that Christ is the 'true Son' of the Father and co-eternal with him.

162 Precursor of the Antichrist: 1.30; imitator of Judas: 2.12, 11.71–2; worm of Arius: 4.31; ulcer: 2.33, 11,1–2; inhuman monster: 5.31–2, 6.16, 9.6; rabid dog: 12.76; devourer of innocents: 6.52; egregious idiot: 6.5.

163 Prudence: 4.13, 7.7; piety: 4.59; most brutal emperor: 2.40; most cruel emperor: 3.22; most ignorant emperor: 4.41 (as well as a similar phrase at 14.1); most unjust persecutor: 14.27.

as are the sufferings of the orthodox, and these are contrasted with the eternal joys that await the blessed in heaven and the eternal punishments that will come to Constantius and the other 'Arians'.

Like Lucifer's other works, the *Moriundum* makes extensive use of quotations from the Bible, although it contains a smaller percentage of scriptural texts than the bishop's other treatises.[164] What is more notable, however, is that Lucifer also incorporated a large number of sentences and phrases from works by, or attributed to, the third-century bishop and martyr Cyprian of Carthage and the early fourth-century Christian rhetorician Lactantius into his text, as well as quoting the same biblical passages that were used by these authors to support their arguments.[165] The writings that he uses here are mostly concerned with the persecution of Christians by secular authorities, especially pagan Roman emperors, and so are well suited to Lucifer's main argument in this text.[166] These largely appear in the same order as they do in the source texts, implying that he was reading the books as he wrote, but he never acknowledges his sources, although he does adapt the grammar of the material to fit his context, such as by changing a third-person reference to a persecutor into

164 On Lucifer's engagement with the Bible, see Piras (2001). His quotations from Scripture across his works are tabulated at Diercks (1978) 331–62, while a list for the *Moriundum* is provided at Laconi (1998) 435–6.

165 These quotations appear in the indices of sources given by Diercks (1978) 363–4 and Laconi (1998) 437–8, as well as being tabulated by Merk (1912) 22–4, 26–32; Ferreres (1977) 110–15, Ugenti (1980) 155–6 and Laconi (1998) 437–8. There are variations between the different scholars' lists, and also between theirs and my own. As well as a few scattered allusions to other texts, there are also five passages that probably draw on a brief section of the *Tractatus Origenis* attributed to Lucifer's contemporary, Gregory, bishop of Elvira in Spain, although there is also the (less likely) possibility that the textual influence may have run in the opposite direction. The relevant section of the *Tractatus Origenis* comes at the end of the discussion of the Book of Daniel and is, like the other texts used by Lucifer, concerned with the celebration of martyrdom. At *Tractatus Origenis* 18.22, there is also the statement *pro deo, pro sacris legibus moriendum est* ('it is necessary to die for God, for the sacred laws'), which bears some resemblance to the title of Lucifer's work.

166 I have provided references and translations for the relevant passages in footnotes at the appropriate points, as well as giving extra information about their original context where necessary. A full list is provided as an index on pp. 224–5. The majority of the passages are drawn from three sources: book 5 and the start of book 6 of Lactantius' *Divine Institutes*, which are mostly concerned with justice, piety and the character of true religious behaviour; Cyprian's *Ep.* 6, 10, 55 and 58, all of which are addressed to confessors and martyrs or discuss their experiences; and the pseudo-Cyprianic *De laude martyrii*, which, as its name suggests, praises Christian martyrdom in the face of imperial persecution and presents it as a sure and certain means of attaining eternal life in heaven.

a second-person jibe at Constantius.[167] Lucifer's work also differs from those of Hilary and Athanasius because of the suggestion that the intended audience for this libellous *libellus* may have been the emperor himself. Jerome claims that the bishop sent polemical writings to the emperor and there is also extant a pair of letters that purport to be between Lucifer and the *magister officiorum* Florentius, in which the former assures that the latter that he is the author of the works transmitted to the emperor under his name.[168] Assuming that these letters are genuine and do indeed refer to Lucifer's more inflammatory works, including the *Moriundum*, it nonetheless seems unlikely that Florentius or any other imperial official deigned to pass them on to Constantius himself. Certainly, Lucifer did not suffer any further harsh punishment from the emperor or receive the martyr's death that he looked forward to with such great enthusiasm throughout this work. It would be sensible to assume that, like Hilary, who also used second-person forms of address extensively, Lucifer's works were circulated to an audience that extended beyond Constantius, if it included him at all.[169]

INVECTIVE, IMPERIAL CRITICISM AND SELF-PRESENTATION

As has already been mentioned, these texts are united not only by their theological opposition to Constantius II but also by their polemical tone and the personal invective that they direct towards the emperor.[170] The *Historia Arianorum* and *In Constantium* have, therefore, tended to be studied less than other works by Athanasius and Hilary, while Lucifer, whose writings are all pervaded by fierce criticism of his opponents, has received relatively little attention at all. Modern scholarship is, in fact, littered with remarks about these texts that range from the embarrassed to the highly critical or

167 On this phenomenon within the *Moriundum* and its significance, see Flower (2013) 115–17, 163–76.

168 Jerome, *De uiris illustr.* 95.2. The exchange of letters can be found at Diercks (1978) 305.

169 Laconi (2002) 227 and (2004) 119–20 accepts the idea that Constantius was the main intended audience for Lucifer's writings.

170 For a more in-depth discussion of the themes and rhetorical tropes of these texts, see Flower (2013) esp. 78–177. Individual examples of all of the points discussed here are highlighted in the notes throughout the translations of the three texts below.

even the outright polemical.[171] Nonetheless, like panegyrics, which used to be dismissed in equally violent terms, these invectives have begun to be taken more seriously and to be understood as engagements with the rhetorical and political culture of the time.[172] Although there are idiosyncrasies in the arguments and rhetoric employed by the three authors, they all take the recognisable tropes of imperial panegyric and invert them to create an image of Constantius as a paradigmatic tyrant. He is therefore presented not as having come from a noble lineage, as he would have been in a speech of praise, but either as the heir to a persecuting genealogy or as standing in stark contrast to his relatives, Constantine I and Constans, who are transformed into paragons of piety.[173] He is also depicted as lacking a number of stock virtues that are recognisable from contemporary panegyrics, including justice, manliness, wisdom and self-control, thereby making him out to be a textbook example of a villain. Just as panegyric created a portrait of an ideal emperor and proclaimed that the current ruler embodied it, so these invectives turned this concept on its head and thus presented Constantius as the epitome of vicious tyranny.

These texts do, however, also represent a departure from the contemporary political discourse of the time, which was still primarily rooted in the 'classical' literary tradition for its *exempla* of heroes and villains. Instead of comparing Constantius and other 'Arians' to figures from 'pagan' mythology or Greek and Roman history, these authors chose examples from the Old and New Testaments, such as Ahab or Judas.[174] When they did mention individuals from Roman history, including those such as Nero who were widely regarded as tyrants, these men were invoked not as exemplifying traditional vices, as they might have been in contemporary

171 A good example is the statement at Hanson (1988) 323 that Lucifer's writings consist of 'one continued shrill monotone of abuse'. For more discussion of such negative responses, particularly to Lucifer, see Flower (2013) 7–8, 85 n. 26.

172 For an eye-opening survey of scholarly attitudes to Roman panegyric since the early twentieth century, see Rees (2012) 15–16.

173 This is one area where a notable difference is visible in the treatment of Constantine I by Lucifer and by the other two authors. While Athanasius and Hilary exalted him as a staunch defender of the Nicene cause who did not interfere autocratically in church affairs, thereby making Constantius an unworthy heir to him, Lucifer focused on Constantine's later years to present him as an impious supporter of 'Arians', which meant that his son could be seen as a chip off the heretical block. On this issue, see n. 86 to Lucifer, *Moriundum* 5 at p. 158 below, as well as Humphries (1997) and Flower (2013) 90–94.

174 Ahab: Ath. *Hist. Ar.* 45.5, 53.3, 68.1. Judas: Ath. *Hist. Ar.* 64.3; Hilary, *In Const.* 10; Lucifer, *Moriundum* 2.12, 11.71–2, 15.53.

political discourse, but specifically as persecutors of Christians, placed alongside figures such as the third-century emperor Decius.[175] Within these texts the classical heritage is replaced by, or sometimes subsumed within, a distinctively Christian conception of history that connects biblical time with the authors' own day, presenting contemporary circumstances as continuations or repetitions of situations and conflicts from a sanctified past. Unsurprisingly, the traditional imperial virtue of *pietas* is also promoted to a prime position in these texts' portraits of the ideal emperor, with an individual ruler's piety being assessed almost exclusively by the criterion of how he treats good, Nicene Christians, especially bishops such as our three authors.

While the negative characterisation of Constantius is a core theme of these works, they are also striking in their promotion of the authors as fearless champions in the fight against heresy and persecution. Writing an invective describing – or even addressed to – a living emperor was a highly unusual action, and these texts represent the earliest surviving examples from the Roman world. The very act of authoring such a work functioned as a proclamation of the writer's brave stand against the oppressive force of tyranny, thereby demonstrating that he possessed the vital characteristic of *parrhesia* ('freedom of speech') that was often prized in antiquity, especially amongst those who wished to be regarded as philosophers.[176] For Athanasius, Hilary and Lucifer, this willingness to speak truth to power was also intrinsically linked to the confessors and martyrs who had opposed a number of persecuting Roman emperors during the preceding centuries, as well as being evident in earlier heroic figures who had objected to impious rulers in the narratives of the Old and New Testaments. Thus, for example, Hilary compared himself to John the Baptist addressing Herod, presenting his own prohibitions to a ruler as paralleling this biblical episode.[177] Much of the rhetoric of these texts centred on portraying Constantius' ecclesiastical policy as equivalent to, or even worse than, the earlier rounds of persecution of the Christians, with detailed claims being made about the violent punishments that had been inflicted on the faithful, or which were being planned by the anti-Christian emperor and his 'Arian' assistants such as Ursacius and Valens. The authors and their theological allies were

175 Nero: Hilary, *In Const.* 4, 7, 8, 11.
176 See, in particular, the numerous references to this quality that are noted in the translations below, especially in Athanasius' work, along with n. 128 to *Hist. Ar.* 34.1 at p. 67.
177 See *In Const.* 6.

therefore cast as successors to the prophets, saints and martyrs who had opposed previous enemies of the true faith, since they too were willing to stand up for their beliefs, even if it meant that they suffered exile and, so they claimed, might even face death.[178] By writing themselves into these recognisable narratives of good versus evil, of piety versus impiety, they therefore invited their audience to perceive contemporary events not as reified theological disputes between groups of Christians but as continuations of the fundamental conflict against the sacrilegious and the heretical that pervaded all of sacred history. Only by choosing to embrace the authors' own positions could their readers be sure of staying on the side of the angels.

NOTES ON THE TRANSLATIONS

The translations in this volume use the texts as printed in the following critical editions, except for a small number of points of variation that are marked in the footnotes:

• Athanasius of Alexandria, *Historia Arianorum*: H. G. Opitz (ed.) (1935–41) *Athanasius: Werke* II.1, Berlin, 183–230.

• Hilary of Poitiers, *In Constantium*: A. Rocher (ed.) (1987) *Hilaire de Poitiers: Contre Constance*, Sources chrétiennes 334, Paris.

• Lucifer of Cagliari, *Moriundum esse pro dei filio*: G. F. Diercks (ed.) (1978) *Luciferi Calaritani opera quae supersunt*, CCSL 8, 265–300. (References to this work are given according to the numbering of chapters and, where appropriate, lines in Diercks' edition. It has not been possible to incorporate these line numbers into the translation owing to the need to restructure many of Lucifer's long and complex sentences.)

Where possible, I have used the King James Version for quotations from the Bible, although sometimes this has been adapted for clarity or to reflect details of the biblical text as reproduced by the three authors. All biblical quotations in the texts appear in italics.

---

178 This expectation of martyrdom is undoubtedly strongest in Lucifer's writings, with the opening of *Moriundum* 14 being particularly striking in this regard.

ATHANASIUS OF ALEXANDRIA

History of the Arians (*Historia Arianorum*)

1.1   Not much later, these men carried out the schemes that they had devised.[1] They laid their plans at once and immediately received the Arians into communion.[2] They disregarded the many judgements against them and also falsely claimed imperial authority for those same men.[3] In their writings, they were not ashamed to say 'Now that Athanasius has suffered punishment, envy has come to an end, so let us now receive the Arians', adding, to frighten their hearers, 'for the emperor has ordered it'.[4] **2** They also were not ashamed to add the claim that these men held correct beliefs, without fearing the words of Scripture: *Woe unto them that call bitter sweet, that put darkness for light.*[5] For they are prepared to do anything for heresy. For doesn't this make it clear to everyone that we suffered before, and are persecuted now, not by an ecclesiastical verdict, but by the emperor's threat,

---

1   The text opens with the events immediately after the Council of Tyre in 335, at which Athanasius had been condemned by his opponents, who are the men referred to here. It is generally assumed that the start of the text has been lost: see Opitz (1935–41) 183; Barnes (1993) 126. However, Robertson (1892) 266 argued that the text is complete and is designed to pick up from the end of Athanasius' *Apologia contra Arianos*, a view which finds approval in Gwynn (2007) 41 n. 96. On the events of the 'Arian controversy' leading up to this point, as well as those narrated in this text, see Introduction pp. 2–14.

2   On the Alexandrian presbyter Arius, treated as the founder of the 'Arian heresy', see Introduction p. 2. The term 'Arians' translates οἱ περὶ Ἄρειον, which could also be rendered as 'associates of Arius'. On Athanasius' polemical construction of both 'Arians' and 'Eusebians', referring to the associates of Eusebius, bishop of Nicomedia, see Gwynn (2007).

3   Arius and his views had been condemned at the Council of Nicaea in 325. Athanasius here seeks to distance the emperor Constantine from any possible accusation of having supported Arians.

4   The statements attributed to Athanasius' enemies in this text should not be taken as quotations, since they reflect Athanasius' own polemical view of events. See, for example, the comments attributed to 'the Eusebians' and 'the Arians' at 9.2–3, 15.5, 30.1–2, 42.2–3 and 45.3, and to Constantius at 33.7.

5   *Isaiah* 5.20.

because of our piety towards Christ?[6] For in fact they plotted against other bishops in the same way, inventing false allegations against them as well: some of them died in exile, with the pride of a confession for Christ, while others are still in exile even now, and are acting even more courageously against the heresy of those men and saying 'nothing will separate us from the love of Christ'.[7]

2.1 It is therefore possible to examine this heresy closely and, indeed, to condemn it: for any friend of these men and comrade in their impiety, even if he is liable to myriad accusations for other offences, even if there is the clearest evidence and proof against him, as soon as he gets their approval, through his impiety he immediately gets an introduction to the emperor and becomes his friend. This man is then granted many gifts and adopts the freedom to do whatever he wants before the judges.[8] **2** But if anyone who refutes their impiety and truly upholds the cause of Christ, even if he is completely innocent, even if he has nothing on his conscience and does not even have an accuser, those men invent false allegations against him and he is immediately seized and exiled by the emperor's judgement, as though he were guilty of whatever they wanted, or as though he insulted the king, like Naboth.[9] **3** An advocate of their heresy is then looked for and immediately sent into the church of the exiled man. Then there are confiscations of property, acts of violence and all sorts of terrible deeds against those who will not

6 On the language of persecution in this and the other texts in this volume, see Introduction pp. 36–7. The reference to an ecclesiastical verdict here is an allusion to Athanasius' condemnation at the Council of Tyre in 335 and subsequent judgements made against him, which he did not regard as valid: see Introduction p. 21. 'Piety' in this context refers to Athanasius' view of his own orthodoxy, while 'impiety' is frequently used by him to refer to the 'heresy' of his opponents.

7 At the time of writing, probably in 357, Athanasius himself was in exile, as were a number of other bishops, including Paulinus of Trier, Lucifer of Cagliari, Eusebius of Vercelli and Dionysius of Milan, all of whom Athanasius mentions at 33.6 and 76.3 below. Hilary of Poitiers was also in exile at this time, although Athanasius seems to have been unaware of him. On the circumstances of these bishops' exiles, see Introduction pp. 10–11.

8 'Freedom' here translates the term παρρησία, which Athanasius often treats as a positive quality possessed by those who speak out against tyranny, although here it is employed pejoratively. See n. 128 to chapter 34.1 below. The term 'judge' is being used to translate δικαστής here, although elsewhere in this text it is rendered as 'local official' based on context.

9 For the story of Naboth, who was falsely accused of insulting God and king Ahab, see *1 Kings* 21 (20 LXX).

accept him.[10] **4** And what is most incredible is that the first man, whom the people want and recognise as blameless, is removed and exiled by the emperor, while the second man, whom they neither want nor recognise, is sent from afar by the emperor with soldiers and his letters.[11] And then they suffer great compulsion to hate the one they love, who taught them and was their father in the worship of God, and to love the one they don't want, and entrust their own children to this man, although they do not know about his lifestyle, his behaviour or who he is, or, alternatively, to suffer retribution if they do not obey the emperor.

3.1 The impious commit these deeds against the orthodox now – and have done so previously as well – supplying evidence of their wickedness and impiety to everyone everywhere. **2** For let us set aside their accusations against Athanasius: what have the other bishops done? What allegations are there or what dead Arsenius has also been found there?[12] What presbyter Macarius is there among them and what chalice has been fabricated?[13] What Melitian has concocted lies?[14] But from the accusations against the others, so it seems, the charges against Athanasius are revealed to be false. So, from their attempts against Athanasius, it is clear that the accusations against the others have also been fabricated. **3** This heresy has emerged onto the earth as some great beast. Not only does it wound the innocent with words that bite like teeth, but it has also purchased secular authority for its plot. It is incredible that, as I said earlier, none of them is formally accused; or, if he is accused, he either is not brought to trial or, after appearing to receive a hearing, he is found innocent against his accusers, and so the

10 Athanasius is probably referring particularly to the events surrounding his expulsion from Alexandria in 356, as part of an attempt to bring in George 'the Cappadocian' to replace him as bishop. See chapters 47–63, 81 below.

11 The description of the intruding bishop as being 'from afar' refers to the fact that, unlike Athanasius, George was not from Egypt, but rather from Cappadocia.

12 Athanasius had been accused of arranging the murder of Arsenius, bishop of Hypsele. In 334 Constantine set up an investigation, which was halted when Arsenius was found to be alive and well, thereby providing Athanasius with this opportunity for sarcasm. This, and the following allegations, were investigated by a commission sent to the Mareotis, a region near Alexandria in Egypt. On these events, see Introduction p. 21 and Ath. *Apol. c. Ar.* 65; Barnes (1993) 21–3.

13 Another accusation made against Athanasius in the 330s was that his presbyter Macarius had smashed a chalice belonging to the priest Ischyras: see Ath. *Apol. c. Ar.* 63–4; Barnes (1993) 21, 27–8.

14 The Melitians were a set of rigorist schismatics in Egypt who were involved in the accusations against Athanasius in the 330s: see Introduction p. 6 n. 16.

prosecutor is plotted against, rather than the guilty man actually shamed. **4** All their people are full of filth, and their 'spies' (for they are not 'bishops') are actually the filthiest of all.[15] If any of them wants to be a bishop, he does not hear '*A bishop must be blameless*',[16] but only 'Hold beliefs that are opposed to Christ and don't worry about your behaviour, for this is sufficient to get you an introduction and the friendship of the emperor.' **5** These are the actions of those who follow the beliefs of Arius; but those who strive for the truth, even if they are seen to be holy and pure, as I said earlier, are transformed into guilty men whenever those other men wish it and with whatever accusation they want to fabricate. As I said earlier, this can be discerned from their actions.

4.1   A certain Eustathius, a confessor and pious in his faith, was bishop of Antioch.[17] Since he strove vehemently for the truth, hated the Arian heresy and would not accept its followers, he was slandered before the emperor Constantine and it was falsely alleged that he had insulted the emperor's mother.[18] He was immediately exiled, as were many presbyters and deacons along with him. **2** Then, after the bishop was exiled, those responsible admitted others into the Church – men that Eustathius had not accepted into the clergy because of their impiety – and even appointed most of them as bishops so that they might have fellow-conspirators for their impiety. Among them were Leontius the eunuch, who is now at Antioch, and Stephen who was there before him, and also George of Laodicea, and Theodosius, who was at Tripolis, and Eudoxius at Germanicia and Eustathius, who is now at Sebasteia.[19]

---

15 Athanasius is here making a pun on the similarity between the words ἐπίσκοπος ('bishop') and κατάσκοπος ('spy'). See also the same pun at chapters 48.3 and 75.3 below.

16 *1 Timothy* 3.2.

17 Eustathius of Antioch, who attended the Council of Nicaea in 325, was deposed at a council held in his city, probably in 327, under the leadership of Eusebius of Caesarea. On these events, including the dating of the council at Antioch, see Barnes (1993) 17; Gwynn (2007) 141–3. The term 'confessor' was used to refer to a person who had confessed their faith under persecution and so had suffered at the hands of the pagan authorities.

18 Constantine's mother was Helena, the first wife of Constantius I. Athanasius consistently portrays Constantine in a positive light, unlike his son Constantius II, with any hostile actions by the former being excused as having been carried out through the trickery of his malicious advisers: see Flower (2013) 90–92.

19 On Athanasius' presentation of a concerted 'Arian' purge of their enemies in this and other passages, see Gwynn (2007) 137–47. Leontius of Antioch died in late 357, so this text must have been written either before then or at least before the news reached Athanasius in Egypt. He was replaced as bishop by Eudoxius of Germanicia, who went on to become

5.1 So did they stop at this point? No. For Eutropius was bishop of Adrianople, a good man and perfect in all respects; because he often refuted Eusebius and advised visitors not to be persuaded by Eusebius' impious words, he suffered the same fate as Eustathius and was expelled from both the city and the church.[20] For Basilina was the one who acted with great zeal against him.[21] **2** Moreover, Euphration of Balaneia, Cymatius of Paltus, Carterius of Antaradus, Asclepas of Gaza, Cyrus of Beroea in Syria, Diodorus of Asia, Domnion of Sirmium and Hellanicus of Tripolis were merely known to hate the heresy, but those men banished them with imperial letters, some with a pretext, some without. They expelled them from their cities and, in place of them, appointed in their churches other men, whom they knew to be impious.[22]

6.1 Perhaps it is unnecessary to talk about Marcellus, the bishop of Galatia, since everyone knows how the Eusebians, after previously being accused of impiety by him, brought a counter-charge against the old man and caused his exile.[23] **2** He went up to Rome, presented his defence and, since they demanded it, he also gave a written statement of his faith, which the council at Serdica accepted;[24] but the Eusebians neither presented any

bishop of Constantinople in 360. On the circumstances of Leontius replacing Stephen in 344, see the story at 20 below.

20 The Eusebius mentioned here is Eusebius of Nicomedia, who was later to become bishop of Constantinople, rather than his namesake, the ecclesiastical historian and bishop of Caesarea. Eutropius of Adrianople is not a very notable figure, although he appears again, alongside Eustathius of Antioch, in a list of exiled bishops at Ath. *De fuga* 3.3.

21 Basilina was the wife of Julius Constantius, one of the sons of Constantius I, as well as being the mother of the emperor Julian. She died soon after Julian's birth in the early 330s: see Julian, *Misopogon* 352b. Eusebius of Nicomedia played some part in Julian's upbringing and was a relative of his, probably on his mother's side: see Amm. 22.9.4; PLRE I 148 (Basilina).

22 These are not famous figures from the controversies of this period. Euphration, Cymatius, Carterius, Asclepas and Cyrus all appear together in Ath. *De fuga* 3.3. Diodorus was bishop of Tenedos: see PCBE III 218 (Diodôros). Honigmann (1953) 36–8 suggests amending Opitz' text to add Cymatius of Gabala to the list of exiled bishops.

23 On Athanasius' designation of his opponents as 'the Eusebians' (οἱ περὶ Εὐσέβιον), see n. 2 to chapter 1.1 above.

24 Marcellus of Ancyra was first deposed at Constantinople in 336, returned to Ancyra after Constantine's death in 337 and was then expelled again shortly afterwards, not arriving in Rome until perhaps 340. He received help from Julius, bishop of Rome, and was exculpated by the 'western' bishops at the Council of Serdica in 343, although the 'easterners' continued to regarded him as a heretic: see Barnes (1993) 56–62, 71–7. On the theological views of Marcellus and his role in the controversies of this period, see Lienhard (1999), Parvis (2006).

defence nor, after they were convicted as impious from their writings, did they feel ashamed, but instead they became more confident against everyone. For they received an introduction to the emperor through the women, and were regarded with fear by all.[25]

7.1 I assume that no one is unaware of Paul, bishop of Constantinople.[26] For the more distinguished a city is, the less hidden are the events there. An allegation was also invented against him. For Macedonius, who is now bishop in place of him, accused him – I was present at the time of the accusation – although he had entered into communion with Paul and was a presbyter under him.[27] **2** Nevertheless, because Eusebius was looking on enviously, wishing to seize the episcopacy of the city (for he transferred from Berytus to Nicomedia in this way), the accusation continued against Paul, and they did not neglect their plot, but kept on slandering him.[28] **3** He was first exiled to Pontus by Constantine, and then on the second occasion he was bound with iron chains and was exiled to Singara in Mesopotamia by Constantius; next he was transferred to Emesa from there, and then on the fourth occasion to Cucusus in Cappadocia, near the wastelands of Taurus, where, as his companions reported, he was strangled by those men

25 On the topos of being controlled by women in invectives against Constantius II, see Flower (2013) 103–4.

26 Paul became bishop of Constantinople either late in the reign of Constantine or early in the reign of Constantius, after the death of the previous incumbent, Alexander. He was soon deposed, but later attempted to return and was ejected from the city on a number of occasions, eventually being imprisoned and then killed in 350, possibly for engaging in correspondence with the western usurper Magnentius. For a detailed reconstruction of his career, revising the traditional chronology and placing his election in mid–late 337, see Barnes (1993) 212–17, largely accepted, but with some caution, at Gwynn (2007) 27 n. 52, 140. The reconstruction of events is complicated further by the fact that this story appears in Athanasius' narrative before the mention of the death of Constantine in May 337 and the recall of the exiled bishops (in chapter 8.1 below).

27 Macedonius became the 'Arian' bishop of Constantinople after the death of the incumbent Eusebius (formerly bishop of Nicomedia) in 341: see Soc. *HE* 2.12; Barnes (1993) 68. Barnes also proposes (at 216) that this passage refers to Macedonius supporting Paul at the time of his first deposition in 337 (when Athanasius was present) and then making an accusation against him in 342, when he was elected bishop himself. This is possible, although Athanasius may also simply be stating that Macedonius had not been an opponent of Paul before the accusation in 337, but had actually been an ally of his, thereby making his betrayal of his bishop an even greater crime.

28 Eusebius of Nicomedia became bishop of Constantinople shortly after the death of Constantine in 337: see Barnes (1993) 36; Gwynn (2007) 118–19.

and died.[29] **4** However, after they had done this, these men, who never speak the truth, were not ashamed to invent another lie after his death, claiming that he died from a disease, even though everyone who lives there knows what happened. **5** And in fact Philagrius, who was then *vicarius* of those regions and was joining them in all their falsehoods in whatever way they wanted, was nonetheless amazed at this.[30] Perhaps he was aggrieved that someone else had performed this evil deed, rather than him. He reported to Serapion the bishop, and also to many others of our friends, that Paul was imprisoned by them in an extremely confined and dark space and left to die of starvation.[31] But when they went in after six days and found him still breathing, they then attacked the man and strangled him. So he ended his life in this way. **6** They said that Philip the prefect was the murderer.[32] But divine justice did not overlook this:[33] for, before a year had passed, Philip was deprived of his position with great dishonour and so, having become a private citizen, he was ridiculed by people that he did not want

29 I have here followed the text of Opitz for the translation, but it is important to note that two emendations have been proposed at Barnes (1993) 215–16 as part of his reconstruction of the career of Paul of Constantinople. Opitz's text states that the first exile was 'by Constantine' (ὑπὸ Κωνστατίνου – with a ν missed out erroneously), but Barnes argues that this must be a corruption of 'by Constantius' (παρὰ Κωνσταντίου), since he believes that Paul did not become bishop until after Constantine's death. His second suggested emendation refers to the second exile, altering 'by Constantius' (παρὰ Κωνσταντίου) to 'to Constantius' (παρὰ Κωνστάντιον), arguing that on the occasion of his deposition in 349 Paul was transferred to Constantius' court, which was then at Singara. Gwynn (2007) 139 regards Barnes' first emendation as plausible (at n. 21), but does not accept either change in the translation given in his main text. Since the chronology of Paul's various exiles is opaque, it is difficult to be certain about this matter and for this reason I have retained Opitz's reading here, but readers should give serious consideration to Barnes' suggestions, especially the first proposed emendation. Taurus is a mountain range in Asia Minor.

30 For the *vicarius*, a late Roman civilian official, see the Glossary. Philagrius had previously been Prefect of Egypt at the time of both the commission in the Mareotis to investigate the early accusations against Athanasius in 335 and also his expulsion from the city in 339: see chapter 9.3 below, as well as Ath. *De fuga* 3, *Apol c. Ar.* 14, 72, 75–6, *Ep. Enc.* 2–3; Barnes (1993) 45–8; PLRE I 694 (Philagrius 5).

31 Serapion was bishop of Thmuis, in Egypt, and a loyal helper and correspondent of Athanasius.

32 The Philip referred to here is the Praetorian Prefect of the East, Flavius Philippus, who had been charged with expelling the bishop Paul from Constantinople on an earlier occasion in the 340s and also sent him into exile for the final time: see Soc. *HE* 2,16, 5,9; Barnes (1993) 214–17. Soon after the death of Paul he was sent on an embassy to the usurper Magnentius in Gaul, but failed in his mission and was detained there, where he died. The reconstruction of the final part of his life depends on this passage: see PLRE I 696–7 (Philippus 7).

33 The same phrase about divine justice can also be found at 14.4 below.

mocking him. And so he was distressed and, like Cain, was *moaning and trembling*,[34] separated from his homeland and his family, expecting every day that someone would finish him off; and so, just as though he had been struck, since he did not want it to happen like this, he died. **7** But if these men have invented allegations against people during their lives, they do not even spare them when they are dead: for they were keen to make themselves appear frightening to everyone; they exiled the living and did not pity the dead. But they, alone of all men, hate the departed and plot against their nearest and dearest, being actually inhuman, hating the good and being crueller than enemies. For the sake of their impiety they have been keen to plot against both us and all the others, on the basis not of truth but of their invented allegations.

8.1   The three brothers Constantine, Constantius and Constans saw this and so, after the death of their father, they made everyone return to their own homeland and church. In the case of the others, they wrote individually to the church of each of them, but in the case of Athanasius they wrote these words, which again both reveal the violence of this affair and also convict the Eusebians of murderous intent.[35]

Transcript

8.2   Constantine Caesar to the congregration of the catholic church of the city of the Alexandrians.
I think that it has not escaped the understanding of your religious sense that on this account Athanasius, the expounder of the worshipful law …
{The text is given below without any alterations in the seventy-fifth book.}[36]

This is what was written, and what other more trustworthy witness of their plot could there be than Constantine? For what he wrote corresponded precisely to what he knew.

---

34 *Genesis* 4.12 LXX.

35 Constantine II, Constantius II and Constans, the sons of Constantine, succeeded their father, Constantine I, after his death in 337. For the circumstances of their accession, together with the dynastic massacre that accompanied it, see n. 252 to chapter 69.1 below.

36 This letter from Constantine II can be found in Ath. *Apol. c. Ar.* 87.4–7. In it, Constantine II claims that he was fulfilling the wishes of his father in returning Athanasius to Alexandria.

9.1 The Eusebians, however, saw that their heresy was losing ground and so wrote letters to Rome, and also to the emperors Constantine and Constans, against Athanasius. But when the envoys sent by Athanasius refuted their claims, the Eusebians were put to shame by the emperors. Julius, the bishop of Rome, also wrote to say that a council ought to be held, wherever we might wish, so that these men might both air their accusations and also have the confidence to defend themselves from the accusations against them;[37] for the presbyters sent by those men, when they saw that they were being refuted, also requested that this should take place. **2** After this, therefore, these men [the Eusebians], who are suspected in all their dealings, saw that they were not going to win in an ecclesiastical trial; so they went only to Constantius and then complained bitterly, as to the protector of their heresy, and said 'Take pity on the heresy: you see that everyone has abandoned us; now only a few of us are left. Start persecuting, because we are being abandoned by those few as well and are left deserted. For after those men [Athanasius and his 'allies'] were exiled, we overpowered others, but the first group have returned home and have now persuaded the rest to be hostile to us again. **3** Write letters against all of them and send Philagrius as prefect of Egypt for a second time; he is capable of persecuting properly, as he has already demonstrated when tested, and particularly since he is an apostate.[38] In addition, send Gregory to Alexandria as bishop, for he is also capable of establishing our heresy.'[39]

10.1 So then Constantius wrote, and he persecuted everyone and sent Philagrius as prefect, together with a certain eunuch called Arsacius, and he also sent Gregory with military support.[40] And the same things happened as before: for, they assembled a mob of herdsmen, shepherds and other thuggish and insolent young men with swords and clubs, and all at once

37 Julius was bishop of Rome from 337 to 352, and was succeeded by Liberius.

38 On Philagrius, who was prefect of Egypt on two occasions, see n. 30 to chapter 7.5 above.

39 Gregory 'the Cappadocian' was appointed as a rival bishop of Alexandria at a council in Antioch in 338/9 and entered the city with the support of Philagrius in the spring of 339: see Athanasius' tendentious account of these events in his *Epistula Encyclica*, with discussion in Barnes (1993) 45–50; Gwynn (2007) 51–7. As mentioned in n. 4 to chapter 1.1 above, this passage provides an excellent example of Athanasius putting impossible words into the mouths of his enemies. Here 'the Eusebians' are cartoonish villains who call their own actions 'persecution' and their own beliefs 'heresy'.

40 No more is known about the imperial functionary Arsacius: see PLRE I 110 (Arsacius 2).

they attacked the church called 'of Quirinus'.[41] **2** Some they killed, others they trampled underfoot; others again they beat up, threw into prison and sent into exile, while they carried off many women, hauled them publicly into court and dragged them by their hair and maltreated them. Some they stripped of their property, while others they deprived of bread for no reason other than to make them join the Arians and accept Gregory, who had been sent from the emperor.[42]

11.1   But before these things happened and as soon as he heard about them,[43] Athanasius sailed to Rome, because he knew the anger of the heretics, and also so that there might be a council, as had been decided. Julius wrote and sent presbyters, Elpidius and Philoxenus, and fixed the appointed day, so that those men [Athanasius' enemies] would either come to the council or else recognise that they were under suspicion in every respect.[44] **2** But the moment that the Eusebians heard that it was going to be an ecclesiastical trial, with no *comes* in attendance,[45] nor soldiers positioned in front of the doors, and nor would the decisions of the council be made in accordance with an imperial command (for through these methods they always prevailed over the bishops, and without them they are not at all confident to prattle away), they were so terrified that they detained the presbyters beyond the appointed day and invented the unseemly excuse that 'we cannot come now because of the war started by the Persians'.[46] **3** This was not true; the real reason was fear of conscience. For what concern is a war to bishops? Or, if they could not come to Rome because of the Persians, even though it is a long way away and across the sea, why did they then travel around the eastern provinces and the lands near the Persians,

---

41 The exact location of the church of Quirinus in Alexandria is unknown.

42 The bread referred to here is probably a reference to the supply that the bishop of Alexandria received from the emperor to distribute to the needy in the city: see Ath. *Apol. c. Ar.* 18.

43 The expression here is confusing, but would seem to indicate that Athanasius left for Rome during the course of the events narrated in the preceding chapter. See also Ath. *Ep. Enc.* 5.1–2.

44 Athanasius also mentions the dispatch of these two presbyters at *Apol. c. Ar.* 20.1. On Elpidius, see PCBE II.1 968 (Helpidius 1). Philoxenus also acted as one of the representatives of Julius at the Council of Serdica in 343: see Ath. *Apol. c. Ar.* 48.2; PCBE II.2 1795–6 (Philoxenus 1).

45 For the imperial rank of *comes*, see the Glossary.

46 On Constantius' long-running military conflict with Persia at this time, see Hunt (1998) 12–14.

and hunt down their opponents like lions, so that they could slander and exile them?

12.1 And so, after they had dismissed the presbyters with this unconvincing excuse, they said to each other: 'Since we can't prevail in an ecclesiastical trial, let's show off our usual reckless behaviour.'[47] They therefore wrote to Philagrius and made him go out into Egypt a little later with Gregory; bishops were then chained up and whipped harshly.[48] **2** For example, they exiled the bishop and confessor Sarapammon; as for Potamon, the bishop and confessor who had lost an eye in the persecution, they struck him with blows to the neck to such an extent that they did not stop until he seemed to be dead.[49] He was thrown to the ground and only just recovered after a few hours of being tended and fanned, because God gave him life. But a little later he died from the injuries sustained in the beating and so achieved in Christ the glory of a second martyrdom. **3** How many other monks were whipped while Gregory sat there with Valacius, the so-called *dux*![50] How many bishops were beaten! How many virgins were struck!

13.1 After this, the wretched Gregory then called on everyone to be in communion with him: and yet, if you wanted communion with them, they did not deserve beatings; but if you beat them as villains, why did you call on them as holy men?[51] But he had no intention other than to fulfil the plans of those who sent him and to establish their heresy. For this reason this foolish man became a murderer, an executioner, violent, treacherous, profane and, in short, an enemy of Christ.[52] **2** He actually persecuted the

47 Many eastern bishops gathered in Antioch at the start of 341 at the 'Dedication Council', which takes its name from the dedication of the city's new church that took place at the same time. They then sent the two presbyters back to Julius with a letter explaining their decisions. See Introduction pp. 6–7.

48 On Philagrius, see n. 30 to chapter 7.5 above.

49 According to Epiphanius of Salamis, Potamon was bishop of Hieracleopolis in Egypt and spoke out in favour of Athanasius at the Council of Tyre in 335: see Epiphanius, *Panarion* 68.8.

50 On the *dux*, a late Roman military commander, see the Glossary. For the career of Valacius (or Balacius), see PLRE I 929 (Valacius).

51 Athanasius here addresses rhetorical questions to Gregory, who had been dead for more than a decade by the time that the *Historia Arianorum* was written.

52 The term Χριστομάχος ('enemy of Christ') was frequently used by Athanasius and others to describe the 'Arians', as well as being employed as a label for other heretical groups and Jews: see Lampe s.v., as well as chapters 33.6, 38.1, 38.2, 39.2, 47.2, 50.1, 53.1, 55.4,

bishop's aunt by refusing permission for her to be buried when she died. This would have happened and she would have been cast out without burial, if those who received her corpse had not then carried her out as one of their own household. And so in this way he maintained his ungodly character. **3** And, after the widows and other needy folk had received their alms, he even gave orders to snatch back these gifts and break the vessels for the olive oil and the wine, so that he might not only use theft to show his impiety but also by his actions show dishonour to the Lord. He will soon hear this from the Lord: *In as much as you dishonoured them, you dishonoured me.*[53]

14.1   He also committed many other crimes that are beyond description; whoever heard about them would think them unbelievable. He acted in this way because he had not been appointed according to the Church's rules, nor was he named as a bishop in the apostolic succession. Instead he was sent out from the palace with military support and a military procession, as though he were being entrusted with some secular office. For this reason he boasted about being the friend of imperial officials, rather than of bishops and monks. **2** Whenever Father Antony wrote to him from the mountains, he [Gregory] found the holy man's letters abominable, just as the worship of God is an abomination to a sinner.[54] **3** But whenever the emperor or a general or some other official wrote to him, he became overjoyed, just like the people in the Book of Proverbs, where the Word complained bitterly and said: *Woe unto those who leave the paths of uprightness, who rejoice to do evil and delight in the forwardness of the wicked.*[55] **4** And while he rewarded these messengers with gifts, when Antony had written to him, he actually made the *dux* Valacius spit on the letter and throw it away.[56] But divine justice did not overlook this: for a little while later this so-called *dux* was sitting on his horse and heading out to the first staging post when the horse turned around, bit him on the thigh and threw him to the ground; in three days he died.[57]

77.2, 77.3 and 79.3 below. Hilary also calls Constantius' pagan predecessors and ancestors 'enemies of Christ' at *In Const.* 9.

53   cf. *Matthew* 25.45.

54   The monk Antony was a revered figure within Egypt and was celebrated in Athanasius' *Life of Antony*, which added to the prestige of both its subject and its author.

55   *Proverbs* 2.13–14.

56   For the *dux* Valacius, see n. 50 to chapter 12.3 above.

57   This story also appeared with slight variations in Ath. *V. Ant.* 86.1–7: see Kannengiesser (2001) 133. The exact date of the death of Valacius is uncertain: see PLRE I 929 (Valacius). For the same expression about divine justice, see 7.6 above. The phrase 'the first staging

15.1 They acted in this way against everyone, but about fifty bishops assembled at Rome and refused to accept the Eusebians, since they were under suspicion and were afraid to come.[58] They [the bishops at Rome] also rejected what those men had written, but they accepted us and embraced our communion. **2** While this was taking place, the council at Rome and the actions against the churches in Alexandria and the whole of the East came to the attention of the emperor Constans. He wrote to his brother Constantius and they both resolved to hold a council and investigate these matters thoroughly, so that the wronged would not suffer any longer, and the wrong-doers would no longer be able to act with such temerity.[59] **3** And so around 170 bishops from both East and West assembled in the city of Serdica.[60] The western delegation was composed solely of bishops, with Ossius as their father, but the eastern delegation brought the *comes* Musonianus and the *castrensis* Hesychius as instructors and advocates.[61] For this reason they came readily, thinking that everything would again be carried out through their authority. With the help of these men they always made themselves terrifying to those they wished to terrify, and plotted against whomever they pleased. **4** But they arrived and saw only an ecclesiastical trial; they saw accusers from every church and city and evidence against them; they saw the honourable bishops Arius and

post' refers to the first stop on the journey inland from Alexandria, at a place called Chaereu on the branch of the Nile that runs to Alexandria: see Ath. *V. Ant.* 86.

58 This council met at Rome in 341 and Julius sent a letter to the bishops who had written to him from the 'Dedication Council' held in Antioch in January 341. Julius' letter can be found at Ath. *Apol. c. Ar.* 20–35.

59 The third brother, Constantine II, had died in 340 after declaring war on Constans, leaving Constans in control of the whole western part of the empire, while Constantius II had the eastern: see Hunt (1998) 5.

60 After Constans wrote to his brother, the Council of Serdica assembled in 343, although the two factions refused to meet together and each issued its own statements, letters and denunciations. See Introduction p. 8 and Barnes (1993) 63–81. Documents from both sides are preserved at Hilary, *Adu. Val. et Ursac.* A.IV, B.II.1–4, *Liber I Ad Constantium* 1–5, as well as Ath. *Apol. c. Ar.* 36–50.

61 Ossius of Cordoba (also known as Hosius) had been an associate of Constantine I and was one of the few western bishops in attendance at the Council of Nicaea in 325. On the *comes* Musonianus, who began his career under Constantine I and went on to be Praetorian Prefect of the East late in the reign of Constantius II, see PLRE I 611–2 (Strategius Musonianus). Hesychius was a *castrensis*, an official in the imperial household, described by Jones as 'majordomo of the palace': see Jones (1964) II 567–9. Hesychius is unattested apart from his role in the Council of Serdica: see PLRE I 429 (Hesychius 1). 'Instructor' here translates παιδαγωγός, which is a term for a person, often a slave, who accompanied a child to school.

Asterius, who arrived with them but then left them and came to us.[62] These bishops described the villainy of these men and related how they were under suspicion for their actions and were afraid there would be a trial, in case they would be convicted both by us, for being false informers, and also by the accusers they had set up falsely, because they themselves had suggested and devised all their lies. They had arrived enthusiastically, because they thought we would be too afraid to attend, but when they saw all this and perceived our eagerness, they locked themselves up in the palace where they were staying. **5** Then they said to each other: 'We came here on certain conditions, but we see that the situation has changed. We came with *comites*, but the trial is happening without *comites*. We're sure to be condemned. You all know your orders. The Athanasians have reports of what happened in the Mareotis, which exonerate him, but put us to shame.[63] So why are we hesitating? Why are we delaying? Let's invent excuses and get away; if we stay we'll be condemned. It is better to run away and be embarrassed than to be convicted and condemned as false accusers. If we run away, we can protect the heresy somehow: even if we run away and they condemn us, the emperor is our protector and will not allow the congregations to expel us from the churches.'[64]

16.1 While they were debating this, Ossius and all the other bishops repeatedly told them that the Athanasians were eager to get started and said, 'They are ready to present their defence and are saying that they will convict you as false accusers' and also 'If you are afraid of a trial, why did you come? You should have either not come at all or come and not run away.' **2** When they heard this, they became even more panic-stricken and used a more shameful excuse than the one in Antioch: they said that they had tried to run away because the emperor had written to them about the celebration of his victory over the Persians.[65] They shamelessly sent this

62 Arius, a bishop from Palestine, and Asterius, from Arabia, left the 'eastern' group at Serdica and joined the 'western' bishops. See 18.3 below.

63 On the commission that investigated accusations against Athanasius in the Mareotis, see n. 12 to chapter 3.2 above. 'The Athanasians' here probably includes not only Athanasius and his supporters, but also the other deposed eastern bishops, including Marcellus of Ancyra and Asclepas of Gaza, who were present at the council and are mentioned in the general letter issued by the 'westerners' at the council: see Hilary, *Adu. Val. et Ursac.* B.II.1.2, B.II.4.

64 On the unrealistic statements put into the mouths of the Arians/Eusebians, see n. 4 to chapter 1.1 above.

65 For the earlier excuse, see 11.2–3 above.

excuse via Eustathius, a presbyter of the church of Serdica.[66] **3** But even so their escape did not go according to plan. Immediately the holy council, with the great Ossius presiding, wrote to them clearly: 'Either come and make your defence for the charges against you and the false accusations you made, or else recognise that the council finds you guilty and declares the Athanasians to be free and innocent of any guilt.' Instead of obeying the letter, they were driven away by fear of conscience: for when they saw the people they had wronged, they did not give a rejoinder to the speakers, but instead ran away all the more quickly.

17.1 While they made this disgraceful and disreputable escape, the holy council, gathered together from more than thirty-five provinces, acknowledged the wickedness of the Arians and allowed the Athanasians to make their defence for their sufferings and the accusations against them. **2** When they had made their defence in the manner we described earlier, the council accepted them and admired them greatly. The council welcomed them and their communion and wrote letters to all places and to the see of each of them, especially to Alexandria, Egypt and the Libyas, to say that Athanasius and those with him were innocent and blameless, while their enemies were false accusers, evildoers and anything but Christians.[67] **3** They dismissed these men in peace, but they deposed Stephen, Menophantus, Acacius, George of Laodicea, Ursacius, Valens, Theodore and Narcissus.[68] As for Gregory, who had been sent to Alexandria from the emperor, they issued a public proclamation that he was not a bishop at all and did not even deserve to be called a Christian. They annulled the ordinations that he had claimed to perform and commanded that these should not be mentioned in the churches at all because of his novel and lawless behaviour.

66 This Eustathius is otherwise unknown.

67 Athanasius refers to the council writing a general letter, as well as then writing specifically to the see of each of the bishops that it had absolved from blame.

68 They were the bishops, respectively, of Antioch, Ephesus, Caesarea, Laodicea, Singidunum, Mursa, Heraclea and Irenopolis/Neronias. These eight bishops are listed as having been condemned in Ath. *Apol. c. Ar.* 36.6 as well as in the 'western' council's letter at *Apol. c. Ar.* 47.3 and Hilary, *Adu. Val. et Ursac.* B.II.1.8 The same list appears, with the exception of Theodore, in their letter to Julius of Rome at Hilary, *Adu. Val. et Ursac.* B.II.3, while all but George appear in the letter to Constantius at *Liber I Ad Constantium* 5. On Menophantus of Ephesus, see *PCBE III* 692–7 (Mènophantos). The episcopal duo of Ursacius of Singidunum and Valens of Mursa feature repeatedly in the later chapters of this text and in the writings of Hilary of Poitiers, where they are presented as leading 'Arians' in the late 340s and 350s: see Introduction p. 9.

18.1   In this way Athanasius and his companions were dismissed in peace (and the letters have been appended to the end because of their length).[69] The council was dissolved; but, although they should have kept quiet, the men who had been deposed, along with those who had returned after their disgraceful escape, performed such terrible deeds that they made their earlier crimes seem small by comparison. **2** When the people of Adrianople refused to enter into communion with them because they had fled the council and had been found guilty, these men appealed to the emperor Constantius. With the help of Philagrius, who was *comes* there again, they had ten members of the congregation from the 'arsenal' beheaded.[70] The funerary monuments of these men stand in front of the city, and we saw them when we passed by. Next, as though they had been victorious, because they ran away to avoid being convicted as false accusers, the emperor told them to do whatever they wanted. **3** So they had two presbyters and three deacons exiled from Alexandria into Armenia. The bishops Arius and Asterius (one from Petra in Palestine, the other from Arabia) who had departed from them were not only exiled into Upper Libya but also subjected to violence.[71]

19.1   When they saw Lucius, bishop of Adrianople, speaking out very freely against them and refuting their impiety, they had his neck and hands bound with iron chains, just as before, and sent him into exile, where he died, as they know.[72] **2** They removed bishop Diodorus and also slandered bishops Olympius of Aeni and Theodoulos of Trajanopolis, both good and orthodox men from Thrace, after they saw that they hated their heresy.[73] The Eusebians had done this first, with the emperor Constantius writing [in support], and these men [who fled the council at Serdica] now repeated it. Their letter said that not only should the orthodox bishops be expelled from their cities and churches, but they should also suffer capital punishment if they were discovered anywhere. **3** If this seems amazing, it is no different

---

69   These letters do not appear at the end of this text, but can be found at Ath. *Apol. c. Ar.* 37–47.

70   Athanasius has here transliterated the Latin word *fabricus*, meaning an arsenal or arms factory, into Greek. On Philagrius, see n. 30 to chapter 7.5 above. On the events described in this and the following chapter, see the discussion in Barnes (1993) 82–6.

71   On these two bishops, who left the 'easterners' at Serdica in 343, see 15.4 above.

72   On the concept of speaking freely, or παρρησία, see n. 128 to chapter 34.1 below.

73   On Diodorus of Tenedos, see 5.2 above. The death of Theodoulos is mentioned in the letter from the 'westerners' at Serdica preserved at Ath. *Apol. c. Ar.* 43.2 and Hilary, *Adu. Val. et Ursac.* B.II.3. Olympius and Theodoulos are also both mentioned at Ath. *De fuga* 3.4–5.

from their usual behaviour; they learned it from the Eusebians and they are heirs of their impiety and attitude.[74] They wanted to appear terrifying in Alexandria, as their fathers had done in Thrace, and they had orders sent that the harbours and entrances of the city were to be watched to stop Athanasius and his associates returning to their churches through the decision of the council. **4** They also had an order sent to the officials in Alexandria, concerning Athanasius and certain named presbyters, saying that an official was authorised to behead the bishop or any of the others if they were discovered having set foot in the city or its surrounding territory. In this way this new Judaic heresy not only denies the Lord, but has also learned to murder.[75]

20.1 Yet even after this they did not stay quiet, but instead acquired the authority to use the *cursus publicus* and travelled around, just as the father of their heresy *goes about as a lion seeking whom he may devour.*[76] Whenever they found someone who criticised them for fleeing the council and hated the Arian heresy, they had them whipped, bound and exiled from their homeland. In this way they made themselves terrifying, and also turned many people into hypocrites and caused many others to run away into the desert to avoid having anything at all to do with them. **2** These were their reckless and insane actions after their escape from the council. They also did something else that was new and entirely appropriate to their heresy, but which had not been heard of before, and will perhaps never happen again, not even among the most shameless of the Hellenes, let alone among Christians.[77] The holy council had sent as its envoys the bishops Vicentius of Capua (which is the metropolis of Campania) and Euphrates of Agrippina (which is the metropolis of Upper Gaul) to ask the emperor

74 Eusebius of Nicomedia had died in 341.

75 On links between Arians and Jews in the polemic of Athanasius, see Lyman (1993) 55; Brakke (2001) 467–75; Gwynn (2007) 172–3; Flower (2013) 189–90.

76 *1 Peter* 5.8. The father of the heresy referred to here is the Devil, who is being described in this biblical passage. The Devil was often regarded as the spiritual father of all heresies. The *cursus publicus*, often referred to as the 'public post', was a system whereby officials, including messengers, could obtain travel and lodgings when moving around the empire on imperial business: see Jones (1964) II 830–34. Constantius was notorious for allowing bishops to use this system when attending councils and is criticised for this practice at Amm. 21.16.18.

77 The term 'Hellenes' here translates οἱ Ἕλληνες, which is also sometimes translated as 'Greeks', 'pagans' or 'gentiles' when it appears in Christian literature. See Johnson (2012) on the semantic range of this term during late antiquity.

to allow the bishops to return to their churches, as the council decided, since he himself had expelled them.[78] The most pious Constans had also written to his brother in support of the bishops. **3** When these staggeringly reckless men saw the envoys in Antioch, they devised a plan together. Stephen alone undertook the deed, since he is suited to such tasks.[79] Even though it was the most holy season of Easter, they hired a public prostitute, stripped her naked and sent her in at night to the bishop Euphrates.[80] **4** At first the prostitute, thinking that a young man had called for her, went along readily. After they had brought her to the room, however, she saw that the man was asleep and unaware of what was happening, and then she saw and recognised the features of an old man and the appearance of a bishop. She immediately called out and complained about this outrageous treatment. They had expected her to keep quiet and then make a false allegation against the bishop. **5** When day came, the story spread quickly and the whole city gathered together. Representatives from the palace were troubled and amazed by the reported story, and so decided that it should not be hushed up. There was an investigation and the pimp gave evidence against the men who had collected the prostitute, and then they in turn gave evidence against Stephen: for they were actually his clerics. Stephen was deposed and Leontius the eunuch was made bishop in his place to ensure that the Arian heresy would not be without a leader.[81]

21.1   Then the emperor Constantius felt his conscience to be pricked a little, and he came to himself and, on the basis of what they did to Euphrates,

78 The council referred to here is the 'western' group at Serdica in 343, while the emperor is Constantius II. Vincentius first appears in the historical record as a presbyter at the Council of Nicaea in 325 and he went on to become bishop of Capua in 341 or 342. He acted as a representative of Liberius of Rome in 353, but eventually agreed to subscribe against Athanasius: see Ath. *Apol. Const.* 27; Hilary, *Adu. Val. et Ursac.* B.VII.5–6; PCBE II.2 2303–5 (Vincentius 1). On Euphrates, bishop of Cologne, see PCBE IV.1 668 (Eufratas). The term 'metropolis' refers to the most important city in a province.

79 For Stephen of Antioch, a leading figure among the 'easterners' at Serdica, see 17.3 above.

80 These events took place at Easter 344, when these two representatives of the 'westerners' at Serdica had arrived in Antioch.

81 On the eunuch Leontius, who was bishop of Antioch at the time that this text was written, see 4.2 above. A fuller, if perhaps rather more fictionalised, version of this episode can be found in Theod. *HE* 2.9–10. For discussion of these events, including the reasonable conclusion that Stephen was deposed at the council held in Antioch in 344 that wrote the 'Long Creed', see Barnes (1993) 87–8. Athanasius may be making a pun when remarking that an ἀπόκοπος (eunuch) had become an ἐπίσκοπος (bishop).

decided that these men's attacks against the others were also of the same sort. He gave orders for the immediate release of the presbyters and deacons who were exiled from Alexandria to Armenia and also wrote a public letter to Alexandria to say that the Athanasian clerics and laity were not to be persecuted any longer.[82] **2** Then, after Gregory died about ten months later, he summoned Athanasius with great honour, and wrote to him in a friendly manner not once or twice, but three times, urging him to take heart and come to him.[83] Constantius also sent a presbyter and a deacon to reinforce Athanasius' confidence and get him to return. He thought that I was neglecting to return because I was afraid after what had happened earlier.[84] **3** In addition, he wrote to his brother Constans so that he would also urge me to return. He affirmed that he had been awaiting Athanasius for a whole year and that he would never permit any innovation or ordination to occur while he was keeping the churches for Athanasius the bishop.

22.1 After he [Constantius] had written and urged him through many others (for he also got his *comites* Polemius, Datianus, Bardio, Thalassius, Taurus and Florentius to write, since Athanasius trusted them more),[85] Athanasius gave the matter over entirely to God, who had

82 This must have taken place in late summer 344, since Gregory, the rival bishop of Alexandria, died on 26 June 345: see *Festal Index* 18. This text, which survives only in Syriac, is translated into English at Robertson (1892) 503–6. There is a critical edition of the text and a French translation in Martin (1985) 224–77.

83 These three letters, written while Athanasius was at Aquileia, are preserved at Ath. *Apol. c. Ar.* 51. There Athanasius presents Constantius' actions as a response to the events at the Council of Serdica in 343. The fifth-century ecclesiastical historians portray Constantius as relenting after a threat of military action by Constans: see Introduction p. 9 and Soc. *HE* 2.22–3; Soz. *HE* 3.20.1–3; Theod. *HE* 2.8.53–5; Rufinus, *HE* 10.20; Philostorgius 3.12, as well as the reconstruction of events at Barnes (1993) 89–91.

84 On a few occasions, such as here and also 7.1 and 18.2, Athanasius slips into the first person, although he usually describes himself in the third person, as he does in most of the rest of this chapter.

85 Polemius is assumed to be the same man who had been consul in 338: see PLRE I 710 (Polemius 4). Datianus was a close adviser of Constantius II and became consul in 358: see PLRE I 243–4 (Datianus 1). Bardio was a court eunuch: see PLRE I 147–8 (Bardio). Thalassius acted as an envoy from Constantius to Constans in 346 and later became Praetorian Prefect of the East: see PLRE I 886 (Thalassius 1). Taurus had a very successful career under Constantius II, becoming Praetorian Prefect of Italy and Africa in the mid-350s and then consul in 361, although he was exiled under Julian: see PLRE I 879–80 (Taurus 3). Florentius went on to be Praetorian Prefect of Gaul during Julian's time as *caesar*, staying loyal to Constantius when Julian rebelled and becoming Taurus' colleague in the consulship of 361, before being condemned *in absentia* under Julian: see PLRE I 365 (Florentius 10).

pricked Constantius' conscience to this end, and so went to him with his companions.[86] Constantius welcomed him affectionately and allowed him to return to his homeland and churches. He also wrote to the local officials in each place and told them to make sure the routes were open, as he had previously instructed them to keep them guarded.[87] **2** The bishop bitterly lamented his sufferings and the hostile things that Constantius had written. He also asked that his enemies should not be allowed to repeat their slanders after his departure, and said 'Summon them, if you wish (for they can stand here on our account), and we will convict them'. The emperor did not do this, but he did order that all the slanderous writings against Athanasius should be destroyed and erased, and declared that he would not put up with slanders any more in the future and that his resolve was firm and unchangeable. **3** He did not simply say this, but also confirmed his words with oaths, calling on God to act as a witness to them. In fact, he encouraged Athanasius with many other statements and exhorted him to be confident, as well as writing these words to the bishops and local officials:

> **23.1**   The victor Constantius the Great, Augustus, to the
> bishops and clerics of the catholic Church.

23.2   The most venerable Athanasius has not been abandoned by God's grace ...
{The text is given below in the sixty-fifth book and is completely identical to this.}[88]

> **23.3**   Another letter

> Constantius to the people of Alexandria.
Keeping watch for your welfare in all respects ...
{The text comes likewise in the same sixty-fifth book and is not reproduced here because there are no differences.}[89]

---

86 This meeting with Constantius took place at Antioch: Ath. *Apol. Const.* 5; Soz. *HE* 3.20.4.

87 See chapter 19.3 above.

88 For the text of this letter, see Ath. *Apol. c. Ar.* 54.2–5. This letter includes the instruction to rescind all earlier rulings against Athanasius. Opitz's text does not include a chapter 23.2, but goes straight from 23.1 to 23.3, so I have inserted this number to fill the gap.

89 For the text of this letter, see Ath. *Apol. c. Ar.* 55. Here Constantius instructs the people of Alexandria to receive Athanasius and not to engage in factional strife.

Another letter

The victor Constantius Augustus to Nestorius, Prefect of Egypt.[90]
It is acknowledged that a previous command was given by us with the consequence that certain letters can be found that are damaging to the reputation of the most venerable bishop Athanasius, and these exist in the register of your sanctity.[91] We therefore wish that your prudence, which has been tested and proved by us, send to our court all the letters that exist in your register concerning the aforesaid individual, in accordance with this our order.

24.1 This is what he wrote after the death of Constans, of blessed memory. It was originally written in Latin and has been translated into Greek:[92]

    24.2 The victor Constantius Augustus to Athanasius.

It will not have escaped your intelligence that it was always my prayer that everything might turn out agreeably for my late brother Constans. Your prudence will also be able to infer how great was my grief when I learned that he had been murdered by extremely irreligious men. **3** Since there are certain people in this present time, this time of mourning, who are trying to frighten you, I have therefore deemed it appropriate that this letter be sent to your fortitude, and I urge you, as befits a bishop, to teach the laity the things that are proper for divine worship and, with them, to devote your time to leading them in the customary prayers, without giving credence to idle rumours, whatever they may be. **4** For it is fixed in our soul that, in accordance with your resolution, you will continue to be bishop in your own place. May divine providence preserve you for many years, most beloved father.

---

90 A different letter to Nestorius, including the instruction to destroy orders that are hostile to Athanasius, can be found at Ath. *Apol. c. Ar.* 56.2–3. Nestorius was Prefect of Egypt from 345 to 352: see PLRE I 625–6 (Nestorius 1).

91 The phrase 'your sanctity' is an example of the elevated forms of address used in exchanges between late Roman officials. See also the phrase 'your prudence' in the following sentence and a number of similar examples in the next letter. More generally, these two letters display the very formal and stilted tone of imperial correspondence, which stands in sharp contrast to the style of Athanasius' own narrative.

92 The term 'of blessed memory' here is used, like 'late' in English, to denote that Constans had died, since he had been killed in 350 after the usurpation of Magnentius in Gaul. This letter can also be found at Ath. *Apol. Const.* 23.

25.1   After these events took place, they said farewell and embarked on their journey:[93] friends were overjoyed to see a friend, but of the rest, some were put to shame when they saw him, others were afraid to speak and hid themselves, while others again repented because of what they had written against the bishop. **2** For example, all the bishops of Palestine (apart from about two or three and the ones who were under suspicion) welcomed Athanasius warmly and embraced communion with him, to the extent of writing and offering as their defence that they had written their earlier statements not of their own free choice but under compulsion.[94] **3** It is unnecessary to speak of the bishops of Egypt and the Libyas, as well as the laity in those regions and in Alexandria: they all hurried together and were filled with indescribable joy, not only because they were recovering their own people alive, contrary to their expectation, but also because they were being rescued from the heretics as though from tyrants and raging dogs.[95] The congregations were filled with joy in their assemblies as they roused each other towards virtue. **4** How many single women, formerly prepared to be married, remained as virgins for Christ! How many young men, seeing the example of others, adopted the monastic life! How many fathers gave encouragement to their children! How many were also asked by their children not to prevent them from taking up the ascetic life in Christ! How many wives persuaded their husbands, and how many were persuaded by their husbands, *to give themselves to prayer*, as the apostle said![96] How many widows, and how many orphans, who had previously been hungry and naked, went away both fed and clothed through the great generosity of the laity! **5** And overall, their desire for virtue was so great that one would believe every household and every home to be a church because of its inhabitants' love of goodness and prayers to God. There was a profound and marvellous peace in the churches, with bishops writing from everywhere and receiving from Athanasius the usual letters of peace.[97]

93 The narrative has now returned to Athanasius' journey back to Egypt in 346, after he was recalled from exile by Constantius.

94 A council was held at Jerusalem and a letter written to the clergy of Egypt and the Libyas: see Ath. *Apol. c. Ar.* 57.

95 Athanasius entered Alexandria on 21 October 346: see *Festal Index* 18. In this passage Athanasius engages in the rhetorical practice of *praeteritio/paraleipsis*, in which an author states that they will not discuss a particular topic, thereby creating a means of introducing it into the piece, often at length.

96 *1 Corinthians* 7.5.

97 The 'letters of peace' referred to here are statements that the author accepts the recipient into communion.

26.1 Moreover, Ursacius and Valens, as though they were being whipped by conscience, had a change of heart and wrote a friendly and peaceful letter to the bishop himself, despite not having received a letter from him.[98] Then they went up to Rome, repented and confessed that everything they had done and said against him was mere lies and false accusations.[99] **2** This was not all they did; they also anathematised the Arian heresy and handed over a written statement of their recantation. They wrote this letter to Bishop Julius in Latin, and it has been translated into Greek. A copy was sent to us in Latin by Paul, bishop of Trier.[100]

26.3 Translation from the Latin

Ursacius and Valens to our lord the most blessed father Julius.
Since it has been established that we previously [laid] many terrible [charges] ...
{The text is given below in the sixty-eighth book and is totally identical.}[101]

26.4 Translation from the Latin

Bishops Ursacius and Valens to our lord and brother, Bishop Athanasius.

An opportunity was given to us through our brother and fellow priest ...
{The text is given below in the same sixty-eighth book and is completely identical.}[102]

26.5 After writing these letters, they subscribed the letters of peace from Peter and Irenaeus, the presbyters of Athanasius, and Ammonius the layman, who were passing through, although Athanasius had not written to them through those men.[103]

---

98 They were the bishops of Singidunum and Mursa respectively: see chapter 17.3 above.

99 This took place in Rome in 347: see Introduction p. 9 and Barnes (1993) 97.

100 This must be an erroneous reference to Paulinus, bishop of Trier, who was exiled in 353/4 at the Council of Arles: see PCBE IV.2 1443–4 (Paulinus 1).

101 This letter is preserved at Ath. *Apol. c. Ar.* 58.1–4. The original Latin text can be found at Hilary, *Adu. Val. et Ursac.* B.II.6. In this document the two bishops rejected Arius, stated that all the accusations against Athanasius were false and declared that they wished to have communion with him.

102 This letter is preserved at Ath. *Apol. c. Ar.* 58.5. The original Latin text can be found at Hilary, *Adu. Val. et Ursac.* B.II.8. This brief letter by Ursacius and Valens asks Athanasius to accept that they are in communion with the Church and to write back to them.

103 Peter, Irenaeus and Ammonius are not mentioned elsewhere.

27.1 Who was not astonished when they witnessed this and the great peace in the churches? Who did not rejoice when they saw the unanimity of so many bishops? Who did not praise the Lord when they beheld the happiness of the congregations in the assemblies? How many enemies recanted! How many former slanderers gave excuses! How many people who had formerly hated Athanasius now loved him! How many people who had written against him now recanted! **2** Many people who had been with the Arians not by choice but by compulsion now came at night, apologised and anathematised the heresy. They asked for forgiveness because, although they had appeared outwardly to side with the Arians because of their plots and slanders, inwardly they had been together with Athanasius and always on his side. Yes, believe me.

28.1 When they heard and saw all this, the heirs of the opinion and impiety of the Eusebians were greatly ashamed. They were Leontius the eunuch, who should not even have been admitted to communion as a layman, because he castrated himself so that he might be free to sleep with a certain Eustolium, who acts as his wife, even though she is called a virgin; and also George, Acacius, Theodore and Narcissus, who had been deposed at the council.[104] **2** Then they saw the harmony and peace towards Athanasius of more than 400 bishops, from great Rome and the whole of Italy, Calabria, Apulia, Campania, Bruttia, Sicily, Sardinia and Corsica, and from all of Africa and from the Gauls, Britain and the Spains, including the great confessor Ossius, and from the Pannonias, Noricum, Siscia, Dalmatia, Dardania, Dacia, Moesia, Macedonia and Thessaly, and from all of Achaea, Crete, Cyprus and Lycia and most of the bishops from Palestine, and Isauria, Egypt, the Thebaid and all Libya and the Pentapolis.[105] **3** When they saw this, they were seized by envy and fear; by envy because of the communion of so many bishops, and by fear in case the men they had deceived were to join in unanimity with so many bishops, because then their heresy would be made an example of and defeated and proscribed everywhere.

104 Leontius had become bishop of Antioch in 344: see chapter 20.5 above. The other bishops had been deposed by the 'westerners' at Serdica in 343: see chapter 17.3 above.

105 In some cases, such as the Gauls, Spains and Pannonias, there was more than one province with the same name at this time, hence the use of plurals here. For Ossius, bishop of Cordoba, see chapter 15.3 above, as well as chapters 42–5 below.

29.1 Firstly they persuaded Ursacius and Valens to change their minds and, like dogs, to return to their own vomit and, like pigs, to wallow again in the former mire of their impiety.[106] They also persuaded them to invent an excuse for their recantation and to say that they had done it because they were afraid of the most pious Constans.[107] Yet even if Ursacius and Valens were afraid, they should not have abandoned those men, if they really had confidence in their actions. **2** But since it was all a lie and they were not actually afraid, how are they not worthy of total condemnation? For there was no soldier present, nor had any *palatini* or *notarii* been sent out, as happens now, and nor did they write in the emperor's presence or after having been summoned by anyone.[108] In fact they willingly went up to Rome themselves and, in the church, where there was nothing to fear from outside, but there is only fear of God and every man has a free choice, they wrote a recantation on their own initiative. And even though they became Arians for a second time and once again contrived such a disgraceful excuse, they still did not feel embarrassed.

30.1 Next they went together to the emperor Constantius and appealed to him, saying: 'When we made our first appeal, we were not believed. For when you were summoning Athanasius, we said that by calling him to court you were expelling our heresy. He has been against it from the beginning and never stops anathematising it. **2** In fact he has already succeeded in this by writing hostile letters against us and sending them everywhere. Most people are now in communion with him, while some of our supposed allies have gone over to his side and others are about to: we've been left on our own. We're afraid that our heresy will be discovered and then we and you will be labelled as heretics. If this happens, watch out or we'll get lumped together with the Manichaeans.[109] Start persecuting again and protect the

---

106 For the images of a dog returning to its vomit and a pig wallowing in a mire, see *2 Peter* 2.22, as well as *Proverbs* 26.11 for the dog.

107 Barnes (1993) 99 dates Ursacius and Valens' change of heart to 350/1. Constans had been killed by the forces of the usurper Magnentius in early 350, leaving Constantius as the last surviving son of Constantine I.

108 On the imperial officials known as *notarii* and *palatini*, see the Glossary.

109 The Manichaeans were a religious group founded in Persia in the third century by the prophet Mani. They were condemned by the Tetrarchy before the Great Persecution and were often criticised by Christians and treated as heretics. Lyman (1993) 53–8 provides a discussion of Athanasius' creation of heretical genealogies for his theological opponents, including labelling them as successors to the Manichaeans. For a selection of Manichaean writings, see Gardner and Lieu (2004).

heresy: you are its emperor.'[110] **3** These were their villainous words. As Constantius was travelling along and hurrying to face Magnentius,[111] he observed the communion of the bishops with Athanasius and, like a man set alight by fire, he changed his mind and did not remember his oaths, as well as forgetting what he had written and disregarding his duty to his brother.[112] For, in fact, when he wrote to him and also when he spoke to Athanasius, Constantius swore on oath that he would only act in accordance with the wishes of the laity and the bishop. **4** Nonetheless, his enthusiasm for impiety suddenly made him forget all this. We should not be surprised that, despite writing many letters and swearing many oaths, Constantius still changed for the worse, since Pharaoh, the former tyrant of Egypt, having made promises many times and so attained respite from his trials, changed his mind, until in the end he was destroyed along with his adherents.[113]

31.1   At first he started forcing people in every city to change their minds; then, after he came to Arles and Milan, he did what the heretics advised and suggested (or, rather, they were given the authority and so did all this themselves and attacked everyone).[114] **2** At once the prefect here [Alexandria] received orders and letters stating that from now on the grain would be taken away from Athanasius and given to those who followed the beliefs of Arius, and that everyone had free rein to abuse Athanasius' associates if they wanted. There were also threats against the local officials

---

110 For Athanasius' tendency to create unrealistic dialogue for his opponents, see n. 4 to chapter 1.1 above.

111 Magnentius had rebelled against Constans in Gaul in 350 and quickly killed him and took control of the western part of the empire. Constantius started his march westwards in late 350 and first engaged Magnentius' forces in the following year. It took until 353 for the usurpation to be suppressed completely, with Magnentius committing suicide in August of that year. See PLRE I 532 (Magnentius), as well as Barnes (1993) 105–6 and Hunt (1998) 10–11, 14–22 for succinct accounts of these events.

112 For Constantius' oaths when he addressed Athanasius, see chapter 22.3 above.

113 For Pharaoh's repeated changes of heart about letting the Israelites leave Egypt, see *Exodus* 7–14.

114 These are the Councils of Arles and Milan, which took place in 353/4 and 355 respectively: see Introduction pp. 10–11. It appears that bishops were being asked to subscribe to a document that included the condemnation of Athanasius, but also incorporated other condemnations and a creed, although in the following chapters Athanasius presents Constantius' campaign as directed primarily against him. For a reconstruction of these events, making significant use of this passage, see Barnes (1993) 109–18. Barnes makes the plausible suggestion that the document that the bishops had to sign was the letter issued by the Council of Sirmium in 351.

if they did not join together with the Arians. This was the prelude to what was done later through the *dux* Syrianus.[115] **3** Orders were sent again to the outlying districts, and *notarii* and *palatini* were dispatched to each city with threats against the bishops and local officials. The officials were told to apply pressure and the bishops had to hold communion with the Arians and write against Athanasius or else themselves suffer the penalty of exile. The laity who followed them were threatened with chains, violence, beatings and confiscation of their property. **4** This order was not neglected: the envoys were accompanied by the clerics of Ursacius and Valens to urge them on and report unco-operative officials to the emperor.[116] They also allowed other heresies, as little sisters of their own, to blaspheme against the Lord, and they only plotted against the Christians and could not stand to hear pious words about Christ. For that reason, how many bishops, in the words of Scripture, *were brought before governors and kings* and heard from the officials: **5** 'Either subscribe or withdraw from the churches, for the emperor has given orders for you to be deposed.'[117] How many were treated violently by these men in every city to stop them censuring them as friends of the bishops! **6** Moreover, instructions were sent to the *decuriones* in each city, and they were threatened with financial penalties if each of them did not force the bishop of his own city to subscribe.[118] Every place and every city was completely filled with fear and upheaval, with bishops being dragged away and officials witnessing the groans and lamentations of the laity.

32.1 While the deployed *palatini* were doing this, those astonishing men were confident in their authority and acted very zealously. They summoned some bishops to the emperor, and dealt with others via letters, inventing allegations against them. They thought that the first group would be cowed by the presence of Constantius, and the others by the messengers and threats, and that, out of fear of the false charges, they would abandon their correct and pious beliefs. **2** Through a mixture of threats and promises,

---

115 Syrianus' outrages appear in the appeal of the people of Alexandria in chapter 81 below and are also described in Ath. *Apol. Const.* 22–5 and *De fuga* 24, as well as Soc. *HE* 2.11 and Lucifer, *De Ath. II* 22. For Syrianus' career in general, see PLRE I 872 (Syrianus).

116 On these two bishops, see chapters 17.3 and 26.1 above.

117 The scriptural quotation is from *Matthew* 10.18.

118 The *decuriones*, also sometimes referred to as *curiales*, were members of the town councils: see Jones (1964) II 737–57. As mentioned in n. 114, the bishops appear to have been instructed to subscribe to the decisions of the Council of Sirmium from 351.

the emperor forced a great number of bishops to say: 'We are no longer in communion with Athanasius.' The ones who travelled to his presence were not permitted to see him, nor were they allowed to rest or even to leave their own houses, until they either subscribed or, if they refused, were exiled. **3** He did this because he saw that everyone hated the heresy, and for this particular reason he compelled so many to be added to a few.[119] He was anxious to gather together a mass of names because of his hatred towards the bishop and to make the Arian impiety look better, because he himself is its leader. He thinks that he will be able to twist the truth in the same way as he does men, for he does not see or recognise that the Sadducees and the Herodians, after taking the Pharisees onboard, could not conceal the truth.[120] **4** Instead, it is made brighter every day because of this. These men have shouted out *We have no king but Caesar* and, possessing the judgement of Pilate, they are equally bereft of any sense of shame, expecting that soon they themselves will be left naked like the partridge, when they see their own protector dying.[121]

33.1   If it is shameful that some of the bishops changed their minds wholly through fear in these circumstances, then to force and compel the unwilling is much more shameful and is the action of people who have no confidence in their beliefs. **2** The Devil, because he possesses no truth, attacks in this way *with axe and stone-cutter* and breaks down the doors of those who will not let him in;[122] but the Saviour is so mild that he teaches *if any man will come after me* and *the one wishing to be my disciple*,[123] and when he comes to each person he does not use force, but instead knocks and says *Open to me, my sister, my bride*.[124] When they open he enters, but when

119 Athanasius is here referring to compelling many bishops to subscribe to a document that had originally been issued by only a small number.

120 These three Jewish groups are depicted as working together to try to entrap Jesus at *Matthew* 22.15–46. The force of this comparison is detrimental to Constantius and the 'Arians', but also exalts Athanasius and his allies as suffering like Jesus. The comparison with the Gospel account continues in the following sentences.

121 The statement attributed to Athanasius' enemies is taken from *John* 19.15, where the Jewish chief priests give this answer to Pilate during the trial of Christ. The comparison with a partridge alludes to *Jeremiah* 17.11, where this bird is castigated for gathering the eggs of others, just like a man who gathers riches unjustly, only to lose them later.

122 For the reference to the axe and stone-cutter, see *Psalms* 74.6 (73.6 LXX).

123 *Matthew* 16.24; cf. *Luke* 14.27. Athanasius' point here is that Christ's teaching was that people should choose freely to follow him.

124 *Song of Songs* 5.2.

they hesitate and are unwilling, he departs. **3** For the truth is proclaimed not with swords and javelins and soldiers, but by persuasion and advice. What sort of persuasion is it when there is fear of the emperor? Or what sort of advice, where anyone who rejects it receives exile and death? **4** When David was king and had his enemy in his power, and his soldiers wanted to kill this man, he prevented them not by his power, but, as Scripture says, by persuading them with arguments and not allowing them to rise up and kill Saul.[125] **5** But this man [Constantius] has no arguments and so he compels everyone through his power, revealing to all that their [the Arians'] wisdom is not in accordance with God, but is merely human, and that those who follow the beliefs of Arius truly *have no king but Caesar*. **6** With his help, the enemies of Christ do whatever they want; they thought that he would enable them to plot against many people and they did not perceive that they were creating many confessors, including the devout men and good bishops who have recently performed a magnificent confession, Paulinus, bishop of Trier, the metropolis of the Gauls, Lucifer, bishop of the metropolis of Sardinia, Eusebius of Vercelli in Italy and Dionysius of Milan, which is the metropolis of Italy.[126] **7** The emperor summoned them and ordered them to subscribe against Athanasius and be in communion with the heretics. When they were amazed at this novel practice and said that it was not an ecclesiastical canon, he immediately replied: 'Whatever I want, let that be deemed a canon. The so-called bishops of Syria allow me to speak in this way. Either obey or be exiled.'[127]

34.1 On hearing these words, the bishops were utterly astonished. Stretching their hands up to God, they employed much freedom of speech towards him [Constantius] as well as arguments, teaching him that the kingdom was not his, but belonged to God, who had given it, and they told him to fear God, because he might suddenly take it away.[128] They

---

125 For this story, see *1 Samuel* 26.

126 Paulinus of Trier was exiled in 353/4 at the Council of Arles: see n. 100 to chapter 26.2 above. Lucifer of Cagliari, Eusebius of Vercelli and Dionysius of Milan were all exiled at the Council of Milan in 355: see Introduction p. 11 for more details.

127 As discussed at n. 4 to chapter 1.1 above, Athanasius frequently places unlikely statements into the mouths of his enemies. The remark about Constantius' wishes being treated as a canon has, rather surprisingly, been accepted as an accurate report by a number of historians. See Barnes (1993) 279 n. 33 for a useful list of those who have taken this view.

128 As elsewhere in this text, the phrase 'freedom of speech' translates the term παρρησία. This fearless outspokenness in the face of tyranny was traditionally associated with philosophers, as well as being present in Christian accounts of martyrdom, and was also adopted

threatened him with the Day of Judgement and told him not to corrupt ecclesiastical affairs, nor to involve the Roman empire in the government of the church, nor to introduce the Arian heresy into the church of God. **2** But he neither listened, nor allowed them to say anything else, but threatened them even more, bared his weapon against them and commanded that some of them be taken away. But, like Pharaoh, he changed his mind yet again.[129] **3** So the holy men shook off the dust, looked up to God and did not fear the emperor's threat or surrender when the sword had been unsheathed.[130] Instead they received exile as the performance of a service in their religious ministry. As they passed through each place and city, they preached the gospel, even though they were in chains. They proclaimed the pious faith and also anathematised the Arian heresy and condemned the change of heart by Ursacius and Valens.[131] **4** This worked against the plotters. For the greater the distance of their [the bishops'] exile, the more did hatred of those villains increase, and the exile of one set of men was a proclamation against the impiety of the other. For who, upon seeing the exiled men passing through, did not revere them as confessors; and who did not shun and loathe the others, no longer calling them simply impious, but also executioners, murderers and anything but Christians.

35.1 It would certainly have been better if, from the very beginning, Constantius had not got involved with this heresy at all; or, once he was involved, if he had not conceded so much to the impious; or, once he had conceded it, if he had stood by them only up to the point where a joint condemnation would come to them all for these actions alone. But by entangling their foolish selves in the chains of impiety, they bring down upon themselves, as is fitting, a greater condemnation. **2** Right from the start they would not leave even Liberius, bishop of Rome, alone. They extended their madness against the people of that city, and they were not ashamed even though this is an apostolic see, nor did they act cautiously because Rome is the metropolis of the Roman world, nor did they remember

by some bishops in late antiquity, especially when seeking to present themselves as standing up to heresy and autocracy: see Brown (1992) 61–70, 117; Rapp (2005) especially 59–60, 75–76, 86–90, 268; Flower (2013) 25–6, 53–61, 129–30, 134–77.

129 On Pharaoh's trademark changes of heart, see n. 113 to chapter 30.4 above.

130 For the notion of shaking off dust when leaving a house or city that did not heed the word of God, see *Matthew* 10.14.

131 On this action by Ursacius and Valens, see chapter 29.1 above.

that they had previously referred in writing to 'those apostolic men'.[132] **3** They jumbled everything together, forgot everything completely and were only concerned with their zeal for impiety. For when they saw that he [Liberius] was orthodox, hated the Arian heresy and was keen to persuade everyone to shun and renounce it, these impious men said to themselves, 'If we persuade Liberius, we will quickly prevail over everyone.' **4** So they slandered him before the emperor. He assumed that he could use Liberius to draw everyone over to himself quickly, so he wrote and sent a certain eunuch called Eusebius with letters and gifts, to seduce Liberius with the gifts and threaten him with the letters.[133] **5** The eunuch went up to Rome and first exhorted Liberius to subscribe against Athanasius and be in communion with the Arians, saying, 'This is what the emperor want and orders you to do.' Then he displayed the gifts, grasped his hands and exhorted him, saying, 'Obey the emperor and take these.'

36.1 The bishop tried to persuade him with an argument and teach him a lesson: 'How can we do this to Athanasius? How can we condemn a man who has been properly acquitted not only by one council but also by a second, which was assembled from everywhere, a man whom the Roman church has dismissed in peace?[134] Who will accept us if, after we greeted him with love and held him in communion when he was present, we then turn away from him when he is absent? This is not an ecclesiastical canon, nor is this the tradition we have from the Fathers, who themselves received it from the blessed and great apostle Peter. **2** If the emperor really cares about ecclesiastical peace, if he gives orders for our writings about Athanasius to be revoked, let the actions that these men

132 The final statement must refer to an earlier document describing the bishops of Rome in this honorific fashion, although it does not appear to be one of the ones preserved in any of the works of Athanasius. Opitz's note to this passage simply reads 'Wo?' Liberius was bishop of Rome from 352 to 366.

133 Eusebius held the post of *praepositus sacri cubiculi*, which placed him in charge of other staff of the imperial bedchamber and so gave him the potential to be very influential with the emperor: see Jones (1964) II 566–70. Eusebius maintained this position throughout the reign of Constantius II and was involved in the fall and execution of the *caesar* Gallus. He was tried and executed in the Chalcedon trials that took place after the death of Constantius and the accession of Julian: see PLRE I 302–303 (Eusebius 11).

134 The first council may be the one held by Athanasius in Alexandria in 338 – see Ath. *Apol. c. Ar.* 3–19; Barnes (1993), 36–40 – although it is probably more likely to be the one assembled in Rome in 341 by bishop Julius: see chapter 15.1 above. The second council is the one held at Serdica in 343: see chapter 15–18 above.

[Athanasius' opponents] took against him also be revoked, let the actions against everyone be revoked, and then let an ecclesiastical council take place far from the palace, with the emperor not present, with no *comes* standing by, with no official making threats, but relying solely on the fear of God and the instructions of the apostles. In this way the ecclesiastical faith will be preserved, just as the Fathers defined it in the council at Nicaea, and those who follow the beliefs of Arius will be driven out and their heresy anathematised.[135] **3** Then when a judgement has been made concerning the accusations against Athanasius and anyone else, as well as those against these men, let the guilty be driven out and let the innocent speak and act freely. For those who are impious in their faith cannot be included in a council, nor can scrutiny of actions take place before scrutiny of faith. **4** All disagreement about faith must be eradicated first of all, and then an inquiry into actions can be conducted. For our Lord Jesus Christ did not attend to the sick until they revealed and professed their faith in him. **5** This is what we learnt from the Fathers, this is what I reported to the emperor, for this is what is beneficial to him and builds up the church. Do not listen to Ursacius and Valens, since they have recanted their earlier views and their words are no longer trustworthy.[136]

37.1 After Bishop Liberius said this, the eunuch became distressed, not so much because the bishop had not subscribed against Athanasius, but because he himself had discovered that Liberius was hostile to the heresy. Then, having forgotten that he was addressing a bishop, he spoke in a very threatening manner and went off with his gifts. Next he did something unlawful that was not only inappropriate for a Christian, but extremely audacious even for a eunuch. Imitating the wrongdoing of Saul, he entered the *martyrion* of the apostle Peter and dedicated the gifts to him.[137] When he learnt about this, Liberius was very displeased with the overseer of the place for failing to prevent this, while he threw out the gifts themselves as an unfit sacrifice, thereby enraging the eunuch still further. In response, Eusebius provoked the emperor, saying: **2** 'Our concern is no longer with

---

135 The characteristic phrase 'those who follow the beliefs of Arius', supposedly uttered by Liberius here, also appears in Athanasius' main narrative in chapters 3.5, 33.5 and 70.3, as well as in the letter of Ossius at chapter 44.1.

136 On Ursacius and Valens' change of heart, see chapter 29.1 above.

137 The 'wrongdoing of Saul' is probably a reference to *1 Samuel* 15, where the king disobeys God's instruction to kill all the Amalekites and their animals, instead bringing some cattle and sheep back as an offering. A *martyrion* is a shrine to a martyr.

getting Liberius to sign, but with the fact that he is so set against the heresy that he anathematises the Arians by name.' He also roused the other eunuchs to help him, since many, or rather the entirety, of those surrounding Constantius are eunuchs, and they control his every action so that nothing happens there without their involvement.[138] **3** So then the emperor wrote to Rome and once again dispatched *palatini*, *notarii* and *comites* with letters for the prefect. They were either to deceive Liberius with a trick, lure him away from Rome and then send him to the emperor at the imperial court, or else drive him out by force.[139]

38.1 Since this was the tenor of the letters, fear and intrigue sprang up throughout the whole city. How many households had threats made against them! How many people received how many instructions against Liberius! How many bishops went into hiding when they saw these events! How many free people withdrew into the rural districts because of slanders uttered by the enemies of Christ! **2** How many ascetics were victims of plots! How many people who lived there and had made it their home were driven out! How assiduously and carefully did they guard the harbour and the entrances of the gates to stop any orthodox people entering to see Liberius! In this way, Rome also gained experience of the enemies of Christ and came to know what she had only previously heard about and not really believed: how these men destroyed the other churches city-by-city. **3** It was eunuchs who set in motion these events, along with the other actions against everyone. What is extraordinary about this plot is that the Arian heresy, which denies the Son of God, receives help from eunuchs, when they, being sterile by nature and having souls that similarly cannot produce virtue, cannot bear to hear anything about a 'Son' at all. **4** The eunuch from Ethiopia, who did not understand what he was reading, was converted by Philip, who taught him about the Saviour;[140] but the eunuchs of Constantius cannot endure the confession of Peter and they turn away when the Father reveals the Son, raging against those who say that the Son of God is genuine and defending this heresy of eunuchs which claims that

---

138 Accusations that powerful people were controlled by eunuchs were not limited to Christian invective: see, for example, Hopkins (1963) esp. 78–80; Long (1996) 97–102; Kelly (2004) 222–4. See also Amm. 21.16.16 for specific criticism of Constantius II for being under the influence of his eunuchs.

139 The verb 'διώκω' is here translated as 'drive out', rather than 'persecute', as is the case in chapter 38.2 below.

140 *Acts* 8.27–39.

there is no genuine and true Son from the Father.[141] **5** For this reason, the law prevents them from being admitted into an ecclesiastical council, but nonetheless Constantius has now given them authority over ecclesiastical judgements, and whatever seems right to them, Constantius decides upon it, while his so-called 'bishops' play along. Oh, who would be the historian of these men? Who would transmit these events to another generation? Who, on hearing this, would believe that eunuchs, who are scarcely entrusted with domestic duties (for their kind are fond of pleasure and they care about nothing except that which nature has removed from them), are now in charge of ecclesiastical matters and that Constantius, being under their control, has plotted against everyone and exiled Liberius?

39.1 It was when Constantius was writing many letters to Rome, threatening, sending messengers and plotting, that persecution also took place in Alexandria.[142] **2** Liberius was dragged before the emperor and addressed him with much freedom of speech, saying 'Stop persecuting Christians.[143] Do not try to use us to introduce impiety into the church. We are prepared to endure anything rather than be called Ariomaniacs.[144] We are Christians; do not force us to become enemies of Christ. **3** We also offer you this advice: Do not fight against the one who has given this empire to you. Do not act impiously against him instead of giving thanks. Do not persecute those who believe in him. Do not find yourself also hearing the words, *It is hard for thee to kick against the pricks*.[145] But would that you did hear them, so that you might also be converted as the holy Paul was! **4** See,

141 'The confession of Peter' probably refers to *Matthew* 16.16, where the apostle Peter calls Christ 'the Son of the living God', while the reference to the Father revealing the Son describes the voice from heaven at Jesus' baptism at *Matthew* 3.17. For the beliefs of the 'Arians' and their representation by opponents, see Introduction pp. 2–3.

142 This refers to the start of the attempts to drive Athanasius out of Alexandria in 355–6, including those that are related from chapter 47 onwards. On these events, see Introduction p. 12 and Barnes (1993) 118–19.

143 A supposed transcript of the conversation between Constantius and Liberius is provided at Theod. *HE* 2.16.

144 The term 'Ariomaniacs' is employed as a pejorative term for the 'Arians' on many occasions in the writings of Athanasius, as well as appearing in Latin in letters written by Eusebius of Vercelli during his exile: Eus. Verc. *Ep.* 2, at 3.1, 5.2, 6.5, 7.2, 8.1 and 11.2, as well as *Ep.* 3.2.1. English translations of these letters can be found at Flower (2013) 242–51. The name of 'Ariomaniacs' for a group of heretics also appears as the title of chapter 69 of Epiphanius' *Panarion*.

145 These words were uttered by Christ when he appeared to Saul on the road to Damascus: see *Acts* 9.5 (repeated by Saul/Paul at *Acts* 26.14).

we are here, we have come before they could invent some allegation.[146] For this reason we have hurried here, knowing that exile awaits us from you, in order that, before we can suffer a false accusation, it might be clearly demonstrated to everyone that all the others have also suffered in the same way as we have, that the allegations made against them were invented by their enemies and that those men deal in nothing except slander and lies.'

40.1 By speaking in this way at this time, Liberius received admiration from everyone. But, instead of replying, Constantius simply gave the order and exiled each of them separately, just as he had done in the earlier cases.[147] He himself came up with this method of exile, so that in his punishments he might be even more savage than the tyrants and persecutors before him. **2** For in the earlier persecution, Maximian gave orders for many confessors to be exiled together and so consoled them with each other's company and lightened the punishment.[148] But this man is more savage than he was: he [Constantius] separated men who spoke out and became confessors together and he divided those men who are bound together in the faith. He did this so that when they die they will not see each other, because he thought that separation of the body would also break the connection of the soul, or that when they had been separated from each other they would forget their agreement and unanimity. He does not realise that, although each man might be alone, he still has with him the Lord, whom they confessed when they were all together and who (as he did with the prophet Elisha) will ensure that the companions of each of them will be more numerous than the soldiers of Constantius.[149] **3** Evil is truly blind. They thought that they could hurt the confessors by separating them from each other, but instead they did great harm to themselves. In fact, if they [the confessors]

146 This claim by Liberius seems to be at odds with Athanasius' earlier statement that the bishop had been dragged before the emperor.

147 This is the first mention here of people accompanying Liberius and suffering exile alongside him.

148 This emperor could be the either Maximian, the co-*Augustus* of Diocletian in the Tetrarchy, or Galerius, their junior colleague who was also known by the name 'Maximianus'. Galerius is usually assigned a greater role in instigating the persecution of Christians, but there is also a reference to persecution taking place under Constantius' grandfather Maximian in chapters 44.1 and 64.2 below, which makes it possible that the former is meant here. On this question generally in presentations of the Great Persecution at this time, see n. 39 to Hilary, *In Const.* 7 on p. 121 below.

149 The reference is to the help that Elisha received from God when faced with the armies of the Syrian king in *2 Kings* 6.16.

had remained together and all gone to the same location, the pollution of the impious would only have become known from that one place; but, by separating them, they [the Arians] have caused their own impious heresy and wickedness to spread everywhere and be recognised in every place.

41.1   Who could hear about their actions in this matter and not realise that they are anything but Christians? For when Lucifer and his companions also made their confession of faith, Liberius sent the presbyter Eutropius and the deacon Hilarius to the emperor with a letter. They exiled the presbyter immediately, but they stripped the deacon Hilarius, flogged his back and then exiled him, exclaiming to him, 'Why did you not oppose Liberius rather than bringing a letter from him?'[150] Ursacius, Valens and their accompanying eunuchs did this.[151] **2** As he was being flogged, the deacon praised the Lord, remembering that he said, *I gave my back to the smiters.*[152] His attackers laughed and jeered at him, and were not ashamed of abusing a Levite.[153] Their mocking behaviour was entirely appropriate to them, but he endured and praised God. It is the lot of Christians to receive a beating, but flogging Christians is the shameless activity of Pilate and Caiaphas.[154] **3** In this way they first tried to corrupt the Roman church and also wanted to introduce impiety into it; the exiled Liberius gave way two years later and subscribed because he was frightened by the threat of death. But this reveals both their violent behaviour and also Liberius' hatred of the heresy and his vote for Athanasius, when he still had a free choice. **4** Statements produced under torture and against a person's original judgement express the wishes not of the intimidated, but of the torturers.

150 This must refer to the Council of Milan in 355, when Lucifer of Cagliari was exiled along with the presbyter Pancratius, the deacon Hilarius and the bishops Dionysius of Milan and Eusebius of Vercelli. See Introduction p. 11. After Hilarius returned from exile, he apparently displayed the same rigorist attitude as Lucifer towards former 'Arians' and so was criticised as a 'Luciferian' by Jerome: see PCBE II.1 985–6 (Hilarius 1). The name 'Eutropius' here must be an error, as the presbyter who accompanied Lucifer and Hilarius is attested elsewhere as being named Pancratius: see Hilary, *Adu. Val. et Ursac.* A.VII.6.2; Lucifer, *De regibus* 5.46; PCBE II.2 1581–2 (Pancratius 1).

151 On the bishops Ursacius of Singidunum and Valens of Mursa, see above, especially chapter 17.3, 26.1–5 and 29.1.

152 *Isaiah* 50.6.

153 The Levites were the priestly tribe of Israel. In Christian usage, 'Levite' gradually came to be employed as a synonym for deacon: see Souter s.v. *levita*; Lampe s.v. λευίτης.

154 Pilate and Caiaphas are, respectively, the Roman prefect and the Jewish High Priest who treat Jesus violently in the Gospel narratives.

These men tried everything for the sake of their heresy. But in every church, men keep to the faith that they learned and wait for their teachers; they have rejected the Christ-fighting heresy and all avoid it like a snake.

42.1 Despite having committed so many crimes of this sort, the impious regarded themselves as having achieved nothing so long as the great Ossius still remained untouched by their wickedness. And so they made plans to extend their madness to reach such a great old man. They were not ashamed, even though he was the father of bishops; they did not act cautiously, even though he was a confessor; they did not respect the length of his episcopacy, where he had remained for sixty years and more, but instead they showed contempt towards everything and only cared for their heresy, as men who were truly *fearing not God nor regarding man*.[155] **2** They went to Constantius and once again spoke in this way: 'We have done everything and exiled the Roman bishop, and we also exiled a great many other bishops before him and filled everywhere with fear. But these great deeds of yours are pointless and achieve nothing for us while Ossius remains. So long as he is amongst his own people and all the others are in their own churches, he can turn everyone against us through his reasoning and faith. **3** He leads councils and gains a hearing everywhere through his writings.[156] He also established the faith at Nicaea and proclaimed the Arians to be heretics everywhere. If he remains, the exile of the others is useless, for our heresy will be routed. So start persecuting and show no mercy, even though he is extremely old. Our heresy does not know to respect even the grey hair of old men.'[157]

43.1 When he heard this, the emperor did not delay because he knew this man and his ability, even in his great age. The emperor wrote and gave him orders to come to him, at the same time when he was starting to put Liberius to the test as well. When he [Ossius] had arrived, Constantius requested and urged him to subscribe against us and enter into communion with the Arians, saying the same things that he had used to try to deceive the others. **2** After listening to this with displeasure and becoming distressed that Constantius had said such a thing at all, the old man rebuked him and,

---

155 *Luke* 18.2.

156 As well as presiding at the Council of Nicaea in 325, Ossius was also the leader of the 'western' delegates at Serdica in 343: see Barnes (1993) 73.

157 This speech is another excellent example of Athanasius presenting his enemies as acknowledging their own heresy and making terrible, immoral statements.

after having gained his permission, left for his homeland and church. When the heretics complained and spurred him [Constantius] on again (and he also had the eunuchs making suggestions and spurring him on even more), the emperor wrote again with a threat. **3** Despite his maltreatment, Ossius was not moved by fear of the plot, but, resolute in his purpose, he built his house of faith upon the rock and he spoke very freely against the heresy, regarding the threats in the letters as nothing more than raindrops and gusts of wind.[158] **4** Constantius actually wrote to him on many occasions, sometimes flattering him by calling him 'Father', sometimes threatening him, naming the other exiles and saying, 'Are you the only one still against the heresy? Yield and subscribe against Athanasius. For the man who subscribes against him will assuredly adopt Arianism with us.' Yet Ossius was not intimidated: he endured these abuses and wrote back these words. I have read the letter and it has been appended at the end.[159]

44.1 I first became a confessor when a persecution arose under your grandfather Maximian.[160] If you persecute me, I stand ready now also to suffer absolutely anything rather than to spill innocent blood and betray the truth, and I do not approve of you writing such letters and issuing threats. Stop writing in this manner and do not follow the beliefs of Arius,[161] and do not listen to the easterners or trust Ursacius and Valens and their associates. They do not make these claims because of Athanasius, but rather to help their own heresy. Trust me, Constantius; I am old enough to be your grandfather.[162] **2** I was at the council in Serdica, when you and your brother Constans, of blessed memory, assembled all of us.[163] By myself I addressed the enemies of Athanasius after they came into the church where I was staying, and I told them that they should say if they had anything against him. I encouraged them to have no fear and not to expect anything other than a fair judgement about everything. **3** I did this not once, but a second time as well, urging them to come to me alone if they did not want to go before

158 For the parable of the wise man who built his house upon the rock, see *Matthew* 7.24–5.
159 In fact, the letter appears here at chapter 44 in the transmitted text, rather than at the end.
160 On the presentation of Maximian, the Tetrarchic emperor and father of Constantius' mother Fausta, as a persecutor, see n. 148 to chapter 40.2 above.
161 On the phrase 'follow the beliefs of Arius', see n. 135 to chapter 36.2 above.
162 Here Ossius offers himself as an alternative, pious grandfather figure for Constantius, replacing the persecutor Maximian.
163 This is the Council of Serdica in 343.

the whole council. I also promised again that, if Athanasius were found guilty, he would be completely rejected by us, but if he were found innocent and convicted them of being false accusers, then, if they still rejected him, I would persuade him to come with me to the Spains.[164] Athanasius agreed to this and did not oppose it, but they rejected it because they were not confident of success. **4** After you sent letters summoning him, Athanasius came to your court again and requested that his enemies, who were present there in Antioch, be sent for, either all at once or individually. He did this so that they might either convict him or be convicted, and might either demonstrate while he was present that he was the sort of man they claimed or else not slander him in his absence. You did not put up with him saying this, and they also rejected it. **5** Why do you listen to the men who speak ill of him? How do you put up with Valens and Ursacius, when they have recanted and confessed in writing that their accusation was false?[165] Despite their allegations, they confessed this without any compulsion, without any soldiers looming over them and without your brother's knowledge (for the kinds of things that happen now did not happen under him – may it never be!). They went up to Rome willingly and wrote in the presence of the bishop and presbyters. They had also previously written a friendly and peaceful letter to Athanasius. If they complain about violence, then they recognise that it is evil, and you do not approve of it either. **6** So stop using force and do not write or send *comites*. Release those who have been exiled, lest, with you accusing them of violence, those men [the Arians] use greater violence against them. For what of this kind was ever done under Constans? What bishop was exiled? When was he [Constans] at the centre of an ecclesiastical trial? What *palatinus* of his ever forced people to subscribe against anyone and so gave Valens and his associates the opportunity to make such an allegation? Stop, I beg you, and remember that you are a mortal man; fear the Day of Judgement and keep yourself pure for it. **7** Do not involve yourself in ecclesiastical matters and do not give us instructions, but learn about these things from us instead. God gave the empire to you; he entrusted church affairs to us. And just as a man who usurps your empire opposes God, since he [God] established your rule, so you ought to be afraid in case, by appropriating church affairs to yourself, you become guilty of a great crime. It has been written, *Render unto Caesar the things which are*

---

164 This is a reference to the multiple late Roman provinces of *Hispania* on the Iberian peninsula.

165 For the episode when the two bishops retracted their accusations against Athanasius, see chapter 26 above.

Caesar's; and unto God the things that are God's.[166] Therefore we are not permitted to rule on earth, and you, emperor, do not have the authority to burn incense.[167] **8** I am writing this out of concern for your salvation; now here is what I think about your orders: I do not agree with the Arians, and I anathematise their heresy; nor do I subscribe against Athanasius, whom we absolved from blame, as did the Roman church and the whole council.[168] Moreover, when you saw this, you sent for Athanasius and let him return to his homeland and church with honour. **9** So what is the pretext for such a great change of heart? He had the same enemies then as now. As for the slanders that they whisper now (for they don't utter them in his presence), they also babbled on about these things before you sent for Athanasius. They spread these claims when they came to the council; but then, after I demanded it, as I said earlier, they could not provide any proof. If they had, they would not have run away so shamefully. **10** Who persuaded you to forget your own letters and words after such a long time? Stop obeying evil men, or you will make yourself guilty through this relationship with them. For you comply with them here, but in the Judgement you will make your defence alone.[169] **11** They want you to help them harm their personal enemy, and they want you to become the assistant of their own wickedness, so that they can use you to implant their abominable heresy into the church.[170] It is not wise to fall into manifest danger for the gratification of others. Stop, I appeal to you, and trust in me, Constantius. For these are things that it is proper for me to write and for you to heed.

45.1   The old man, the truly holy Ossius, was like Abraham.[171] He believed and wrote these things, but the other man [Constantius] did not refrain from his plotting, nor did he stop looking for a pretext to attack him. He kept on making terrible threats against Ossius, intending either to change his mind

---

166 *Matthew* 22.21.

167 This is a reference to *2 Chronicles* 26.16–21, where King Uzziah usurped the position of the priests by burning incense as an offering to God, resulting in him being punished with leprosy. This passage is also used in Lucifer's criticism of Constantius at *De non parc.* 6.

168 This is the 'western' Council of Serdica in 343, where Ossius was in attendance.

169 The point being made here is that, unless Constantius dissociates himself from the Arians now, he will be found equally complicit with them in the Last Judgement and he will not be able to argue that he was merely following their lead.

170 The word translated as 'assistant' here is διάκονος, which is also the term for a deacon.

171 After the text of Ossius' letter Athanasius has now returned to his narrative. Here and in 45.2 Athanasius puns on the name Ὅσιος, which is both an alternative version of the name 'Ossius' and also a Greek word meaning 'holy'.

by force or else exile him if he did not comply. **2** Just as the ministers and satraps of Babylon sought a pretext and *did not find one against Daniel except concerning the laws of his God,*[172] so too these current satraps of impiety could not concoct any pretext against the old man except his hatred of heresy, because the truly holy Ossius and his blameless life were well known to everyone. **3** So they slandered him, not in the way that Daniel was slandered to Darius (for Darius listened unwillingly to the accusations against Daniel), but rather as Jezebel slandered Naboth and as the Jews did to Herod,[173] saying, 'Not only does he not subscribe against Athanasius, but he also condemns us for that man's sake and hates our heresy so much that he writes to other people and says that he would rather suffer death than become a traitor to the truth. He says that it is because of the heresy that "our beloved Athanasius" is persecuted and that Liberius, bishop of the Romans, and all the others are the victims of plots against them.' **4** When the champion of impiety, the emperor of heresy, Constantius, heard this, and especially when he discovered that there were others in the Spains who held the same views as Ossius, he tried to get them to subscribe. When he could not force them, he sent for Ossius. Instead of exiling him, he kept him in Sirmium for a whole year. This godless man revered neither God nor his own father's respect for Ossius; this unholy man did not respect his [Ossius'] old age (for then he was a hundred years old); this heartless man felt no shame.[174] **5** He disregarded all this out of impiety, since he was a new Ahab and another Belshazzar of our own times.[175] He was so violent towards the old man and placed him in such narrow confinement that he [Ossius] broke and reluctantly agreed to enter into communion with Valens and Ursacius and their associates, although he still would not subscribe against Athanasius. But even so the old man was not negligent: when he was about to die, as though making a will, he testified to the violence that he had been subjected to, anathematised the Arian heresy and encouraged everybody to reject it.[176]

---

172 *Daniel* 6.5.

173 For these two biblical parallels, see *1 Kings* 21.1–16; *Luke* 23.10.

174 The description of Constantius as ἀνόσιος ('unholy') is another pun on the name Ὅσιος, with Constantius here being described as the opposite of the venerable old bishop.

175 For the Old Testament impious characters of Ahab, king of Israel, and Belshazzar, king of Babylon, see *1 Kings* 16.29–22.40 and *Daniel* 5 respectively. Both suffered violent deaths that could be seen as divine retribution for their actions.

176 Ossius probably died in late 357, fairly soon after subscribing to the theological statement known as the 'Blasphemy of Simium' and shortly before Athanasius composed the *Historia Arianorum*: see Barnes (1993) 126. On the 'Blasphemy', see Introduction p. 12.

46.1   Upon seeing all this – or even just hearing about it – who is not astonished and will not himself cry out to the Lord and say *wilt thou wipe out Israel?*[177] Who, when they perceive this, will not himself justifiably call out and say *A terrible and fearful thing has been committed in the land* and *Heaven is astonished at this and the earth is horribly afraid even more?*[178] The fathers of the congregations and the teachers of the faith are being removed and impious men are being brought into the churches. **2** When Liberius bishop of Rome was exiled, as was the great Ossius, the father of bishops, was there anyone who [saw him suffering in this way, or] saw so many bishops exiled from Spain and other regions, but still did not observe, even if he was not very perceptive, that the accusations against Athanasius and the others are false allegations, all packed with malice and slander?[179] It is for this reason that they put up with all their sufferings, for they recognised that the plot arose from the slander of those men. **3** For what formal charge was there against Liberius? Or what accusation was there against the old man Ossius? Who would have spoken falsely against Paulinus, Lucifer, Dionysius and Eusebius? What fault could be used to accuse the other exiled bishops, presbyters and deacons? There was none – may it never be! – since these plots did not proceed by means of formal charges, nor was each man exiled because of an official accusation. In reality, this is a rebellion of impiety against piety; this is both zeal for the Arian heresy and a prelude to the coming of the Antichrist, with Constantius preparing the way for him.

47.1   Once he had accomplished all he wanted in the churches of Italy and the other regions, and after he had exiled some people and used force against others, and had instilled fear everywhere, Constantius then turned his anger towards Alexandria, like some form of plague. **2** This arose through the malicious cunning of the enemies of Christ. In order to give the appearance of a formal subscription by many bishops and to prevent the persecuted Athanasius from complaining to any bishop, they moved swiftly and instilled fear everywhere.[180] The idiots kept this up as a support

---

177 *Ezekiel* 11.13, 9.8.

178 *Jeremiah* 5.30, 2.12.

179 Opitz believes that the section in square brackets represents an interpolation from a marginal gloss.

180 Athanasius had been condemned by the hostile Council of Sirmium in 351, while the Councils of Arles in 353/4 and Milan in 355 were asked to assent to this condemnation, possibly along with the theological formula approved at Sirmium. See chapters 28–34 above

for their plot, since they did not realise that what they were displaying publicly was not a reasoned decision by bishops but rather the violence that they themselves had inflicted. Nor did they realise that, even if Athanasius' brethren were to abandon him, or his friends and companions were to keep their distance from him and no one could be found to sympathise with his plight and comfort him, more than anything else it is instead refuge in God that suffices for him. **3** For the persecuted Elijah was alone, and God was all and in all for the holy one.[181] And the Saviour, who was alone, abandoned and plotted against by his enemies, has given us this model for imitation, so that, if we find ourselves persecuted and abandoned by men, we may not lose heart, but instead may retain hope in him and not abandon the truth.[182] Although it may seem to be under threat initially, the truth will be recognised eventually, even by its persecutors.

48.1 So they [the heretics] spurred the emperor on and he began by writing a threatening letter and sending it to the *dux* and the soldiers. The *notarii* Diogenes and Hilarius and the *palatini* with them were the envoys.[183] Very terrible and savage deeds were committed against the church; these were briefly related a little earlier and are known by everyone from the appeals that the laity made. These can be found appended to the end of this text.[184] **2** When Syrianus had performed these actions and after such terrible events had taken place, including outrages against virgins, Constantius gave his approval to these and similar crimes. Then he wrote again to the council and people of Alexandria, inciting the young men to all come together and either persecute Athanasius or at least recognise

for Athanasius' tendentious account of these events, emphasising both the unwillingness of other bishops (including Lucifer) to condemn him and also the importance of Athanasius as the most vehement opponent of heresy. Athanasius warned other bishops not to subscribe to the decisions of Sirmium in his *Ad Ep. Aeg.* 5–6. On this series of events, see Barnes (1993) 109–20 and Introduction pp. 10–11.

181 For the story of Elijah's persecution by Ahab and Jezebel, during which he fled to the desert and was supported by God, see *1 Kings* 19. This episode suits Athanasius' self-presentation very well.

182 On Athanasius' deployment of imitation of biblical models and use of the term τύπος for a 'model', see Ernest (2004) 183–268; Flower (2013) especially 178–207. Athanasius devoted his *De fuga* to arguing that his retreat from Alexandria was not an act of cowardice but the proper action of a persecuted Christian. Chapters 11–22 of the *De fuga* expand on the theme of flight as biblical re-enactment touched upon here.

183 For Diogenes, see PLRE I 255 (Diogenes 2). For Hilarius, see PLRE I 434 (Hilarius 2).

184 This account of the actions of the *dux* Syrianus is appended to the end of the text as the 'second appeal' in chapter 81 below.

that they were his enemies.[185] **3** In fact, before these instructions reached them, Athanasius withdrew after Syrianus entered the church, recalling the words of Scripture: *But hide for a little while, until the anger has passed.*[186] A certain Heraclius, who held the rank of *comes*, was the bearer of this message, paving the way for a certain George, a spy despatched by the emperor.[187] For no one sent by him could be a bishop (may it never be!), as is shown by his actions and the preliminaries to his arrival.[188]

49.1   Then he [Heraclius] displayed the message publicly and revealed the great shame of its author. For although he [Constantius] could not come up with a plausible pretext for his change of heart when the great Ossius wrote to him, he now invented one that brought much more disrepute to him and his advisors. **2** For he said, 'Showing respect for love towards my brother of divine and pious memory, for a while I put up with the return of this man [Athanasius] to you.'[189] This reveals both that he lied in his proclamation and also that he was ungrateful towards his brother after his death. Then Constantius calls him worthy 'of divine and pious memory', which he certainly is, and says that he [Constantius] <shows respect for> his command and 'love', as he himself says. Nonetheless, even if he only acquiesced on account of Constans, of blessed memory, he ought to have acted in a manner not unworthy of his brother, by becoming heir to his opinion just as to his empire.

50.1   But, when he wanted to demand his rights, he deposed Vetranio, saying 'Who receives the inheritance after the death of brothers?'[190] In

185 The 'council' referred to here is the city council, or *boule*, of Alexandria, rather than an ecclesiastical council.

186 *Isaiah* 26.20. Syrianus entered the church on the night of the 8/9 February 356, causing Athanasius to flee: see chapter 81 below.

187 For Heraclius, see PLRE I 418–9 (Heraclius 3). For Athanasius' play on the similarity between the Greek words for 'bishop' and 'spy', see n. 15 on chapter 3.4 above.

188 On the actions of George, the rival bishop who arrived in Alexandria to replace Athanasius in 357, see *De fuga* 6–7 and *Apol. Const.* 28. The phrase 'preliminaries to his arrival' echoes the description of Constantius preparing the way for the Antichrist at the end of chapter 46.3.

189 The brother is the emperor Constans, who died in 350.

190 Vetranio, the former *magister peditum* of Constans in the Balkans, had been proclaimed emperor there after the murder of Constans by the usurper Magnentius. Constantius soon forced Vetranio to abdicate in his favour. On these events, see Hunt (1998) 15–17. The reference to 'brothers' here must include both Constans and also the emperor Constantine II,

contrast, because of this abominable heresy of the enemies of Christ, he does not recognise rights, but instead acts in an unworthy manner towards his brothers. Because of this heresy he showed no concern for maintaining his father's wishes intact. Instead he pretends to preserve it in order to please the impious, but, in order to cause distress to everyone else, he does not accept that he should maintain respect for his father. **2** For after he [Athanasius] had been falsely accused by the Eusebians, he [Constantine I] sent the bishop to Gaul for a while because of the savagery of the plotters. He rejected the Eusebians' request to send them the bishop, and he hindered their desires and frustrated their attempts with a terrifying threat. Constantine [II], of blessed memory, Constantius' brother, made this clear after his father's death, as is demonstrated by his letter.[191]

51.1 If Constantius wanted to maintain his father's policies, as he claims, how come he sent first Gregory and now George, this devourer of the treasury?[192] Or why is he keen to bring the Arians, whom Constantine labelled 'Porphyrians', into the church and, after becoming their leader, why does he exile others?[193] Even if his father gave an audience to Arius, nonetheless when Arius committed perjury and burst he lost Constantine's benevolence.[194] In fact, when he learned about this he then condemned him as a heretic. **2** How is it that, although he [Constantius] claims to respect

who had been killed in 340. After Constans' death in 350 Constantius was the last surviving son of Constantine I and thus could claim to be heir to the whole empire.

191 Athanasius is here providing a relatively positive account of his first exile, in 335, on the orders of Constantine I. The letter of Constantine II referred to here, which supports this interpretation of these events, is preserved in Ath. *Apol. c. Ar.* 87.4–7. On the circumstances surrounding this event, including the fact that no bishop was appointed to replace Athanasius at this time, see Barnes (1993) 24–5. Constantine II had died in 340 in a civil war with his brother Constans: see Hunt (1998) 5. For the term 'the Eusebians', see n. 2 to chapter 1.1 above.

192 On Gregory 'the Cappadocian', an earlier rival claimant to the Alexandrian see, see n. 39 to chapter 9.3 above. On claims that George 'the Cappadocian', the 'Arian' bishop of the city at the time that this text was written, misused public funds and was involved in various business dealings, see Barnes (1993) 284 n. 6. The fact that both of Athanasius' episcopal rivals were referred to as 'the Cappadocian' and had quite similar names creates substantial potential for confusion.

193 In a letter, preserved at Soc. *HE* 1.9, Constantine had labelled the Arians as 'Porphyrians' because they were said to be imitating the anti-Christian philosopher Porphyry in their impiety.

194 On the circumstances of Arius' death in 336, see Introduction p. 6 and also n. 57 to Lucifer, *Moriundum* 4 at p. 153 below.

ecclesiastical rules, he has contrived to do everything in contravention of them? For what canon says that a bishop is sent from the palace? Or what canon says that soldiers attack churches? Or who has handed down that *comites* and senseless eunuchs should rule over church matters and that the decisions of so-called 'bishops' are to be proclaimed by an edict? He falsifies everything for the sake of his unholy heresy. Against his father's wishes, he sent Philagrius to be prefect of Egypt for a second time and so created the current situation.[195] **3** Nor does he speak the truth for his brother's sake. For after Constans' death he wrote to the bishop not once, not twice, but three times.[196] Yet again he promised that he would not change his mind, and even encouraged Athanasius to be confident that he would not be troubled by anyone and could remain in his church with complete freedom from anxiety. **4** With Asterius the *comes* and Palladius the *notarius* as his envoys, he also sent orders to Felicissimus, who was *dux* at that time, and to Nestorius the prefect, to prevent Philip the prefect or anyone else from daring to plot against Athanasius.[197]

52.1   For this reason, when Diogenes arrived and Syrianus lay in ambush for us, they and we and the people demanded to see the emperor's letters. Since it has been written, *Let no falsehood be spoken by the king from his mouth*, we thought that the king, once he had made a promise, would not lie or change his mind.[198] **2** If he acquiesced on account of his brother, how come he wrote again after Constans' death? And if he wrote then on account of Constans' memory, why did he completely disregard him later by persecuting Athanasius and writing letters in which he used the judgement of bishops as a pretext, when he was actually doing whatever he

195 On Philagrius and his previous stint as Prefect of Egypt, see n. 30 to chapter 7.5 above.

196 See chapter 21.2 above.

197 As well as holding the rank of *comes*, Asterius also had the military position of *dux Armeniae*: see PLRE I 119 (Asterius 3). Palladius went on to hold the important administrative post of *magister officiorum* under the *caesar* Gallus and, like a number of other officials from Constantius' regime, was tried at Chalcedon in 361, although he was not executed, instead being exiled to Britain: see PLRE I 658–9 (Palladius 4). Papyrological evidence indicates that Flavius Felicissimus had held the post of *dux Aegypti* since 347: see PLRE I 331 (Felicissimus 3). On Nestorius, Prefect of Egypt, see n. 90 to chapter 23.3 above. On the Praetorian Prefect Philip, see n. 32 to chapter 7.6 above.

198 This quotation is from a passage in the Septuagint version of *Proverbs*, at the end of chapter 24. On Diogenes, see n. 183 to chapter 48.1 above. On Syrianus, see n. 115 on chapter 31.2 above.

liked? He did not escape detection, however, and proof of his villainy was at hand. **3** For if a judgement is made by bishops, what interest does the emperor have in it? If a threat comes from the emperor, what need is there then of the so-called 'bishops'? When since the dawn of time have such things ever been heard of? When has a judgement of the church received its authority from the emperor or, actually, when was his verdict recognised [by the Church]? Many councils have taken place before this, and there have been many decisions by the church, but the fathers never prevailed on the emperor about them, nor did the emperor meddle in church affairs. **4** The apostle Paul had friends in the household of Caesar and he sent greetings from them when he wrote to the Philippians, but he did not invite them to be partners in making decisions.[199] **5** Now a new wonder has appeared, the invention of the Arian heresy. The heretics and the emperor Constantius have united for this purpose: he, with the bishops as a pretext, can do whatever he wants with authority and can persecute without being called a persecutor, while they, with the power of the emperor, can plot against whomsoever they wish. For they want to plot against anyone who is not impious like them. **6** Someone might think that this was a comedy written for these people to perform on the stage, with the so-called 'bishops' acting out roles and Constantius being the producer for their performance; once again he makes promises, as Herod did to the daughter of Herodias, and once again they dance their slanders to bring about the exile and death of those who are pious towards the Lord.[200]

53.1 Who have they not harmed with their slanders? Who have the enemies of Christ not plotted against? Who has not been exiled by Constantius after being accused by these men? When has he not listened to them with pleasure? And, incredibly, what opponent of theirs has he ever given an audience to, rather than admitting those men to say whatever they might say? What church now worships Christ with freedom? If it is pious, it is in danger; if it plays along with him, it lives in fear. **2** As far as he could, he has filled everything with pretence and impiety. If anyone

---

199 See *Philippians* 4.22.

200 This passage employs not only the concept of pretence through acting, but also the idea of re-enactment, in which Constantius becomes Herod, while the 'Arian' bishops act out the role of Salome, who bewitched the emperor with her dancing and thus brought about the execution of John the Baptist: see *Matthew* 14.6–11; *Mark* 6.22–8. I have kept the literal (and pleasingly vivid) phrase 'dance their slanders' in the translation to reflect the direct equation of the bishops with Salome.

anywhere is pious and loves Christ (and in every place there are many people who resemble the prophets and the great Elijah), they go into hiding if they can find a trustworthy man like Obadiah and either head off into a cave or cracks in the earth, or else spend their time wandering around the deserts.[201] **3** These idiots utter the same sorts of slanders as Jezebel concocted against Naboth and the Jews did against the Saviour.[202] Then Constantius, the protector of the heresy, who wants to change the truth just as Ahab changed the vineyard into a garden of herbs, carries out their wishes, since what he has heard from them is what he himself wants.[203]

54.1   So, as I said above, he exiled the true bishops, because they did not act impiously as he wanted, and then he sent the *comes* Heraclius against Athanasius. Heraclius displayed the edicts publicly and announced the emperor's orders that, unless they obeyed his letter, the bread would be taken away, the idols would be overturned and many of the *decuriones* and others of the population would most certainly be imprisoned.[204] **2** As he made these threats, he was not ashamed to say publicly in a loud voice, 'The emperor dismisses Athanasius and has ordered that the churches be handed over to the Arians.'[205] **3** Everyone was astounded by this, turning to each other and saying, 'Has Constantius become a heretic?' Although he should have been blushing with embarrassment, Heraclius instead compelled the city councillors and the common pagan wardens of the idols to subscribe to these decisions and to agree to receive whomever bishop the emperor chose to send. **4** Constantius was certainly obeying the canons of the church when he caused this to happen![206] For he demanded written statements not from the church but from the agora, and not from the congregations but from the temple wardens. He realised that he was not sending him [George] as a bishop to Christians but rather as a troublemaker to the men who had subscribed.

---

201 See *1 Kings* 18.3–4, where Obadiah hid fifty prophets in a cave to protect them from Ahab and Jezebel. In the following chapter, Elijah himself fled into the desert to avoid persecution.

202 These two biblical examples of slander also appear in chapter 45.2 above.

203 For Ahab's desire to turn Naboth's vineyard into a garden of herbs, see *1 Kings* 21.1.

204 On the *comes* Heraclius, see chapter 48.3 above. *Decuriones* were members of the city council. The threats are clearly presented as being directed towards the whole population of Alexandria, including pagans.

205 Constantius would not, of course, have referred to these men as 'the Arians'.

206 This line contains heavy sarcasm.

55.1 So the Hellenes subscribed, as though they were buying the safety of their idols by doing so, as did some members of the guilds, albeit unwillingly, because of Heraclius' threats, just as if it were a governor or some other official who was being sent. For, being Hellenes, what were they going to do other than what the emperor wanted? **2** In contrast, after the congregation had assembled in the Great Church (as it was the fourth day of the week), on the next day the *comes* Heraclius took with him Cataphronius the Prefect of Egypt, Faustinus the *rationalis* and Bithynus the heretic.[207] They raised a mob of common young men and idol-worshippers and told them that the emperor has given orders to attack the church and throw stones at the congregation. **3** As the dismissal [at the end of the service] had taken place by this point, most of the congregation had already departed, but there were a few women still present when these orders were put into effect. It was a pitiable sight: a few who had just come from prayer were sitting down when these naked young men attacked them with stones and clubs. These godless men threw stones at some of them and they also beat the holy bodies of the virgins, dragged off their veils and uncovered their heads; when the women resisted, these wretches kicked them. **4** And these things are terrible, very terrible indeed; but what happened afterwards was even more terrible, and harder to endure than any outrage; for, because they knew about the revered status of the virgins and the purity of their ears, and also that they could endure stones and swords more than foul language, they attacked them with words of this sort. The Arians suggested this idea to the young men, and laughed while these things were being said and done. When the holy virgins and the other revered women fled from these shouts, as they would from the

---

207 Not much more is known of Cataphronius, who was Prefect of Egypt from 356 to 357: see PLRE I 186 (Cataphronius 1). The *rationalis rei priuatae* was an important financial official and was in charge of imperial property in Egypt and its revenue: see Jones (1964) I 412–14; Kelly (2004) 202. Faustinus went on to become Prefect of Egypt in 359–361, during which time he is reported to have continued to seek out Athanasius, who was in hiding until after the death of Constantius: see PLRE I 326–7 (Faustinus 2). Bithynus is not mentioned elsewhere. The so-called 'Great Church' had been created within the large Caesareum complex, which had been begun at the end of the Ptolemaic period and consisted of numerous buildings, porticoes and gardens. It had been handed over to Gregory 'the Cappadocian' by Constantius II, although the bishop did not live to see the church's construction completed. See Epiphanius, *Panarion* 69.2.2–3; Haas (1997) 26, 210–11. In *Apol. Const.* 14–15, Athanasius defended himself against the charge of having used this church before it had been completed. The church is also mentioned in chapter 74.2 below. Barnes (1993) 119 dates this attack to June 356.

bites of asps, the enemies of Christ gave assistance to the young men and maybe even joined them in shouting. For they were delighted by the obscene language that they were yelling.

56.1   In order to complete their orders (for they were keen to do this and had been commanded to by both the *comes* and the *rationalis*), they then seized the stalls, the throne, the altar table (which was wooden) and the church curtains, as well as whatever else they could, carried them outside, set fire to them in front of the entrance in the great main street and threw on frankincense.[208] **2** Oh, who could hear this and not weep? He might even stop up his ears,[209] so as not to experience someone else relating it, thinking it harmful even to hear about such an event. They also praised their idols and said, 'Constantius has become a Hellene and the Arians have given their approval to our beliefs'. These men do not have any scruple about acting out Hellenism, so long as it helps their heresy. **3** They even attempted to sacrifice a heifer that was used in irrigating the garden areas at the Caesareum, and they would have done this if it had not been female.[210] For they said that they are not allowed to sacrifice these animals.[211]

57.1   The impious Arians went along with the Hellenes in doing this because they thought that it would harm and injure us. But divine justice[212] convicted them of wickedness and provided a great and remarkable sign, thereby revealing clearly to everyone that, just as these men are rashly insulting none other than the Lord with their impiety, so by committing these crimes they tried to harm him again. And there is even clearer proof of this from the amazing thing that happened: **2** a young man from this shameless mob ran in and dared to sit down on the throne.[213] When he had

---

208 The great main street referred to here is probably the central east-west arterial road through the centre of Alexandria, also known as the Via Canopica: see *RE* I 1383; Haas (1997) 29–32, 81–90. The accusation that frankincense was thrown onto the flames is presumably part of the claim by Athanasius that this attack on the church was turning into a 'pagan' ritual, as he continues to argue in the rest of this chapter.

209 Possibly an allusion to *Isaiah* 33.15.

210 On the large Caesareum complex, where the Great Church had been built, see n. 207 to chapter 55.2 above, as well as chapter 74.2.

211 This Egyptian taboo against sacrificing cows, which were sacred to Isis, is mentioned at Herodotus 2.41.

212 Other interventions by 'divine justice' have already been described in chapters 7.6 and 14.4 above.

213 This is a reference to the episcopal throne in the church.

sat down, this wretch hummed a filthy tune through his nostrils. Then, after he stood up, he used force to detach the throne and pull it towards himself, unaware that he was bringing down justice on himself. **3** For the earlier inhabitants of Azotus dared to touch the ark, although they were not even permitted to look at it, and were immediately annihilated by it, having first had their backsides destroyed by excruciating pain;[214] in the same way, this wretch, when he dared simply to pull the throne, brought down upon himself the thing that he was pulling. Just as if justice itself were driving the wood into him, he struck his own belly and, instead of detaching the throne, he detached his own entrails with the blow, and so the throne took away his life, rather than being taken away by him. **4** In fact, as Scripture states about Judas, he poured out his innards and, after falling to the ground, he was carried off and died a day later.[215] And another man entered with branches and he waved them about like a Hellene and made jokes. He was immediately blinded and could no longer see or know where in the world he was. He was about to fall over, but his companions took him by the hand and he left supported by them. The reckless man recovered with difficulty the next day and he could not recall either his actions or his affliction.

58.1 When they saw this, the Hellenes were afraid and did not dare to do anything more. But the Arians were still not ashamed and, like the Jews who saw the signs, these faithless men did not believe. Instead, they were hardened like Pharaoh and they kept their hopes somewhere below, in the emperor and his eunuchs.[216] **2** They allowed the Hellenes, or, rather, the more contemptible Hellenes, to do the things related above. They got Faustinus to play along with this and incite the Hellenes; he was called the *rationalis*, but in fact he was base in his behaviour and shameless in his soul.[217] The Arians decided to do the same things themselves, so that, just as they modelled their heresy on other heresies, so they might also

---

214 See *1 Samuel* 5.6.

215 *Acts* 1.18. This comparison with Judas is also used by Athanasius when recounting the death of Arius in his *De morte Arii*. See Introduction p. 6.

216 The hardening of Pharaoh's heart occurs on a number of occasions in *Exodus* 7–14. The sub-divisions of this chapter are misnumbered in Opitz's edition, with the final three parts being numbered as 3, 3 and 4. I have amended these to 3, 4 and 5.

217 On Faustinus and the title *rationalis*, see n. 207 to chapter 55.2 above. Athanasius is here punning on the word καθολικός, which is the Greek version of the title *rationalis*, but which also means 'universal' and 'orthodox' in Christian contexts. In Athanasius' judgement, the *rationalis* Faustinus is far from orthodox.

share their wickedness with the more shameless people. **3** I have already described what they got those men to do, but surely the wrongs that they committed themselves exceed all wickedness and surpass the evil of any executioner! What house did they not plunder? What household did they not despoil under the pretext of carrying out a search? What garden did they not trample and what tomb did they not open? The hunt for Athanasius was a pretext; their real desire was to plunder and despoil everyone they met. **4** How many people's houses were sealed? How many people had the contents of their lodgings distributed to the soldiers who were helping them? Who did not experience their wicked behaviour? Who, having met them, did not then hide himself in the agora? Who did not leave his home because of these men and spend the night in the desert? Who, while endeavouring to guard his possessions from these men, did not lose most of them? **5** Who, despite never having been to sea, did not choose to take to it and risk its dangers rather than to watch these men issuing their threats? Many people changed house and moved from alley to alley and even from the city to the suburbs. How many people paid over how many fines or, if they did not have the money, borrowed it from others, just so that they might escape from their plots?

59.1 They made themselves terrifying to everyone and behaved arrogantly towards all, always referring to the emperor and using the terror of him in their threats. They also had assistants in their wickedness: the *dux* Sebastian, a Manichaean and a shameless young man, and the prefect, the *comes* and the one who claims to be *rationalis*.[218] **2** In fact, when many virgins condemned their impiety and acknowledged the truth, these men took them from their houses. They also committed outrages against others as they walked along the street and got their gang of young men to uncover the virgins' heads. And the women who were with them were also given licence to maltreat anyone they wished. **3** The revered and faithful women turned aside and gave way to them on the road; but these women, like maenads and furies, thought themselves unlucky if they could not do wrong and they were miserable on any day when they could not commit

218 The unnamed officials are Heraclius, Cataphronius and Faustinus: see 55.2 above. The comment about the *rationalis* Faustinus is another use of the double meaning of καθολικός. Sebastian held the office of *dux Aegypti* from 356 to 358, after which he went on to have a long military career, eventually becoming *magister peditum* in 378, shortly before his death at the battle of Adrianople: see PLRE I 812–13 (Sebastianus 2). On the Manichaeans, see n. 109 to chapter 30.2 above.

evil.[219] In fact, they were so wild and vindictive to everyone that they were universally called executioners, murderers, lawless, troublemakers, evil-doers and anything but Christians.

60.1 Furthermore, they imitated the Scythians and seized Eutychius the subdeacon, a man who served the church well, and they caused his back to be flogged with ox-hide whips and left him almost dead.[220] Then they asked for him to be sent to the mines, and not just to any mines, but to the ones at Phaeno, where even a condemned murderer can scarcely survive for a few days.[221] **2** And the extraordinary thing was that they would not even allow him a few hours to be treated for his injuries. Instead, they had him sent away immediately, saying 'If this happens, everyone will be frightened and will then join us.' Not much later, he was unable to reach the mines because of the pain of his injuries and died on the road. **3** When he met his end, he rejoiced and obtained the glory of martyrdom; but the impious men felt no shame even then and, as Scripture says, *having innards without mercy* and having planned this, they did something else diabolical.[222] For when the people tried to intercede for Eutychius and were pleading with them on his behalf, they had four respectable and free men taken into custody, including Hermias, who used to wash beggars. These men were beaten very violently and thrown into prison by the *dux*. **4** But the Arians were more savage then Scythians, and when they saw that these men had not

219 Furies were terrifying avenging female deities that punished men, while maenads were female followers of Dionysus and were famous for their out-of-control behaviour. Haas (1997) 284 describes this passage as containing 'some measure of hyperbole on the part of the patriarch', but nonetheless regards it as evidence that worshippers of Dionysus were involved in this incident. It does, however, seem more likely that Athanasius' mention of 'maenads and furies' is merely a way of describing the women as raving and destructive, rather than a specific reference to the involvement of these actual religious adherents.

220 The Scythians lived in lands to the north of the Black Sea and the Persian empire. Ever since Herodotus, they were a by-word in Greek literature for fierce and savage behaviour.

221 Phaeno in Palestine was the location of remote copper mines to which criminals might be sent: see *Barrington Atlas* Map 70 G4; http://pleiades.stoa.org/places/697726. The use of Phaeno for this purpose is mentioned in the Tetrarchic letter against the Manicheans (*Collatio* 15.3.7) and it was also a place of exile for Christians during the Great Persecution: see Eus. *Mart. Pal.* 7.2–3, 13.1; Epiphanius, *Panarion* 68.3.6. For discussion of the evidence for Phaeno, as well as the suggestion that some people sent there during the Great Persecution enjoyed more liberty (and so may have had a greater chance of survival than Athanasius suggests here), see Millar (1984) 140–41. On the punishment of being condemned to the mines more generally, see n. 35 to Lucifer, *Moriundum* 3 at p. 148 below.

222 See *Proverbs* 12.10.

died from their injuries, they complained and uttered threats, saying 'We're writing to the eunuchs to say that you're not flogging people in the way we want.'[223] When he [Sebastian] heard this, he became frightened and was forced to beat the men a second time. **5** As they were being beaten, these men knew why they were being beaten and who had spoken against them, and yet they said nothing other than 'We are being beaten because we defend the truth, but we refuse to be in communion with heretics. Beat us more, as you wish, and God will judge you for it.' The impious men wanted them to be in danger of actually dying in the prison, but the people of God saw an opportunity and interceded on their behalf. After seven days or more, they were released.

61.1   Those men [the Arians] were distressed by this and tried to do something even more savage and unholy, something that seemed savage to everyone, but which was entirely in keeping with their Christ-fighting heresy. For the Lord instructed us to remember the poor, saying *Sell what you have and give alms* and *I was hungry, and you gave me food. I was thirsty, and you gave me drink. For inasmuch as you have done it unto one of these little ones, you have done it unto me.*[224] **2** But these men are actually opposed to Christ and they have dared to act against his will in this matter. For after the *dux* had handed the churches over to the Arians, the needy and the widows could no longer spend time in them. They then sat down in places marked out by those clerics who had been entrusted with the widows. When they [the Arians] saw the brothers feeding the widows and looking after them eagerly, they persecuted the women by beating them on their feet and they also made accusations to the *dux* against those who were caring for them. **3** This they did with the help of a certain soldier called Dynamius, but Sebastian also approved.[225] For there is no compassion among Manichaeans, and showing compassion to a poor man is something they detest.[226] And so there appeared a new ground for complaint and a new court was now contrived by them for the first time: one could be tried for kindness, a compassionate person was accused, a beneficiary of kindness was beaten. They preferred a poor man to go hungry rather than

223 Having set up the 'Arians' as being like the Scythians, Athanasius now claims that they surpass these paradigmatically savage people in their savagery. He makes a similar comparison between his enemies and the 'pagans' at 64.1 below.
224 *Luke* 12.33; *Matthew* 25.35, 40.
225 Dynamius appears again in chapter 81.10 below, but he is not mentioned elsewhere.
226 On the Manichaeans, see n. 109 to chapter 30.2 above.

be provided for by a compassionate volunteer. **4** These men are new Jews, who have learned this from the ancient Jews. For when the Jews of old saw that the man who had been blind from birth could now see and that the man who had been paralysed long before was now healthy, they accused the Lord because he had done these good deeds, and they condemned the healed men as transgressors.[227]

62.1 Who was not amazed at these events? Who did not denounce the heresy and its supporters? Who did not recognise that the Arians are more ferocious than wild animals? For these blood-stained men did not profit from this as they had planned, but instead they made everybody hate them even more. They thought that their plotting and terror would force some people to become heretics and join up with them. **2** But they got the opposite result instead. The people who were suffering endured this treatment as martyrdom, and refused to abandon or renounce their piety towards Christ; and people outside who witnessed this, and even the Hellenes who saw it, all denounced the Arians as antichrists and executioners. Human beings love the poor and are sympathetic to them. But these men have even lost human reason. If they were suffering, they would have prayed for help from others; but they would not allow others to be helped, and they wielded the oppressive authority of the officials, particularly the *dux*.

63.1 They even committed crimes against the presbyters and deacons; they got the *dux* and the officials to banish them; they used soldiers to drive their relatives from their homes, while the *strategos* Gorgonius also beat them; and (which is the crueller than anything else) they violently snatched the loaves from these men and from those who had already died.[228] It is impossible to put all this into words because their savagery surpasses the very power of language. **2** How might someone think of a way to describe this? For whatever they described first, they would then discover that the second set of events was more terrible, and the next ones even more terrible still. All the irreligious actions of these men have been full of murder and impiety. They are so wicked in their desires and so wily in their behaviour that they attempt to deceive people with a promise of patronage or a

227 For these stories, see *John* 9.1–41; *Matthew* 9.1–8.
228 The two men who held the title of *strategos* of the city of Alexandria had responsibilities for maintaining law and order: see Haas (1997) 76. Gorgonius is otherwise unknown.

payment of money. Because they cannot gain support through reasonable and honourable means, they do this to create a false appearance and trick the unwary.

64.1   Who would still call these men gentiles even, let alone Christians?[229] Who would interpret their behaviour as human rather than bestial because of the savagery and ferocity of their actions? In fact they are more wicked than executioners and more reckless than the other heresies. And they are vastly inferior to the Hellenes and also very different from them.[230] **2** For I heard from our fathers – and I believe that their story is trustworthy – that in the beginning, when persecution arose under Maximian, the grandfather of Constantius, Hellenes hid our Christian brothers when they were being hunted down.[231] And the Hellenes themselves often lost money and suffered imprisonment, purely to avoid betraying these fugitives. They protected those who sought refuge with them as they would have protected themselves, and they wanted to face danger in their place. **3** But now these extraordinary men, these inventors of a new heresy, do the complete opposite, and are recognisable from nothing other than their plotting against others. They have appointed themselves executioners, they seek to betray everyone and they plot against those who conceal others, regarding both the concealers and the concealed as their enemies. In this way they are murderers and evil-doers who have imitated the wickedness of Judas.[232]

65.1   It is impossible to adequately describe their evil deeds, except to say only that, as I write and seek to recount their wicked actions, it occurs to me to consider whether this heresy is not *the fourth daughter of the horse-leach* in *Proverbs*, since after so many injustices and so many murders it has not said *It is enough*.[233] For it still acts insolently. It goes around hunting

---

229 The term 'gentile' here translates the Greek word ἐθνικός.

230 Having linked the Arians with 'pagans' and their practices elsewhere in the text, Athanasius here strengthens his rhetorical denunciation of his enemies by presenting them as surpassing the impiety of the impious.

231 On the presentation of Maximian, the Tetrarchic emperor and maternal grandfather of Constantius, as a persecutor, see n. 148 to chapter 40.2 above. Athanasius is here referring to the 'Great Persecution' in the early fourth century.

232 Opitz here prints the verb ἐξήλωσαν, which does not make sense in this context. Presumably, instead of ξ, Opitz meant to print ζ (as Migne does in PG), giving the verb 'imitated'.

233 See *Proverbs* 30.15.

down people that it has not yet found, while it is eager to inflict yet more hurt on those it has already harmed. **2** Look! After the night attack, after all the evils that followed, after the persecution under Heraclius, they still continue uttering slanders before the emperor.[234] Because they are impious, they are confident that they will get a hearing so that a worse punishment than exile may be imposed and then those who will not convert to their impieties may be done away with. **3** Because they were now so confident, Secundus, that most utterly evil man from Pentapolis, and Stephanus, his fellow conspirator, realised that, if they ever did any harm, they had their heresy as a defence.[235] When they saw a presbyter in Barca who refused to obey them, a man who was also called Secundus (he had the same name, but not the same faith as the heretic), they kicked him to death.[236] While he was being killed, he imitated the holy one by saying, 'Let no one avenge me before judges. I have the Lord to avenge me, and for him I suffer this at the hands of these men.' But they neither showed mercy to him as he spoke nor did they feel ashamed because of the time of year: for they kicked and killed this man during Lent itself.

66.1 O new heresy, totally clothed in the Devil in its impiety and its behaviour! This evil is a new invention. If some people seemed to have thoughts about it before, they hid them and were not discovered to be holding these beliefs. **2** But Eusebius and Arius went out from their lair like serpents and spat out the venom of this impiety.[237] Arius had the audacity to commit open blasphemy, while Eusebius gave it patronage. But he could not support the heresy until he found the emperor to act as its protector, as I said above. **3** Our fathers held an ecumenical council, where 300 bishops, more or less, came together, condemned the Arian heresy and unanimously declared it to be alien and foreign to the ecclesiastical faith; but when its protectors saw that they were now in disgrace and had no reasonable arguments, they devised another route and tried

---

234 On the *comes* Heraclius, see chapter 48.3 above. There is no number to denote chapter 65.2 in Opitz's edition, but the spacing of the text makes it clear that it should fall at this point.

235 Secundus, bishop of Ptolemais, is also criticised by Athanasius at *Ad Ep. Aeg.* 7.3. 19.8; *De synodis* 12.3. He was one of the two Libyan bishops who were exiled at the Council of Nicaea in 325: *Urk.* 23.5. The Libyan Stephanus is also mentioned at Ath. *De synodis* 12.3.

236 Nothing more is known about this presbyter. Barca was a city in Pentapolis, not far from Ptolemais.

237 As above, this is Eusebius, bishop of Nicomedia.

to vindicate it using external authority.[238] At this point, someone might marvel at their novel and wicked behaviour that surpasses other heresies. **4** For the madness of the other heretical inventions consisted in persuasive words that trick the unwary. The Hellenes, as the apostle said, attack with elevated and persuasive words and plausible sophisms, while the Jews, who abandoned the divine scriptures, conduct their wrangling from now on *in fables and endless genealogies*, as the apostle said.[239] Along with them the Manichaeans and Valentinians and the others corrupt the divine scriptures and invent fables from their own false texts.[240] **5** But the Arians are more daring than other heresies and have proved that these others are their little sisters. For they are more impious than the others, as I have said, and they compete with all of them, especially the Jews, in their wickedness. For just as they [the Jews], when they could not refute Paul using their false claims, led him at once to the military commander and the governor, so these men, who invent even more than they did, have relied solely on the authority of officials.[241] Anyone who merely answers them back is dragged before the governor or the general.

67.1   When other heresies are convicted with evidence by the truth itself, they do not say anything further, because they have been put to shame by the refutations. In contrast, whenever this new and abominable heresy of theirs is overturned by arguments, whenever it collapses, shamed by the truth itself, then, because it cannot persuade people through reasoned argument, it tries to compel them through violence, beatings and prison sentences, thereby revealing that it is anything but pious towards God. **2** For it is characteristic of piety not to force people, but to persuade them,

---

238 The concept of an 'ecumenical' or 'worldwide' council began with presentations of the Council of Nicaea from the late 330s onwards, but Athanasius was very keen to use this term in order to present Nicaea as more authoritative than other councils: see Chadwick (1972). The number of bishops who attended Nicaea in 325 is uncertain, although the earliest estimates are around 250–300. Hilary, *In Const.* 27 gives the figure of 318, which was also the number of Abraham's servants in *Genesis* 14.14. The acceptance of this number became standard by the late fourth century: see Hanson (1988) 155–6.

239 The first of these references may be an allusion to *1 Corinthians* 2.1. The second is a quotation from *1 Timothy* 1.4.

240 On the Manichaeans, see n. 109 to chapter 30.2 above. On Valentinus, a second-century theologian often referred to as a 'Gnostic' by his opponents, see Iren. *Haer.* 1.1–9, 1.11; Hippol. *Haer.* 6.21, 6.29–37, 10.13; Epiphanius, *Panarion* 31; Markschies (1992); Brakke (2010) 99–105, 115–19.

241 For this story, see *Acts* 21–25.

as we said.[242] For the Lord himself did not force people; instead he gave them a choice, saying to everyone, *If any man wishes to come after me*,[243] and to his disciples, *Do you also wish to go away?*[244] But this heresy is utterly alien to piety. **3** What could it do except be hostile to the Saviour, when it has enrolled Constantius as the Christ-fighting leader of impiety, as the Antichrist himself? At first he was eager to help the heresy by competing with Saul in savagery. For when the priests had given provisions to David, Saul gave the order and had all 305 of them done away with; but when everyone flees from the heresy and when the sound faith in the Lord is confessed, Constantius does away with a council of a whole 300 bishops.[245] He exiles the bishops themselves, while he stops the congregations from assembling, in order to prevent them from practising piety and praying to God. **4** As Saul obliterated *Nob, the city of the priests*, so this man has become even more evil and has handed over the churches to the impious; and just as that man [Saul] preferred the accuser Doeg to the true priests, persecuted David and listened to the Ziphites, so this man prefers heretics to the pious, continues to persecute people who flee from him and listens to his eunuchs, who slander the orthodox.[246] He cannot see that whatever he does or writes for the Arian heresy constitutes an attack on the Saviour.

68.1 Ahab did not treat the priests of God in the way that this man has dared to treat the bishops. After Naboth had been murdered, that man [Ahab] actually *felt compunction*, and when he saw Elijah, he was frightened;[247] but this man [Constantius] neither respected Ossius, despite his great age, nor, after exiling so many bishops, did he go numb or feel compunction, but, as another Pharaoh, he is afflicted and hardened all the

242 See chapter 33.1–4 above.
243 *Matthew* 16.24.
244 *John* 6.67.
245 The story about Saul and David is from *1 Samuel* 22.10–18 and there are more references to it in the next part of this chapter. The figure of 305 priests (as opposed to eighty-five) is found in the Septuagint version of *1 Samuel* 22.18. On the number of bishops at the Council of Nicaea in 325, see n. 238 to chapter 66.3 above. Athanasius clearly found the similarity in the two numbers to be very useful for his argument that Constantius is a new Saul.
246 Doeg and the city of Nob appear in *1 Samuel* 22.9–19, with the quotation coming from verse 19. Saul listens to the Ziphites at *1 Samuel* 23.19, 26.1.
247 *1 Kings* 20.27 LXX.

more, and invents worse crimes on a daily basis.[248] **2** Here is an extraordinary example of his wickedness: after the bishops were exiled, some other people received sentences on charges of murder or sedition or theft, according to the nature of the offence. After a few months he released these men in response to a request, as Pilate released Barabbas,[249] but he did not let the servants of Christ go, and instead he became an imperishable evil towards them and punished them even more pitilessly in their exile.[250] He was friendly to the first group of men because of their bad character, but hostile to the orthodox because of their piety towards Christ. **3** Has it not been clearly revealed to all from this that the Jews, who once asked for Barabbas and crucified the Lord, were the same as these men who now join Constantius in fighting against Christ? He is probably more vicious that Pilate. For while he [Pilate] recognised the injustice and washed his hands, this man gnashes his teeth even more and exiles the blessed.[251]

69.1   Why is it amazing if, having strayed into impiety, he is so savage towards the bishops, since he did not spare his own family as a human being would? He murdered his uncles; he did away with his cousins; he showed no mercy to his father-in-law, even though he had married his daughter, or to his suffering relatives, and he has always been a breaker of oaths towards all.[252] He has even dared to be impious towards his brother [Constans]: although he pretends to construct a memorial to him, he has actually

248 For the treatment of Ossius, see chapters 42–5 above. For comparisons between Constantius and Pharaoh, including the repeated occasions when Pharaoh's heart was hardened, see also chapters 30.4, 34.2 and 58.1 above.

249 See *Matthew* 27.16–26; *Mark* 15.7–15; *Luke* 23.18; *John* 18.40.

250 This may be a reference to changes that were made in the locations where exiled bishops were held. At *In Const.* 11 Hilary states that Constantius kept moving Paulinus of Trier around while he was in exile. Eusebius of Vercelli was also sent first to Scythopolis in Palestine, then to Cappadocia and finally to the Thebaid in Egypt: see PCBE II.1 693 (Eusebius 1). On Lucifer's movements during exile, see Introduction p. 32. The phrase 'imperishable evil' is used in Homer, *Odyssey* 12.118 to describe the monster Scylla.

251 On the gnashing of teeth as a biblical characteristic of villains, see n. 264 to chapter 72.5 below.

252 Athanasius here assigns to Constantius the blame for the dynastic massacre of 337, in which many of the male relatives of Constantine I were killed shortly after this emperor's death, leaving his sons Constantine II, Constantius II and Constans as joint rulers of the empire. The 'uncles' mentioned here were two half-brothers of Constantine I, named Flavius Dalmatius and Julius Constantius, the latter of whom was also the father-in-law of Constantius II. A number of cousins of Constantius II were killed, including Flavius Dalmatius' two sons (Dalmatius and Hannibalianus), Julius Constantius' eldest son and four

handed over Constans' fiancée Olympias to barbarians [to be married], even though Constans had protected her until his death and brought her up to be his own wife.[253] **2** He also tried to set aside Constans' wishes, despite professing to be his heir, and he writes the sorts of things that anyone with even the slightest sense would be ashamed of. In reviewing all his letters, I discover that he does not have his own wits in accordance with nature, but instead he is driven solely by people who make suggestions, having no mind of his own whatsoever. For Solomon says, *If a ruler hearkens to injustice, all his servants are wicked*, and by his actions this man reveals that he himself is unjust and his associates are wicked.[254]

70.1 Because he is this sort of man and delights in the company of such people, when could he ever believe in anything just or rational? He is a man shackled by the wickedness of his associates, who enchant him, or, rather, trample his brain under their heels. For this reason he writes, and writing he repents, and repenting he becomes angry, and then he goes back to lamenting; not knowing what to do, he reveals his witless soul. **2** Because he is like this, one should more properly pity him, since, although he has a free appearance and name, he is the slave of men who drag him around for their own pleasure in impiety. In fact, because he wishes to yield his stupidity and folly to others, as Scripture has said, he has handed himself over to condemnation, as something to be destroyed in the coming judgement of fire.[255] He is already doing their bidding and giving his approval to their plotting against the bishops and to their authority over the churches. **3** See now that he has once again disrupted all the churches in Alexandria and in Egypt and Libya! And he has openly given orders that the bishops of the catholic church and of piety should be expelled from the churches, and that all these should be handed over to those who follow the beliefs of Arius. **4** The general started to implement this. Then the bishops were chained up

others whose names are not known. A number of other high-ranking officials were also executed at the same time. On these events, see Barnes (1993) 34–5; Burgess (2008).

253 Constantius was apparently engaged at this time in the construction of a tomb for his brother, who had been killed by the usurper Magnentius in 350. This monument has sometimes been identified with a mausoleum at Centcelles, near the Spanish city of Tarragona. For discussion of this structure, see Johnson (2009) 129–39. Olympias was the daughter of the Praetorian Prefect Ablabius (who also died in the massacre of 337) and was given in marriage to Arsaces, king of Armenia: see Amm. 20.11.3; PLRE I 642 (Olympias 1).

254 *Proverbs* 29.12.

255 This is not a direct quotation from Scripture, but may be an allusion to *Proverbs* 7.22 LXX.

and the presbyters and monks were clapped in irons. They were beaten until they were almost dead and then escorted away. Everything everywhere has been thrown into chaos. The whole of Egypt and Libya is in danger, and the congregations are finding it hard to endure this lawless command and are watching this preparation for the Antichrist and seeing their property being seized from them and handed over to the heretics.

71.1   When has such great lawlessness ever been heard of before? When has anything so evil ever happened during persecution? The earlier persecutors were Hellenes, but they did not bring their idols into the churches. Zenobia was a Jewess and championed Paul of Samosata, but she did not hand the churches over to the Jews to be used as synagogues.[256] This is a new abomination. This is not simply a persecution: it is more than a persecution – it is the prelude and preparation for the Antichrist. **2** Let us accept that they invented false allegations to use against Athanasius and the other bishops they exiled; what has this got to do with their new activity? What pretext have they got to use against all Egypt, Libya and the Pentapolis? They are no longer just plotting against individuals, so that they can tell lies against them; now they have started to attack everyone at once, so that, whenever they want to invent an accusation, all are condemned. **3** Evil has blinded their intellect in these matters and they have not hesitated to demand the expulsion of all the bishops. They thereby reveal that, in the case of Athanasius and the other bishops who were exiled, they invented false allegations for no other reason than to aid the blood-stained heresy of the Christ-fighting Arians. This is no longer a secret, but is now completely obvious to everyone. **4** For he gave an order for Athanasius to be expelled from the city, while he handed the churches over to those men. Athanasius' presbyters and deacons, who were ordained by Peter and Alexander, are expelled and banished, while, at the same time, the true Arians have got possession of the churches. These are men who are not under suspicion for any external reasons but ones who, along with Arius himself, were expelled by Bishop Alexander at the beginning because of their heresy: in Upper Libya, Secundus; in Alexandria, Euzoius the Chananaian, Julius,

---

256 Zenobia was queen of Palmyra, ruling for her son after her husband's death in 267. She gradually increased the territory that Palmyra controlled, including taking over Egypt in 270, but was defeated by the emperor Aurelian two years later. On Paul of Samosata, a third-century bishop of Antioch who was deposed for his beliefs and came to be regarded as a heretic, see Introduction n. 68. For the modern debate about whether Zenobia really was a patron of Paul, see Potter (2014) 631 n. 31.

Ammon, Marcus, Irenaeus, Zosimus and Serapion surnamed Pelycon; and in Libya, Sisinnius and the young men who join him in impiety.[257]

72.1 The general Sebastian wrote to the *praepositi* and the military authorities in every place.[258] This led to the true bishops being persecuted and the impious being brought in to replace them. **2** They exiled bishops who had grown old in their office and had been in the episcopacy for many years, having been appointed by Bishop Alexander: they banished Ammonius, Hermes, Anagamphus and Marcus to the Upper Oasis and Muis, Psenosiris, Neilammon, Plenes, Marcus and Athenodorus to Ammoniaca for no other reason than to finish them off by the journey through the desert.[259] **3** They showed no pity to the sick, and they drove these men along when they moved off with difficulty because of their infirmity. They therefore had to be carried in litters, and, because of their illness, materials were brought along for their burial. One of them actually died, but they would not allow his body to be released to his own people. **4** For this reason they also exiled Bishop Dracontius to the deserts around Clysma, and they exiled Philo to Babylon, Adelphius to Psinabla

257 Peter was bishop of Alexandria from around the start of the fourth century until his execution in 311. Alexander was the immediate predecessor of Athanasius, occupying the see from 313 to 328. On Secundus of Ptolemais, see chapter 65.3 above. Euzoius and Julius are both named by Alexander of Alexandria as deacons who had joined Arius in heresy: see *Urk.* 4b. Euzoius went on to become bishop of Antioch in 360: see Ath. *De synodis* 31.3. Ammon is probably the same figure named by Athanasius in *Ep. Enc.* 7.6 as being the secretary of Gregory 'the Cappadocian', the 'Arian' bishop of Alexandria. Opitz (n. ad loc.) suggests that he may be identical with the deacon Parammon deposed by Alexander for agreeing with Arius: see *Urk.* 4a. No Marcus is listed in *Urk.* 4a or 4b, but Irenaeus, Zosimus and Serapion are all deacons deposed by Alexander in *Urk.* 4a. Sisinnius is otherwise unknown.

258 On the *dux* Sebastian, see chapter 59.1 above. The *praepositi* were commanding officers of military units: see Jones (1964) II 640. Athanasius uses a Greek transliteration of the Latin term here.

259 All of these bishops appear in the list of exiles given by Athanasius at *De fuga* 7.4. Ammonius is probably the bishop of Pachnamunis who appears as a signatory to the *Tomus ad Antiochenos* in 362. He is also a signatory to the 'western' letter from Serdica in 343 at Ath. *Apol. c. Ar.* 49.3, as are Anagamphus, Muis, Psenosiris and Neilammon. The two Marci are probably the bishops of Zygra and Philae, who signed the *Tomus ad Antiochenos*. Athanasius' Festal Letter for 347 provides the details that Neilammon was bishop of Latopolis, while Psenosiris may also be the figure named as bishop of Coptos in the same letter. The 'Upper Oasis' is probably the so-called 'Greater Oasis', which was in southern Egypt, while Ammoniaca was the city of Ammon at the Siwa Oasis: see *Barrington Atlas* Map 73 C4; http://pleiades.stoa.org/places/716520. As Athanasius states, travel to either of these locations would have involved a journey through the desert.

in the Thebaid and the presbyters Hierax and Dioscorus to Soene.[260] They banished Ammonius, Agathus, Agathodaimon, Apollonius, Eulogius, Apollo, Paphnutius, Gaius and Flavius, very old bishops, and Dioscorus, Ammonius, Heracleides and Psais, also bishops.[261] **5** They transferred some people to public service; they persecuted others, wishing to do away with them, and robbed many more.[262] They also exiled forty members of the laity and some virgins who had previously stood firm through fire.[263] They beat them with blows from rods made from palm trees. After five days, some of them died, while others had to be operated on because of the spines stuck in their limbs, which caused them tortures worse than death. And here is something that is even more shocking to everyone in their right mind, but is characteristic of these impious men: when the women were being beaten and were calling out to Christ, these men gnashed their

260 All of these figures appear in the list of exiles given by Athanasius at *De fuga* 7.4. Dracontius was bishop of Hermupolis Parva and was a signatory of the *Tomus ad Antiochenos*, as well as the recipient of an extant letter by Athanasius. His place of exile was near Clysma at the northern end of the Gulf of Suez (*Barrington Atlas* Map 74 H5; http://pleiades.stoa.org/places/727101) and is referred to as *castrum Thaubastum* in Jerome, *Vita Hilarionis* 20. Philo may be one of the two Egyptian bishops of that name who were signatories to the 'western' letter from Serdica in 343 at Ath. *Apol. c. Ar.* 49.3. The fortress of Babylon on the Nile is also mentioned in Jerome, *Vita Hilarionis* 20.10: see *Barrington Atlas* Map 74 E4; http://pleiades.stoa.org/places/727082. Adelphius is described as 'bishop of Onuphis in Lychni' in the signatures to the *Tomus ad Antiochenos*. Hierax and Dioscorus appear in a list of presbyters from the Mareotis at Ath. *Apol. c. Ar.* 75.6. Soene is probably Syene in the far south of Egypt: see *Barrington Atlas* Map 80 Inset; http://pleiades.stoa.org/places/786123.

261 As at *De fuga* 7.4, two bishops named Ammonius are mentioned here, one of whom may be the bishop of Pachnamunis just mentioned in chapter 72.2. Agathus also appears at *De fuga* 7.4 and is also called bishop 'of Phragonis and part of Helearchia in Egypt' in the signatures of the *Tomus ad Antiochenos*, where Agathodaimon, Paphnutius and Gaius are also listed as bishops of Schedia, Sais and Paratonium respectively. Apollonius, Paphnutius, Gaius, Dioscorus, Heracleides and Psais may be the Egyptian bishops of those names listed as having signed the 'western' letter from Serdica in 343 at Ath. *Apol. c. Ar.* 49.3.

262 The phrase 'public service' here refers to the system of 'liturgies', which were financially onerous obligations placed on members of city councils. In the later Roman empire, wealthier citizens frequently sought immunities from these burdens, including by entering the imperial bureaucracy or the Christian clergy: see Jones (1964) II 734–57; Kelly (2004) 146–7. 'Public service' is a translation of the Greek term λειτουργία, which Opitz prints here. This would suggest that Athanasius is here referring to clergy losing their exemptions from performing liturgies. The PG text of Migne has λιθουργία here, which is rendered into English as 'work in the stone-quarries' in Atkinson's translation in Robertson (1892).

263 This mistreatment of virgins is also described by Athanasius at *De fuga* 6.6.

teeth against them even more.[264] **6** They would not even hand the bodies of the departed over to their nearest and dearest for burial. Instead, they hid them, in the hope that their murders might avoid detection. But they failed in this: the whole city saw and everyone turned away from them as executioners, as evil-doers and robbers. What is more, they overturned monasteries, tried to throw monks into fire and plundered houses; they entered the homes of free people and then robbed and despoiled the items placed there by the bishop; they beat widows on the soles of their feet and prevented almsgiving.

73.1 Such are the wicked deeds of the Arians. Who will not shiver when they hear about the other godless crimes that they attempted? They caused very old, long-standing bishops to be exiled, and in their place they appointed young, shameless men and Hellenes who had not even been catechumens (since they thought it was a good idea to promote them straightaway), as well as others who had been married twice and people accused of even greater offences.[265] They appointed them because of their wealth and political power, and then, after these men had given them gold, the Arians sent them out as though from an auction-room and called them bishops. **2** Then an even more terrible disaster befell the congregations: when they [the congregations] turned away from these men for being hired servants of the Arians and completely alien to themselves, they were flogged, arrested and imprisoned by the general. Being a Manichaean, he did this eagerly, so that they would not request their own [bishops], but would instead accept those they had rejected, men who were performing the same games that they previously played among their idols.[266]

74.1 Could anyone see or hear about these things, or witness the arrogance of the impious and such great injustice, and not groan, if he

264 See also chapter 68.3 above for this image of Constantius gnashing his teeth against the righteous. This activity is often attributed to enemies and villains in the Bible: see *Job* 16.9 (16.10 LXX); *Psalms* 35.16 (34.16 LXX), 37.12 (36.12 LXX); *Lamentations* 2.16; *Mark* 9.18; *Acts* 7.54.

265 Catechumens were people who were receiving instruction in Christianity in preparation for baptism. The instruction that a bishop should be the husband of one wife is based on *1 Timothy* 3.2.

266 On the Manichaean *dux* Sebastian, see chapter 59.1 above. At the end of the sentence Athanasius is being dismissive of traditional 'pagan' worship by referring to it as 'playing games'.

himself were just? For *in the places of the impious, just men groan.*[267]
Now that this has happened and their impiety has become so utterly
shameless, who still dares to say that this Costyllius is a Christian and not
rather the likeness of the Antichrist?[268] For what marks of the Antichrist
are absent? How will he [the Antichrist] not be thought to be this man
[Constantius] in every respect, and how would this man not be assumed to
be the same as him?[269] **2** Have the Arians and Hellenes not had sacrifices
carried out in the Great Church in the Caesareum and blasphemies uttered
against Christ, as though by his command?[270] Does the vision of Daniel
not identify the Antichrist in this way, saying that *he will make war with
the saints and prevail against them* and will surpass in evils all those
before him; *and he shall subdue three kings and he shall speak words
against the most High, and think to change times and laws?*[271] **3** Who
has ever attempted to do these things except Constantius? For he is the
kind of person that the Antichrist would be: he speaks words against
the most High when he supports this impious heresy and he makes war
against the saints by exiling bishops, even though he possesses authority
only for a short time and for his own destruction. **4** He has surpassed his
predecessors in evil, because he has contrived a new form of persecution.
After he deposed the three kings Vetranio, Magnentius and Gallus, he
immediately gave support to impiety.[272] And, like a giant, he has in his
arrogance dared to rise up against the most High.[273] **5** He has thought
to change laws by annulling the instruction that the Lord gave through
the apostles, changing the customs of the church and himself devising
a new form of appointments: from other places and fifty stopping posts

---

267 *Proverbs* 28.28 LXX.

268 Costyllius is a diminutive form of the name Constantius. Athanasius uses it again at
chapter 80.1 below.

269 A rather difficult sentence that seeks to express the similarity between Constantius and
the Antichrist.

270 On the Great Church in the Caesareum in Alexandria, see n. 207 to chapter 55.2 above.

271 *Daniel* 7.21; 7.24–5.

272 On Vetranio, who was emperor for only a short time in 350, see chapter 50.1 above. On
the usurper Magnentius, who ruled in the West from 350 until his death in 353, see n. 111 to
chapter 30.3 above. Gallus was a cousin of Constantius who survived the massacre of 337.
He was raised to the rank of *caesar* in 351 and married Constantius' sister Constantina,
but fell out of favour and was removed and executed three years later: see PLRE I 224–5
(Constantius 4).

273 Although giants are mentioned in *Genesis* 6.4 just before God decides to flood the
earth, Athanasius' description fits better with the Giants of classical mythology, who waged
war against the Olympian gods.

away, he sends bishops to unwilling congregations, accompanied by soldiers; instead of a letter of introduction to the congregations, they bring threats and letters to the officials.[274] This was how he sent Gregory from Cappadocia to Alexandria, and also summoned Germinius from Cyzicus to Sirmium and dispatched Cecropius from Laodicea to Nicomedia.[275]

75.1 Constantius also sent Auxentius – a troublemaker, not a Christian – from Cappadocia to Milan. After he exiled Dionysius, the bishop there and a reverent man, because of his piety towards Christ, he gave orders for Auxentius to take his place, even though he did not yet know the Roman language or anything except how to be impious.[276] Now once again he has ordered George, a Cappadocian who was an official at the treasury in Constantinople, where he appropriated everything and then ran away, to come into Alexandria with a military procession and the authority of the general.[277] **2** Then, when he found Epictetus, a new convert and an insolent young man, he was very fond of him, because he saw that he was ready to do evil, and he made use of him to plot against selected bishops.[278] For Epictetus is ready to do anything the emperor wants. In fact, Constantius

274 The stopping posts mentioned here refer to lodgings where people would rest at the end of a day's journey. Athanasius' point is therefore that bishops are not only being imposed on communities from outside, but are also figures who have come from far distant locations, as they take so long to reach their new sees. As these lodgings were often part of the empire's *cursus publicus* system for official communications, Athanasius may also be emphasising his claim that these bishops are imposed by the imperial authorities. On these stopping places, see Jones (1964) II 831–4; Leyerle (2009) 117–18; Sotinel (2009) 130–32. Opitz (1935–41) 224 interprets the figure of fifty stopping points as a specific reference to George's journey from Cappadocia to Alexandria.

275 On Gregory 'the Cappadocian', see chapter 9.3 above. Germinius became bishop of Sirmium in 351 and features as a heretical villain in the dialogue known as the *Altercatio Heracliani cum Germinio*: see PCBE III 430 (Germinios); Simonetti (1967); Hanson (1988) 528–9; Williams (1996); Flower (2013) 1–6, 230–37. Cecropius is included by Hilary of Poitiers in his list of heretical bishops who attended the Council of Sirmium: see *Adv. Val. et Ursac.* B.VII.9; PCBE III 574 (Kékropios). Both bishops are criticised by Athanasius at *Ad Ep. Aeg.* 7.4–5.

276 Auxentius became bishop of Milan in 355, after the exile of Dionysius, and held the see until his death in 374, when he was succeeded by Ambrose. In the mid-360s Hilary of Poitiers made an unsuccessful attempt to unseat him by appealing to the emperor Valentinian I, as recounted in Hilary's *Contra Auxentium*. See PCBE II.1 238–41 (Auxentius 1); McLynn (1994) 13–43; (1997), Williams (1995) 76–83, 102–27; (1997); Kaufman (1997); Durst (1998); Flower (2013) 207–17, 252–60. The 'Roman language' here is Latin.

277 On the bishop George, see chapters 48.3 and 51.1 above, as well as Introduction p. 12.

278 Epictetus was bishop of Centumcellae in Italy from the middle of the 350s and

has used this underling to do something extraordinary in Rome, something that accurately resembles the Antichrist's perversity. **3** He prepared the palace instead of a church; he made three of his eunuchs attend instead of a congregation; and then he compelled three malicious spies (for who would call them bishops!) to 'ordain' a certain Felix, a man worthy of them, as bishop in the palace.[279] All the congregations saw this transgression by the heretics and would not allow them to enter the churches, but instead withdrew far away from them.

76.1   What of the Antichrist's actions has this man omitted? What would the Antichrist do, when he comes, beyond what that this man has done? When he comes, how will he not find the way ready for deceit and prepared for him in advance by this man? Once again he [Constantius] transfers trials to himself in the palace, instead of in the churches. **2** And he directs them himself. Astonishingly, whenever he observes that the prosecutors are at a loss, he takes up the prosecution himself, so that the wronged parties cannot present a defence because of his violence. **3** He also acted in this way in the proceedings against Athanasius: he saw the freedom of speech employed by the bishops Paulinus, Lucifer, Eusebius and Dionysius; and he also saw that, on the basis of Ursacius and Valens' recantation, these four bishops refuted Athanasius' opponents and advised that Valens and his associates were not to be trusted, because they had already changed their minds about what they were now saying. At this, Constantius immediately stood up and said 'I am now the prosecutor of Athanasius and so you are to believe whatever they say because of me'.[280] **4** Then they said, 'How can you be a prosecutor when the accused man is absent? If you are a prosecutor but he is absent, he cannot be judged.

---

was treated as a functionary of Constantius by pro-Nicene authors, including Lucifer at *Moriundum* 7.4–5: see PCBE II.1 634–6 (Epictetus 2); Barnes (1993) 274–5 n. 28.

279 For Athanasius' play on the similarity between the Greek words for 'bishop' and 'spy', see n. 15 on chapter 3.4 above. The archdeacon Felix was made bishop of Rome after Liberius was sent into exile, with Acacius of Caesarea acting as another of the three bishops who consecrated him: see Jerome, *De uiris illustr.* 98; PCBE II.1 770–71 (Felix 7); Barnes (1993) 118.

280 On the exile of these bishops at the Councils of Arles in 353/4 and Milan in 355, see chapter 33.6 above. For the change of mind by Ursacius and Valens, see chapter 29.1 above. The dialogue between Constantius and the four bishops in this chapter is almost certainly a rhetorical invention by Athanasius, not only because Paulinus was tried and exiled on a different occasion to the other three but also because the speakers, especially Constantius, make statements that perfectly accord with Athanasius' narrative of events.

This is not a Roman trial, where your word as emperor would be accepted: it is a decision concerning a bishop.[281] This judgement has to be fair to both the prosecutor and the defendant. And how can you prosecute him? You could not have had dealings with him when he was so far away. If you speak merely from hearsay, you ought to trust what he says; but if you do not trust him, but trust those men instead, it is clear that they are making these claims for your benefit and accusing Athanasius to please you.' 5 He heard this and regarded their statement, accurate though it was, as outrageous. So he exiled them and was also moved to be even more ferocious towards Athanasius: he wrote to say that Athanasius should suffer what he has now suffered, that the churches should be handed over to the Arians and that they should be allowed to do whatever they wanted.

77.1 Such actions are terrible, and beyond terrible, but this behaviour is nevertheless appropriate for someone who is assuming the attributes of the Antichrist. Who could see him ruling over the supposed bishops and presiding over ecclesiastical trials and then not say that this was what Daniel called *the abomination of desolation*?[282] After clothing himself in Christianity, he enters the holy places, stands in them and makes the churches desolate, annulling their canons and using force to make his own ideas prevail. 2 Who still dares to say that the present time is peaceful for Christians and not rather a persecution? And it is a persecution the like of which has never occurred before and will probably never be perpetrated by anyone else, except the son of lawlessness, who is already revealed by the enemies of Christ, who create an image of him in themselves.[283] This heresy is utterly shameless; it is spread out like *the poison of an adder*, as is written in Proverbs, and it teaches people to oppose the Saviour.[284] It is therefore absolutely right for us to be sober, since otherwise this heresy might somehow be that *falling away* after which the Antichrist will be revealed, with Constantius evidently being his precursor.[285] 3 For why does

281 'Roman' here is used to mean a 'secular' case, in which the emperor would be the highest authority.
282 *Matthew* 24.15, quoting *Daniel* 9.27 or 12.11.
283 The phrase 'son of lawlessness' seems to be a conflation of the neighbouring phrases 'man of lawlessness' and 'son of perdition' in *2 Thessalonians* 2.3. This claim that Constantius' actions represent an unprecedented persecution also appear at Hilary, *In Const* 1.
284 *Proverbs* 23.32.
285 This 'falling away' or 'apostasy' is predicted as a precursor to the Antichrist in *2 Thessalonians* 2.3.

he rage against the pious in this way? Why does he champion this as his personal heresy and say that whoever refuses to follow the madness of Arius is his personal enemy, while happily accepting statements from the enemies of Christ and dishonouring so many and such great councils? Why has he given orders for the churches to be handed over to the Arians? Has he not done all this so that when the Antichrist comes, he [the Antichrist] may discover how to enter the churches and accept the man who has prepared these places for him? **4** For the aged bishops, from the time of Alexander and (before him) the time of Achillas and (back before him) the time of Peter, have been driven out; and they have been replaced by men who were nominated by these followers of the soldiers.[286] They nominated men who promised to follow their beliefs.

78.1   This was an easy task for the Melitians.[287] Most of them, or, rather, all of them have not had a pious education nor have they come to know the sound faith in Christ or what Christianity actually is or what scriptures we Christians have.[288] Some of these men have come from worshipping idols, while others have come from the council chamber and high office just to get patronage and a miserable exemption from public service.[289] They gave bribes of money to the Melitians who preceded them, and so came to this [place in the episcopacy] even before they had received instruction as catechumens.[290] And even when they do seem to have received instruction, what sort of instruction do Melitians get? They certainly did not appear to have received instruction, since they arrived at once and were called bishops immediately, like children taking names. **2** Being people of this sort, they regarded this matter as unimportant and saw no difference between piety and impiety. So they quickly and readily went from being Melitians to being Arians. And if the emperor were to order anything else, they are ready to switch again to that. Their ignorance of piety quickly brings them down to the habitual recklessness that they learned from the beginning.

286 On Peter and Alexander, earlier bishops of Alexandria, see n. 257 to chapter 71.4 above. Achillas was bishop of Alexandria after Peter and before Alexander, holding the see from 311 to 313.

287 On the Melitian schismatics, see n. 14 to chapter 3.2 above.

288 The phrase 'sound faith' may be an allusion to the idea of being 'sound in the faith' from *Titus* 1.13.

289 On the exemption from the system of liturgies and public service that came with clerical office, see n. 262 to chapter 72.5 above.

290 Catechumens were people who were in training about Christianity in preparation for baptism.

3 They do not care if they are *carried about with every wind and wave*,[291] so long as they are exempt from public service and enjoy the patronage of men. It would probably not bother them to switch back again to their earlier way of life, which they had when they were Hellenes. **4** In fact, being, by character, easily led, they treat the church like the government of a town council and believe in worshipping images like the gentiles. This is how, through coming into *the worthy name* of the Saviour, they have defiled the whole of Egypt, simply by causing the Arian heresy to be spoken of there.[292] **5** The freedom to express orthodoxy still remained intact only in Egypt, and so the impious were eager to introduce malice there as well – or rather it was not them, but the Devil. He roused them so that his herald, the Antichrist, could arrive and discover that the churches in Egypt had become his and that the Melitians had already been instructed in his ideas, as well as finding his own form already present in them.

79.1 These were the results of the wicked command of Constantius. There was an eagerness for martyrdom among the congregations and, even more, there was a hatred of this most impious heresy. But there was also grief for the churches and groaning from everyone as they cried out to the Lord, '*Spare your people, O Lord, and give not your heritage to reproach* with your enemies, but hurry to rescue us from the hands of the lawless.'[293] For behold, they have not spared your servants, and they are preparing the way for the Antichrist.' **2** The Melitians will never stand against him, nor will they be concerned about the truth or think it wrong to renounce Christ. These are men who have certainly not come to the word sincerely, and they take on different forms in each situation like a chameleon and are mercenaries for anyone who wants to employ them. They have no desire for the truth; in its place they prefer momentary pleasure, and they merely say, *Let us eat and drink; for tomorrow we die.*[294] **3** This is the disposition and faithless attitude of hypocrites.[295] In contrast, the faithful servants of the Saviour

291 *Ephesians* 4.14.
292 For the term 'worthy name', see *James* 2.7.
293 The phrase 'spare your people, O Lord, and give not your heritage to reproach' is taken from *Joel* 2.17. Elsewhere, Athanasius presents bishop Alexander of Constantinople as uttering a variation on these words as a prayer to prevent Arius from being readmitted to communion, resulting in Arius' sudden and grisly death: see Ath. *De morte Arii* 3.2.
294 *1 Corinthians* 15.32.
295 I have omitted the words πικριτιανῶν ἀντὶ Μελιτιανῶν, placed in square brackets by Opitz, who regarded them as a corrupt gloss on the preceding word 'hypocrites' (which can also mean 'actors').

and the true bishops hold their faith sincerely, and they are living not for themselves but for the Lord. These men are faithful and pious towards our Lord Jesus Christ and they recognise, as I said before, that the allegations against the truth are false and have clearly been fabricated to help the Arian heresy. After Ursacius and Valens recanted, the faithful came to understand that false accusations had been concocted against Athanasius to get him out of the way and to bring the impiety of the enemies of Christ into the churches. When these defenders and heralds of the truth saw this, they chose to allow themselves to be abused and exiled rather than to subscribe against Athanasius and enter communion with the Ariomaniacs.[296] **4** They have not forgotten what they had taught, but instead they recognise that there is great disgrace for traitors, while the kingdom of heaven awaits those who are confessors of the truth. Nothing good will come to those who are faint-hearted and afraid of Constantius; but just as a calm harbour comes to sailors after a storm, just as a crown comes to athletes after the competition, so a great and eternal joy and gladness will come in heaven to those who have endured afflictions here. It will be the same as Joseph received after his afflictions; the same as the great Daniel received after the temptations and the many plots of the members of the royal court; the same as Paul now has, receiving his crown from the Saviour; the same as the people of God everywhere were looking forward to, when they saw these events and did not weaken in their resolve, but were instead strengthened in their faith and increased their eagerness even more.[297] **5** They have been reassured about the false accusations and the impiety of the heretics, and so they condemn the persecutor and join with the persecuted in resolve and unity of mind, so that they themselves may receive the crown of confession.

80.1 Someone could certainly say a lot against this abominable and Christ-fighting heresy, and could also offer extensive proof that the actions of Constantius are a prelude for the Antichrist. For, as the prophet said,

---

296   On the term 'Ariomaniacs', see n. 144 to chapter 39.2 above.

297   Joseph: *Genesis* 41. 38–46; Daniel: *Daniel* 6. Paul was believed to have died as a martyr under Nero and so received the 'crown' of martyrdom, just as athletes received crowns for their victories, as is mentioned in the preceding sentence. For a crown or garland of triumph as the achievement of the martyr, see, for example, *Acts of Marian and James* 11.9; *Martyrdom of Montanus and Lucius* 2.1, 4.6, 14.5; *Acts of Maximilian* 3.2 (see Musurillo (1972) for editions and translations of these texts). On athletic imagery in martyr literature more generally, see, for example, Castelli (2004) 117–18, 151–2.

from the feet even unto the head there is no soundness in it,[298] and it has been filled with all filth and all impiety. So one must flee from even hearing about it, as one would from the vomit of a dog or the venom of dragons, and it is clear that Costyllius bears the image of the adversary.[299] **2** So that my argument does not become too long, it is good to be satisfied with divine Scripture and for everyone to obey its command concerning both other heresies and this one in particular. This is what it commands: *Depart, depart, go out from thence, touch no unclean thing; go out of the midst of them; set yourselves apart, you that bear the vessels of the Lord.*[300] **3** This is a sufficient instruction for everyone. So if someone has been deceived by them, he should depart, as though from Sodom, and not turn back to them, lest he suffer the fate of the wife of Lot; but if someone has remained pure from this impious heresy from the beginning, he should have pride in the Lord, saying, *we have not stretched out our hands to a strange god,* nor *worshipped the works of our own hands,* nor *served the creature more than you, the creator* of all things, God, through your Word, the only-begotten Son, our Lord Jesus Christ, through whom to you the Father and with the Word in the Holy Spirit there is glory and power for ever and ever.[301] Amen.

4 {This is the complete work composed against Constantius by the father Bishop Athanasius to the monks everywhere, concerning the actions of the Arians under Constantius.}[302]

The second appeal[303]

81.1 The congregation of the catholic church in Alexandria, which is

---

298 *Isaiah* 1.6.

299 For Costyllius as a diminutive form of Constantius, see chapter 74.1 above. For the concept of a dog returning to its vomit, see *Proverbs* 26.11; *2 Peter* 2.22. The 'venom of dragons' appears at *Deuteronomy* 32.33.

300 *Isaiah* 52.11.

301 For the story of the destruction of Sodom and the transformation of Lot's wife into a pillar of salt, see *Genesis* 19.1–26. The quotations are from *Psalms* 44.20 (43.20 LXX); *Jeremiah* 1.16; *Romans* 1.25.

302 This manuscript comment, as well as the placement of the text directly after the *Epistula ad monachos*, is the basis for the assumption that this work was primarily intended for a monastic audience. On this issue, see Introduction p. 25.

303 This text, which describes events at Alexandria in February 356, has already been mentioned at chapter 48.1 above.

under the most venerable bishop Athanasius, makes this appeal publicly through the people who have subscribed in order.

2 We have already made an appeal about the nocturnal attack that we and the Lord's house suffered, even though there was no need for an appeal about things that the whole city perceived and perceives; for the bodies of the victims have been discovered and exhibited publicly, and the weapons and the bows and arrows in the Lord's house have proclaimed the transgression. **3** After the appeal, the *clarissimus dux* Syrianus has forced everyone to come to terms with him, as though there has been no uproar and no one has died.[304] This is significant proof that these events did not take place in accordance with the will of the most philanthropic *augustus* Constantius. **4** For, if Syrianus had acted in obedience to a command, he would not have been frightened when things turned out like this. Moreover, after we went to him and requested that he neither commit violence nor deny what had happened, he gave orders for us Christians to be beaten with clubs, and so revealed by these actions that a war had been waged against the church at night. **5** We now, therefore, make an appeal concerning these events, and some of us are already about to travel to the most pious *augustus*. By almighty God and for the salvation of the most pious *augustus* Constantius, we adjure Maximus, the Prefect of Egypt, and the *curiosi* to report everything to the piety of the *augustus* and the authority of the *clarissimi* prefects.[305] We also adjure all the captains of ships to publicise it everywhere and to report it to the ears of the most pious *augustus* and to the prefects and the officials in every place so that it may become known that a war has taken place against the churches, and that, in the time of the *augustus* Constantius, Syrianus has caused virgins and many others to become martyrs. **6** For, at the beginning of the fifth day before the Ides of February, that is the fourteenth day of the month of Mechir, we were keeping a vigil in the Lord's house and

---

304 On the *dux* Syrianus, see n. 115 on chapter 31.2 above. The title *clarissimus* denoted a person of senatorial rank in the later Roman empire, although it was gradually extended to more and more imperial officials, especially from the second half of the fourth century onwards, meaning that it lost some of its earlier prestige: see Jones (1964) I 143, II 527–30.

305 Maximus was Prefect of Egypt from 355 to 356: see PLRE I 582 (Maximus 13). For the imperial officials known as *curiosi*, see the Glossary. The prefects mentioned are the Praetorian Prefects, distinguished here from ordinary governors such as the Prefect of Egypt, and often referred to as *clarissimi et illustres* at this time, although the title *clarissimus* would later be extended to all provincial governors: see Jones (1964) I 143, 379.

devoting ourselves to prayers (for the assembly on the day of preparation was about to take place).[306] Suddenly around midnight the *clarissimus dux* Syrianus attacked us and the church with many legions of soldiers carrying weapons, naked swords, spears and other military equipment and with helmets on their heads. While we were actually at prayer and the reading was taking place, they broke down the doors and, as soon as the doors had been opened by the force of the crowd, he gave the order. Some of them fired arrows, others raised war-cries, and a crash of arms erupted and the swords were illuminated by the light from the lamps. **7** Following this, virgins were killed and many people were trampled and crushed against each other when the soldiers attacked, and men were struck by arrows and died. Some of the soldiers turned to looting and also stripped the virgins, because the women's fear that some of them might simply be touched was greater than their fear of death. **8** While the bishop sat on his throne urging everyone to pray, the *dux* directed the attack, accompanied by Hilarius the *notarius*, whose actions were made clear by their result: the bishop was dragged down and almost torn apart.[307] He was seriously paralysed and became like a dead man; and we do not know where they carried him off to out of sight, for they were eager to kill him. **9** When those men saw that many people had been killed, they ordered the soldiers to hide the bodies of the dead. The most holy virgins who had died were left behind and were buried in tombs, with the pride of having become martyrs in the time of the most pious Constantius. The deacons in the Lord's house were beaten up and shut in. But this was not the end of the matter. After this happened, anyone who wanted to do so proceeded to break down any door he chose, opened it, searched around and looted the contents, and they entered the places which not even all Christians are allowed to enter. **10** Gorgonius, the *strategos* of the city, knows about these things, for he was there.[308] Substantial proof of this warlike attack can be found in the weapons, spears and swords of the attackers that were left in the Lord's house. They have remained hung up in the church until now, so that those men cannot deny what happened. He has very frequently sent Dynamius from the garrison and also the *strategos*, because he wants to remove the weapons, but we will not allow it until everyone knows what happened.[309] **11** If there really is a command

---

306   The date is 9 February 356. The 'day of preparation' is Friday.
307   On Hilarius the *notarius*, see chapter 48.1 above.
308   On Gorgonius, see chapter 63.1 above.
309   On Dynamius, see chapter 61.3 above.

that we should be persecuted, we are all ready to become martyrs; but if this is not the command of the *augustus* we request that Maximus, the Prefect of Egypt, and all the *decuriones* should request him to stop making these attacks.[310] **12** We also request that this petition of ours be referred up, so that they do not try to impose any other bishop here. For we stand firm even unto death and we long for the most venerable bishop Athanasius. God gave him to us from the beginning, in accordance with the succession of our fathers, and the most pious *augustus* Constantius himself sent him with letters and oaths.[311] **13** For we have faith that, if his piety [Constantius] learns about what has happened, he will be extremely angry about it and will also do nothing contrary to his oaths, but will once again give orders that our bishop Athanasius should remain with us.

14 Written on the seventeenth day of Mechir, which is the day before the Ides of February, in the consulship of those who will have been appointed after the consulship of the *clarissimi* Arbitio and Collianus.[312]

310 On *decuriones*, who were members of the town council, see n. 118 to chapter 31.6 above.

311 See chapters 21–4 above.

312 The date is 12 February 356. The name 'Collianus' is a corruption of Lollianus, who was consul alongside Arbitio in 355. On the title *clarissimus*, see n. 304 to chapter 81.3 above. It would appear that the names of the consuls for 356 had not reached the authors before they wrote this appeal. This way of referring to the year 356 also appears at *Historia acephala* 1.10, although the consuls for 356 are named shortly afterwards at 2.1. Atkinson's translation in Robertson (1892) incorrectly assumes that the consuls are the addressees of the petition, since their names appear in the dative. The dative was, however, often used in Greek translations of the regular ablative absolute construction employed in Latin consular dating formulae: see Adams (2003) 504.

HILARY OF POITIERS

Against Constantius (*In Constantium*)

1 It is time for speaking, since the time for being silent has now passed.[1] Let Christ be expected, because the Antichrist has assumed power.[2] Let the shepherds shout, because the hired men have fled.[3] Let us lay down our lives for the sheep, because the thieves have entered and the raging lion prowls.[4] Let us advance to martyrdom by these words, because the angel of Satan has transformed himself into an angel of light.[5] Let us enter through the door, because nobody comes to the Father except through the Son.[6] Let the false prophets be revealed in their peace, because the approved will be made manifest through heresy and schism.[7] Let this tribulation be endured, a tribulation such as there has never been since the creation of the world; but let it be understood that the days are to be shortened for the sake of God's elect.[8] The prophecy is fulfilled that

---

1 See *Ecclesiastes* 3.7. The first chapter of Hilary's text is filled with quotations from and allusions to biblical passages, particularly prophecies and warnings concerning persecution and the End of Days.

2 See *1 John* 2.18; *Daniel* 7.20–2. The eschatological rhetoric of the coming of the Antichrist appears frequently in this short text, sometimes with him explicitly identified as Constantius himself: see chapters 2, 5, 6, 7 and 11. In contrast, Lucifer only links Constantius with the Antichrist, rather than equating the two: see *Moriundum* 1 and 11. From *Hist. Ar.* 67 onwards Athanasius discusses resemblances between Constantius and the Antichrist, sometimes identifying the two, sometimes saying that the former is preparing the way for the latter.

3 See *Jeremiah* 25.34; *John* 10.11–13.

4 See *John* 10.8, 15; *1 Peter* 5.8.

5 See *2 Corinthians* 11.14.

6 See *John* 10.1–9, 14.6.

7 See *Matthew* 24.11, 24; *1 John* 4.1; *1 Corinthians* 11.19. This concept of the superficially attractive but ultimately false peace brought about by heretics also appears in Hilary's later work *Contra Auxentium*, written in the middle of the 360s: see *Contra Auxentium* 1 and 12.

8 See *Matthew* 24.21–2. This image of a time of unprecedented tribulation also appears at Ath. *Hist. Ar.* 77.2.

says: *The time will come when they will not endure sound doctrine, but according to their own desires they will heap up teachers for themselves, having itching ears: and indeed they will turn from hearing the truth and will be turned to fables.*[9] But let us await the promise of him who pronounced: *Blessed are you, when they will slander and persecute you, and will speak every evil against you for righteousness' sake. Rejoice and exult, because your reward is great in heaven. For in this way did they persecute the prophets who were before you.*[10] Let us stand before judges and powers for the sake of Christ's name, because blessed is he who will endure even unto the end.[11] Let us not fear the man who can kill the body, but not the soul: but let us fear the one who can kill both body and soul in hell.[12] Let us not be anxious for ourselves, because the hairs of our head have been numbered.[13] And let us pursue the truth through the Holy Spirit, lest we believe falsehood through the spirit of error.[14] And let us die with Christ, so that we may reign with Christ.[15] For to be silent any longer is a sign of unbelief, not a plan of restraint, because there is no less danger in always having kept silent than in never having done so.

2   As for myself, brothers, as all my listeners and friends can testify, I foresaw long ago the gravest danger to the faith and so, more than four years ago, after the exile of the holy men Paulinus, Eusebius, Lucifer and Dionysius, I, together with the Gallic bishops, withdrew from communion with Saturninus, Ursacius and Valens;[16] the rest of their colleagues were

9 *2 Timothy* 4.3–4.

10 *Matthew* 5.11–12; see also 5.10.

11 See *Matthew* 10.18; *Matthew* 10.22.

12 See *Matthew* 10.28. The original biblical passage makes reference to 'those' who could kill the body on earth, but Hilary has substituted the singular for the plural, probably to make the phrase refer to Constantius specifically. See also Lucifer, *Moriundum* 3, where the same change has been made, along with n. 41 on the translation of 'Gehenna' as 'hell'.

13 See *Matthew* 10.19; *Luke* 12.11; *Matthew* 10.30–1.

14 See *1 John* 4.6.

15 See *2 Timothy* 2.11–12.

16 The four orthodox bishops mentioned here are Paulinus of Trier, who was exiled in 353/4 at the Council of Arles, and Eusebius of Vercelli, Lucifer of Cagliari and Dionysius of Milan, who were all exiled at the Council of Milan in 355. See Introduction p. 11 on these events, as well as pp. 31–32 on the career of Lucifer. For the careers of the other bishops, see PCBE IV.2 1443–4 (Paulinus 1); PCBE II.1 692–7 (Eusebius 1); PCBE II.1 563–5 (Dionysius 1). The excommunicated bishops are Saturninus of Arles, Ursacius of Singidunum and Valens of Mursa. On Ursacius and Valens, who were regularly invoked as

granted the opportunity to recover their senses, so that the option of peace might still exist, while those limbs, which were putrid with deadly diseases and spreading to infect the whole body, might be amputated, if the most blessed confessors of Christ really did decide to abide by the decrees we had issued. A faction of these false apostles then compelled me to attend a synod at Béziers, where I proposed a hearing to reveal this heresy.[17] But they were afraid that it might become public knowledge and so refused to hear any of the issues I had raised, believing that they would be able to feign innocence before Christ if they wilfully ignored what they would later knowingly do. Kept in exile ever since then, I have resolved neither to desert the confession of Christ nor to reject any honest and commendable method of achieving unity.[18] Finally, I have neither written nor uttered any reproach against these present times, nor anything defamatory and appropriate to their impiety against that body which was then claiming to be the church of Christ, but is now a synagogue of the Antichrist.[19] During this time I have not considered it an offence for anyone to speak with them or attend the house of prayer (although the fellowship of communion has been withdrawn) or hope for circumstances conducive to peace, until we

leading 'Arians' by both Hilary and Athanasius, see Introduction pp. 9–10. On Saturninus, see PCBE IV.2 1714–16 (Saturninus 1). The phrase *quinto abhinc anno*, which I have rendered as 'more than four years ago', would suggest 359 or 360 as the date of composition, although the reference to the capitulation of the 'Homoiousian' delegates from the Council of Seleucia in chapter 15 means that work cannot have been completed before early 360. On the issue of the date and process of composition, see Rocher (1987) 29–38 and Barnes (1988), as well as Introduction pp. 29–30.

17 Hilary appeared at a council in Béziers (Biterrae) in southern Gaul, probably in 356. The circumstances and proceedings of this event are obscure. See Introduction p. 26 and Sulpicius Severus, *Chronicle* 2.39. The term 'false apostle' (*pseudoapostolus*) comes from *2 Corinthians* 11.13.

18 After the council at Béziers, Hilary went into exile in the eastern part of the empire, including attending the Council of Seleucia in 359 and then travelling to Constantinople, where he was when the council approved the 'Homoian' creed in January 360. Probably quite soon afterwards he returned to Gaul, although it is unclear how he obtained permission for this, or even that he did obtain it. See Introduction p. 28.

19 See *Revelation* 2.9, 3.9, where there are references to the 'synagogue of Satan'. Chapters 2 and 3 function as a double apology, in which Hilary both explains that he does not write immoderate and extreme invective and simultaneously claims that his silence on this issue so far was not because of a lack of righteous anger about the injustices suffered by the Church. He thus attempts to defend himself against charges of saying either too much or too little. See also the opening of *Moriundum* 1, where Lucifer also justifies his decision to speak out against Constantius again.

might prepare forgiveness of error and a return from the Antichrist to Christ through repentance.[20]

3   Therefore, if any astute man understands the reason for my silence, he undoubtedly affirms that, as my faithful freedom of speech in Christ bears witness, it is not through any vice of human passion that, having restrained until now my bitterness for this recent injustice, I have now at last been roused to write these words.[21] I, who have remained silent for so long, will not speak too soon; nor did I, who now at last speaks, remain silent without discretion; nor do I, who kept quiet about a recent injustice, complain of any now; I devoted so great a time to silence for that period so that no one would think that I speak for my own cause. Now I speak for no other cause than that of Christ: it is for him that I had to keep silent until now, and I understand that I must be silent no longer.[22]

4   O omnipotent God and creator of all things, and also Father of our one Lord Jesus Christ, if only you had granted to my age and time the opportunity to have fulfilled this task of mine – to confess you and your only-begotten Son – during the reign of Nero or Decius![23] Fervent in the Holy Spirit and through the compassion of our Lord and God your Son

20 The phrase 'considered it an offence' translates *criminis loco duxi*. For the use of the phrase *criminis loco* in forensic oratory, see Cicero, *Pro Caelio* 4.

21 The Latin word *libertas*, here translated as 'freedom of speech', can be seen here as analogous to the Greek concept of *parrhesia* (παρρησία), which could mean speaking out boldly against those in authority: see n. 128 to Ath. *Hist. Ar.* 34.1 at p. 67.

22 Hilary had not remained completely silent during his exile, as he had written his *De synodis*, which was addressed to the bishops of a number of provinces in Britain and Gaul, and probably started compiling his *Against Valens and Ursacius*. He had also written his deferential *Ad Constantium*, although it is unlikely that any of his audience for this invective would have read it. Hilary's claim here is that he had previously remained silent about the great impieties of Constantius, while he was still hopeful that reconciliation could be effected. Now, he claimed, the circumstances were such that it was his duty to speak out. On a more practical note, it is possible that his return to Gaul, probably fairly soon after Julian's usurpation, had provided him with a fortuitous opportunity to indulge in an attack on Constantius. On the circumstances of the composition of this text, see Introduction p. 27.

23 The term 'only-begotten' translates the word *unigenitus*. This is a Latin rendering of the Greek term *monogenes* (μονογενής), which appears in *John* 1.14, 1.18. Lucifer used the Latin term *unicus* as a translation of the same Greek word: see n. 4 to *Moriundum* 1 on p. 142. Nero (AD 54–68) and Decius (AD 249–51) are here used as examples of Roman emperors who persecuted Christians. On Hilary's use of the tropes of persecution and martyrdom in this text, see Introduction pp. 33–4.

Jesus Christ,[24] I would not have feared the rack, knowing that Isaiah was sawn asunder;[25] I would not have shuddered at the fires, remembering the Hebrew boys singing in their midst;[26] I would not have fled from the cross and the breaking of my legs, after recalling the robber carried over to Paradise;[27] I would not have trembled at the depths of the ocean or the submerging tide of the waves of Pontus, since you have taught us, through Jonah and Paul, that survival at sea is granted to the faithful.[28] My battle against your evident enemies would have been blessed, because there would be no doubt that they were persecutors, compelling people to deny you through tortures, swords and fire, nor could we pay out more than our deaths in bearing witness to you. We would be fighting openly and with confidence against deniers, against torturers, against cutthroats; and your people, knowing that it was a public persecution, would accompany us as their leaders to the rite of confession.[29]

5   But now we are fighting against a deceptive persecutor, a flattering enemy, Constantius the Antichrist, who does not strike the back, but rather caresses the belly;[30] does not proscribe people to life but rather enriches

24 For the concept of being 'fervent in the spirit', see *Acts* 18.25; *Romans* 12.11.

25 The *eculeus* was clearly an instrument of torture and execution, probably a rack, which is how it is translated here: see OLD *s.v.* See also *Hebrews* 11.37, which appears to allude to the tradition that Isaiah was martyred by being sawn in half on the orders of king Manasseh, as well as Justin, *Dialogue* 120.5; Tert. *De patientia* 14.1; Tert. *Scorpiace* 8.3; *The Lives of the Prophets* Isaiah 1.1 (Charlesworth [1983–85] II 385). See also the pseudepigraphic *Martyrdom and Ascension of Isaiah* 5 (Charlesworth [1983–85] II 163–4) for a fuller version of this story.

26 The boys Shadrach, Meshach and Abed-nego were said to have survived unscathed after being cast into the fiery furnace by King Nebuchadnezzar II of Babylon: see *Daniel* 3. The same *exempla* appear at Lucifer, *Moriundum* 2.58–60.

27 For the story of the robber who was crucified beside Christ and brought to Paradise with him, see *Luke* 23.40–43. For the breaking of the robber's legs, see *John* 19.32.

28 See *Jonah* 1–2; *Acts* 27; *2 Corinthians* 11.25.

29 'Confession' here refers not the modern admission of sins to a priest but to the act of confessing or professing of one's Christianity to pagan persecutors, even when tortured and threatened with execution. Individuals who had maintained their faith in this way were often referred to as confessors.

30 This chapter uses the paradoxical language of salvation through suffering, which is a common feature of Christian persecution literature. See, for example, Lucifer, *Moriundum* 4, reworking a phrase from [Cypr.] *De laude martyrii* 7: 'For death makes life more complete, death leads away rather to glory.' Here this rhetoric is balanced with the parallel claim that earthly wealth and power under a tyrannical emperor leads to everlasting death, since Constantius means the opposite of what he says. This idea also appears throughout

them to death; does not drive them to freedom in prison, but rather burdens them to slavery within the palace:[31] instead of torturing flanks, he invades the heart; instead of cutting off the head with a sword, he destroys the soul with gold; instead of openly threatening flames, he secretly kindles hell.[32] He does not fight to avoid defeat, but rather fawns in order to dominate; he confesses Christ so that he might deny him, he promotes unity to prevent peace, he suppresses heresies to eliminate Christians, he rewards priests to preclude bishops, he constructs buildings for the Church to demolish its faith. He proclaims you in words and in speech, but he does absolutely everything to prevent you being believed to be God, as the Father is.[33]

6   And so let the accusation of slander and suspicion of falsehood vanish. For ministers of truth ought to utter true statements. If we speak falsely, may our slanderous speech become infamous; but if we demonstrate that everything we say is clearly true, then we do not exceed the apostolic freedom of speech and moderation in making these accusations after a long silence.[34] But perhaps someone will think me rash, because I call Constantius the Antichrist. Whoever judges this to be impudence rather than fearlessness should first read again what John said to Herod: *It is not lawful for you to do that.*[35] Let him know what was said by the martyr to king Antiochus: *You unjustly banish us from this present life, but the*

Lucifer's *Moriundum*. On the concept of Constantius as a man who hides his persecution under speciously beneficial actions, see also Lucifer, *Moriundum* 6.24–7.

31   The verb *onero* is here translated as 'burden', since Hilary is writing negatively about Constantius loading people up with gifts so that they do his bidding. It can also have the sense of overloading or gorging: see OLD and Lewis & Short s.v. See also chapter 10 below: 'You burden God's sanctuary with the empire's gold.'

32   See n. 41 on Lucifer, *Moriundum* 3 below on the translation of *Gehenna* as 'hell'.

33   In this sentence Hilary employs the rhetorical technique of apostrophe to address Christ himself. The argument that 'Arians' denied that Christ was truly God, in the same manner as the Father, was a common feature of polemics against them. On this issue, see Introduction p. 3.

34   On the term *libertas*, here translated as 'freedom of speech', see n. 21 to chapter 3 above.

35   There is no biblical passage where John the Baptist says these precise words in his confrontation with Herod Antipas. The closest is *Matthew* 14.4: *it is not lawful for you to have her* (*non licet tibi habere eam*); see also *Mark* 6.18: *it is not lawful for you to have your brother's wife* (*non licet tibi habere uxorem fratris tui*). It would appear that Hilary has altered the passage to better suit his circumstances, as he sought to present himself as a fearless prophet of God opposing the wrongdoing of an impious ruler, even though it could lead to his death.

king of the world shall raise us up at the resurrection, who have died for his laws, unto eternal life.[36] And again another one reproached him with a blessed and faithful pronouncement: *Having power over men*, he said, *you do whatever you want, even though you are mortal; but do not think that our race has been abandoned by God. Wait patiently and see how his awesome power will torture you and your seed.*[37] This is how boys responded, but a woman also spoke no less well than these blessed, perfected men, saying: *You, who have become the author of every crime against the Hebrews, will not escape the hand of God. For although the Lord is angry towards us for a little while, while we are alive, for our chastening and correction, he will yet be reconciled again to his servants.*[38] This is not rashness, but faith; not thoughtlessness, but reason; not madness, but confidence.

7 I proclaim to you, Constantius, what I would have said to Nero, what Decius and Maximian would have heard from me:[39] you fight against God,

---

36 *2 Maccabees* 7.9. This passage from *2 Maccabees*, along with the two that follow, also provides Hilary with examples of opposition to persecuting authorities, in this case the Seleucid king Antiochus IV Epiphanes (175–164 BC), against whom the Maccabean revolt took place. The celebration of the Maccabees by Christians developed during the course of late antiquity, including with a site of veneration at Antioch from the fourth century onwards: see Vinson (1994), especially 177–8.

37 *2 Maccabees* 7.16–17.

38 *2 Maccabees* 7.31, 33. Hilary's quotation from *2 Maccabees* 7.33 deviates from the Septuagint in referring to *nobis uiuis* (translated here as 'while we are alive'). The original Greek of this passage applies the term 'living' (ζῶν) not to 'us' but to 'the Lord'. This variant form of the passage is also quoted at Lucifer, *De non parc.* 22.55, but is not found elsewhere. It is well suited to the rhetoric of persecution and martyrdom that appears both here and in the works of Lucifer, because it suggests that suffering in this world will bring a reconciliation with God for his servants.

39 Alongside the two persecuting emperors Nero (AD 54–68) and Decius (AD 249–51), who have already appeared in chapter 4, the identity of 'Maximian' is uncertain. Humphries (1998) 213 identifies him as Galerius (AD 305–311), whose full name was Gaius Galerius Valerius Maximianus: see PLRE I 574–5 (Maximianus 9). He was often referred to as 'Maximianus', including in Lactantius' account of this emperor's crimes and grisly death: Lact. *Mort. pers.* 10.6, 20–26, 33–35. This is a plausible explanation, as Galerius was widely regarded as a major instigator of the 'Great Persecution', especially in Lactantius' account. It is, however, also possible that Maximian (AD 286–305), the father of Constantine's wife Fausta and grandfather of Constantius II, is meant here, as he was Diocletian's co-Augustus at the start of the persecution: see PLRE I 573–4 (Maximianus 8). This argument gains strength from the fact that Athanasius refers to the persecutor Maximian on three occasions in his *Historia Arianorum* (40.2, 44.1, 64.2) and explicitly calls him Constantius' grandfather in two of these passages. From this point until the end of chapter 11 Hilary addresses Constantius directly in the second person, as though delivering an invective to

you rage against the Church, you persecute the saints, you detest those who proclaim Christ, you abolish religion, you are now a tyrant not just in human matters but also divine.[40] The characteristics that I describe are common to both you and those persecutors. Accept them now as your own: you pretend that you are Christian, although you are actually a new enemy of Christ; you are a precursor of the Antichrist and perform the rites of his mysteries; you establish statements of faith while living against the faith; you are a teacher of impieties while being ignorant of all piety. You make episcopal sees your gifts; you replace good men with evil. You consign priests to prison; you dispatch your armies to terrorise the Church; you summon councils and force the faith of the Westerners into impiety; having shut them up together in one city you then terrify them with threats, weaken them with starvation, destroy them with cold, corrupt them with trickery.[41] Among the Easterners you artfully foment discord; you entice sycophants; you incite partisans; you overturn what is old and corrupt what is new. You commit the most savage atrocities without the invidiousness of glorious deaths. In a new and unheard of triumph of ingenuity you conquer with the Devil and persecute without martyrdom.[42]

him personally. On the possible circumstances of the text's publication and circulation, see Introduction pp. 29–31.

40 As Timothy Barnes has argued, in the political discourse of this period the Latin term *tyrannus* ('tyrant') incorporated a sense of moral criticism and could also, in the works of Christian authors, carry a strong association with persecution: see Barnes (1996) especially 57–60, with discussion of this passage at 59.

41 The description here of the summoning of councils and the coercion of western bishops could be a general reference to Constantius' policy in the 350s, including the Councils of Arles in 353/4 and Milan in 355. At Milan, which was convened by Constantius at the suggestion of Liberius of Rome, the delegates were instructed to subscribe to certain decisions, possibly from the Council of Sirmium in 351, including deposing Athanasius of Alexandria. Eusebius of Vercelli, Lucifer of Cagliari and Dionysius of Milan all refused and were sent into exile. Hilary's more specific description of the confining of the western bishops and the creation of dissent among the easterners seems, however, to be better suited to the specific context of the twin councils of Seleucia and Ariminum in 359, since (according to Sulpicius Severus 2.41, 2.43–4) the Praetorian Prefect Taurus did not allow the western delegates to leave Ariminum until they had agreed to the Homoian creed. The gathering of easterners at Seleucia was also divided between 'Homoians' and their opponents. On these events, see Introduction p. 17.

42 The accusation that the emperor was even worse than earlier persecutors, because he contrived his attacks so that he did not give the Church any martyrs, was also made against Julian the Apostate by Gregory of Nazianzus a few years later: see Greg. Naz. *Or.* 4.58.

8   We are more indebted to your cruelty, Nero, Decius, Maximian, since through you we defeated the Devil.[43] The holy blood of the blessed martyrs has everywhere been gathered up and their venerable bones provide daily testimony, while through them demons cry out, diseases are cured, miracles are witnessed with wonderment:[44] bodies are raised up without ropes; women are hung by their feet, but their clothes do not fall down over their faces; spirits are burnt without fire; the tormented confess without interrogation; all of which contribute no less to the benefit of the questioner than to the advancement of the faith.[45] But you, cruellest of the cruel, cause us more destruction in your raging, but with less excuse. You insinuate yourself with a name, you kill with a compliment, you promote impiety under the guise of religion, as a false herald of Christ you extinguish the faith of Christ. You do not even leave the wretched any excuses, so that they might display to their eternal judge their punishments and some scars on their lacerated bodies, so that their weakness might excuse their yielding to necessity. You, most wicked of men, moderate all the evils of your persecution in such a way as to exclude both pardon for a lapse and martyrdom for a confession. But your father, the author of human deaths,[46] has taught you to conquer without facing defiance, to slaughter without a sword, to persecute without becoming infamous, to hate without arousing mistrust, to lie without detection, to profess without faith, to flatter without generosity, to do whatever you want without revealing what that is.

9   But the only-begotten God himself,[47] whom you persecute in me,[48] warned me not to believe you and not to be deluded by the false and

43 On this trio of persecutors, see n. 39 to chapter 7 above.

44 Rocher's text prints *dum admirationem opera cernuntur* here, although the note at 235 makes it clear that *admirationem* is a slip for *admirationum*.

45 The 'tormented' here is a reference to those possessed by demons, who are being exorcised by the relics of the martyrs. For examples of such miracles being attributed to relics, see Ambrose's letter on the discovery of the bodies of Gervasius and Protasius in Milan in 386, in which he describes a possessed woman flung through the air by their power and demons confessing that they could not stand being tortured by the presence of the martyrs: Ambr. *Ep.* 77.2, 77.16.

46 Here the reference is to Constantius' 'spiritual' father, i.e. the Devil, rather than to his actual father, Constantine. For the description of enemies of Christianity as children of the Devil, see *John* 8.44; *Acts* 13.10; *1 John* 3.10.

47 On the importance of Christ as true God in Hilary's anti-Arian polemic, see n. 127 to chapter 23 below and Introduction p. 3.

48 This may be an allusion to Christ's words to Saul during his vision on the road to Damascus in *Acts* 9.4.

fabricated name you adopt,[49] when he said: *Not everyone who says unto me 'Lord, Lord' shall enter into the kingdom of heaven; but he who does the will of my Father, that man will enter the kingdom of heaven.*[50] Do you now recognise in yourself the truth of divine prophecy and the trustworthiness of the Lord's statement, that it is not profession of his name but obedience to the Father's will that brings admission to the heavenly kingdom? Examine whether, while professing the Lord's name in words, you actually carry out the will of God the Father in deeds. He proclaims: *This is my beloved Son, in whom I am well pleased.*[51] But you decree that there is no Son and no Father, but rather names of adoption and titles tacked on:[52] as a new persecutor of divine religion today, you install a God who counterfeits everything about himself. Previously your ancestors were enemies of Christ alone: but you fight against God the Father, saying that he is a liar, that he has deceived, that he has made statements about himself that are not true, and could not even be true.[53] The Son proclaims: *I and the Father are one;*[54] and: *Believe my works, that the Father is in me and I am in the Father;*[55] and: *All things that are the Father's are mine.*[56] You criticise Christ for telling the truth; you accuse the Father for his declaration. Though you are a man, you correct God; though you are corruption, you govern life; though night, you illuminate the day;[57] though faithless, you promulgate the faith; though impious, you feign piety; and you engage the whole world in a sacrilegious conflict, denying about God what he himself has said about himself.

49 This 'name' is Constantius' claim to be a Christian, which Hilary rejects. See also Lucifer, *Moriundum* 5.3–4.

50 *Matthew* 7.21.

51 *Matthew* 3.17.

52 It was often said that the 'Arians' did not regard Christ as being 'properly' the Son of the Father, but rather that this was merely a name applied to him. See chapter 13 below, as well as Introduction p. 3.

53 Hilary is contrasting Constantius' 'ancestors', the pagan persecutors of earlier centuries such as Nero, Decius and Maximian, identified as enemies of Christ in their opposition to Christianity, with Constantius, who attacks God the Father and accuses him of having lied in the quotation from *Matthew* 3.17. Athanasius also described many of his opponents, including his episcopal rival, Gregory 'the Cappadocian', as 'enemies of Christ': see, n. 52 to *Hist. Ar.* 13.1.

54 *John* 10.30.

55 *John* 10.38.

56 *John* 16.15.

57 See *1 Thessalonians* 5.5. Hilary's point here, as elsewhere in this passage, is that Constantius claims to perform actions for which he is singularly unqualified.

10 As well as this correction of deception, the Lord has also taught me another saying for recognising you, for he said: *Beware of false prophets, which come to you in sheep's clothing, but inwardly they are ravenous wolves: you shall know them by their fruits.*[58] There is something in the heart that is disguised in the face and veiled in the mind. What they thought to be a sheep they found to be a wolf. If people act like sheep, may they be believed to be sheep; but if they perform the deeds of rapacious wolves, they are recognised as wolves through their deeds, and the appearance of their garments is confuted by the fruit of their actions. We see your sheep's clothing, rapacious wolf. You burden God's sanctuary with the empire's gold and you heap up for God property that has been stripped from temples, confiscated with edicts or exacted through punishments.[59] You receive priests with the kiss by which Christ was betrayed;[60] you bow your head for a blessing in order to trample the faith underfoot; you regard yourself worthy of that banquet from which Judas departed to commit betrayal;[61] you remit the poll tax that Christ paid to avoid scandal;[62] as Caesar, you remit public revenues in order to lure Christians to deny their faith; you cede what is your own to purloin what is God's.[63] These are your garments, false sheep.

11 But now hear the fruits of your deeds, rapacious wolf. I do not record any actions except those performed in the Church; otherwise I would be mentioning a tyranny other than that against God.[64] I do not make a formal complaint, because I do not know the judicial process; however, the grievance is well known: bishops, whom no one dared condemn,

---

58 *Matthew* 7.15–16. See also Lucifer, *Moriundum* 5.26–8, where the same imagery is employed.

59 Hilary is complaining about imperial euergetism towards churches, which is described as the bribing of Christians to accept heresy, made even worse by the measures by which the emperor obtained these funds in the first place.

60 See *Luke* 22.48–9 on Judas' betrayal of Christ with a kiss.

61 See *John* 13.30 on Judas' departure from the Last Supper. Constantius is here said to regard himself as worthy of receiving the re-enactment of this meal in the Eucharist.

62 This is a reference to *Matthew* 22.17–22, where Christ stated that people should pay tribute to the Roman empire. See also *Matthew* 17.24–7. Hilary here presents the tax exemptions, which were granted to Christian clergy from the reign of Constantine onwards, as part of Constantius' plot to destroy the Church.

63 See *Matthew* 22.21. *Render therefore unto Caesar the things which are Caesar's; and unto God the things which are God's.*

64 On the use of the concept of 'tyranny' and the term 'tyrant' in fourth-century political discourse, see n. 40 to chapter 7 above.

have been deposed by you, and even now those who are inscribed on the facades of churches are listed as persons condemned to the mines.[65] Near to me is Alexandria, shaken by many wars and terrified by the great commotion of the military operations launched against her.[66] A shorter war was fought with Persia than against that city.[67] Prefects were changed, commanders chosen, populations bribed, legions mobilised, all to prevent Christ being preached by Athanasius.[68] I remain silent about the smaller cities and communities who throughout the whole East are subjected to either terror or war. Afterwards, you directed all your arms against the faith of the West and turned your armies on Christ's flock: under Nero, I would have been allowed to flee. But, having solicited him with flattery, you then exiled Paulinus, a man who has undergone blessed suffering, and robbed the holy church at Trier of such an exceptional priest.[69] You terrorised the faith with edicts.[70] You kept changing his place of banishment and wore him out until he died; you even exiled him beyond the borders of Christendom, lest he receive any bread from your granary or look for any that had been desecrated from the cave of Montanus and

65 Here Hilary gives another example of the inverted and paradoxical nature of Constantius' rule. While the names of bishops should be displayed in honorific inscriptions on churches, they are instead written up in public lists of condemned criminals. The punishment of being sent to the mines could be regarded as tantamount to a death penalty. It is attested as having been used during the earlier persecutions under pagan emperors: see n. 35 to Lucifer, *Moriundum* 3, where the claim that Constantius used it against his theological opponents also appears, as well as Ath. *Hist. Ar.* 60, with the latter providing the specific example of a sub-deacon named Eutychius who died on his way to the mines.

66 If this statement about Alexandria is taken to be geographical rather than metaphorical, it would suggest that Hilary was still in the East when he wrote this text. The proximity of the city may, however, not be meant literally. Hilary is probably referring to the imperial action surrounding Athanasius' flight from Alexandria in 356, which started his third period of exile. This is described in colourful terms at Ath. *Hist. Ar.* 47–63, 81, as well as being mentioned in Lucifer, *Moriundum* 2, 8.

67 During the reign of Constantius there were numerous battles between Rome and Persia: see Dignas and Winter (2007) 88–90.

68 Athanasius wrote dramatic accounts of two occasions on which he was expelled from Alexandria by force. The first, in 339, is described in his *Encyclical Epistle*, while the second expulsion, in 356, appears in *Hist. Ar.* 48.2–3, 81. Hilary is probably referring specifically to the latter episode. On these events, see Introduction p. 24.

69 On Paulinus of Trier's exile, see n. 16 to chapter 2 above.

70 This may not be a reference to 'edicts' in a technical legal sense, but rather to imperial orders, which were frequently conveyed in letters to specific officials. Barnes (1993) 273 n. 9 provides the argument that an edict led to the Councils of Arles in 353/4 and Milan in 355.

Maximilla.[71] With what great terror of your fury did you disturb the most pious people of Milan![72] Your tribunes approached the holy of holies, forcing a path for themselves through the congregation with every form of cruelty, and dragged the priests from the altar. Do you think, wicked man, that you have sinned less than the Jews in their impiety? For they poured out the blood of Zachariah, but you, as far as you can, have separated from Christ those who are incorporated in Christ.[73] Then you directed your war against Rome herself and snatched the bishop away;[74] O you wretch, I do not know which was the greater impiety, your banishment of him or your restoration of him! What frenzy you then let loose against the church of Toulouse![75] Clerics were beaten with clubs, deacons were crushed with leaden whips, and (let the most holy join me in recognising this) hands were laid on the anointed one himself.[76] If my account is a lie, Constantius, then you are a sheep; but if these are truly your actions, then you are the Antichrist.

12 Now, because these matters that I have described are public knowledge and are not slanders, but rather the truth, if anyone still has hope in Christ, if anyone fears the day of judgement, if anyone has renounced the Devil, if

71 Paulinus was exiled to Phrygia, where he died in 358. Montanus and Maximilla were two leading figures within Montanism, a Christian movement which emerged in Phrygia in the late second century. It was an enthusiastic movement, placing a great focus on prophecy, and was regarded as being ascetic and eschatological. See Trevett (1996). The reference to the 'cave' may be a general comment about the landscape of Phrygia or could be a specific allusion to a rock-cut shrine at the Montanist centre of Pepouza.

72 On the Council of Milan in 355, see Introduction p. 11.

73 For the story of Zachariah, see 2 *Chronicles* 24.20–1. See also *Matthew* 23.35; *Luke* 11.51. Zachariah represents a useful Old Testament example for Hilary here because he was killed at the Temple.

74 This is Liberius of Rome, exiled in 355, but allowed to return in 357 after subscribing to the condemnation of Athanasius. See Ath. *Hist. Ar.* 35–41 and Introduction pp. 11–12, as well as Barnes (1993) 130.

75 Rhodanius of Toulouse was exiled with Hilary at the Council of Béziers, which probably took place in 356: see Introduction p. 26. Sulpicius Severus, *Chronicle* 2.39.4 claims that Rhodanius was a weak man, but was emboldened by Hilary. On his career, see PCBE IV.2 (1610) (Rhodanius 1).

76 See *1 Samuel* 24.6 (24:7 LXX): *The Lord forbid that I should do this thing unto my master, the Lord's anointed, to stretch forth my hand against him, seeing he is the anointed of the Lord.* The Latin term for 'the anointed one' is *christus*, so while the passage refers literally to the bishop Rhodanius, it also conjures up the image of Constantius' men attacking Christ himself. See Rocher (1987) 240 for a note on this passage, rejecting the alternative suggestion that this passage describes the profanation of the Eucharist.

anyone remembers being reborn to life, let him accept what I say and from it judge with the judgement by which he himself must be judged.[77] For what I am about to relate has not come to me second-hand; I heard it myself and was present when it happened. Therefore in Christ I do not lie,[78] for I am a disciple of the truth, and also now present myself as a witness of the truth. I discovered a council of Easterners at Seleucia, where there were as many blasphemies as Constantius desired.[79] For when I first withdrew I had found that 105 bishops preached *homoiousios*, i.e. of like essence, and nineteen bishops preached *anomoiousios*, i.e. of unlike essence; only the Egyptians, with the exception of the Alexandrian heretic, unwaveringly maintained *homoousios*.[80] They had all gathered together under pressure from the *comes* Leonas.[81] Out of those who were preaching *homoiousios*, some expressed in words certain propositions that were orthodox:[82] that the Son was from God, i.e. from the substance of God,[83] and had always

77 See *Matthew* 7.2.
78 See *Romans* 9.1: 'I say the truth in Christ, I lie not'.
79 The Council of Seleucia was called by Constantius and met in 359, with a parallel council for Western bishops taking place at Ariminum: see Introduction p. 17; Barnes (1993) 144–51.
80 The term *homoiousios* ('of like essence') was suggested by many eastern bishops at this time, including Basil of Ancyra, and is presented as inferior to *homoousios* ('of the same essence') but not heretical in Ath. *De synodis* 33–54 and Hilary, *De synodis* 72–91. The definition *anomoiousios* ('of unlike essence') represents the group at Seleucia led by Acacius of Caesarea, which also included Eudoxius of Antioch (who became bishop of Constantinople soon afterwards). As the following chapters show, rather than supporting 'of unlike essence' itself during the council, they actually rejected any use of *ousia* ('essence') terminology as unscriptural, instead propounding a 'Homoian' Christology that the Son is *homoios* ('like') the Father. The term *homoousios* is the Nicene formula professed by Hilary. See the Introduction pp. 2–18 and the Glossary for more discussion of the theological details discussed in this chapter, including these different ways of defining the relationship of the Son to the Father. The 'Alexandrian heretic' is George 'the Cappadocian', Athanasius' rival for the see at this time: see Introduction p. 12.
81 On Leonas, see PLRE I 498–9 (Leonas). Soc. *HE* 2.39–40 presents him as having been placed in charge of the organisation and running of the Council of Seleucia by Constantius. On the imperial rank of *comes*, sometimes translated as 'count', see the Glossary.
82 The Latin word rendered into English here as 'orthodox' is *pie*, used (like the Greek *eusebes*) to mean in a manner that is pious in belief. As noted above, in his *De synodis*, written before the *In Constantium*, Hilary defended *homoiousios* as orthodox, but inferior to *homoousios* as a theological definition.
83 This picks up the language of the Nicene Creed, in which Christ was described as 'begotten from the Father, only-begotten, that is, from the *ousia* of the Father': see Kelly (1972) 215. Hilary has here moved to using the Latin term *substantia* ('substance') to gloss the Greek term *ousia*; he had previously been using the Latin word *essentia* ('essence').

existed. Those who were defending *anomoiousios* asserted nothing but the most sacrilegious ideas, denying that anything could be like the substance of God, or that there could be generation from God, but saying instead that Christ is a creature; and so his creation could be reckoned to be his 'birth', but he is from nothing, and therefore he is not a Son and is not like God.

13 But I am telling you what I personally heard read publicly in an assembly and which was reported to have been preached by the bishop of Antioch.[84] These are what were related as his words: 'God was what he is now; he was not a Father because he had no Son: for if there is a Son, then there would have to be a woman, a conversational exchange, a marital bond, alluring words and, finally, the natural equipment for begetting children.' O my poor ears that heard the sound of this deadly statement – these words being spoken about God by a man and preached about Christ in a church! And after many impieties of this kind, when he had judged 'Father' and 'Son' to be mere titles rather than expressions of a natural relationship, he said: 'For however much the Son exerted himself to know the Father, so much the more did the Father exert himself further not to be known by the Son.'[85] When he had said this, uproar erupted.

14 When even these men who call God 'unlike' realised that human ears could not accept words of such impiety, they – who are really bishops of the palace, not of the Church – once again wrote a creed, condemning *homoousios, homoiousios* and 'unlikeness'.[86] Since in the judgement of the hearers this was self-contradiction, I pretended to be ignorant of proceedings and asked one of them, who happened to have come over to

84 Eudoxius of Antioch, who became bishop of Constantinople in early 360: see Introduction p. 14.

85 See *Matthew* 11.27, where Christ states that 'no man knows the Father, except the Son'.

86 Here Hilary moves into discussing the details of the arguments about how to define the relationship between the Son and the Father. While the first two terms are transliterated from Greek, for the third Hilary uses the Latin word *dissimilitudo*, which translates the Greek concept of *anomoios* ('unlike'). Hilary is here presenting his opponents at Seleucia as being Anomoians, but abandoning their position because they realised that they could not get away with it. The creedal formula put forward at Seleucia by Acacius of Caesarea and his supporters declared that *homoousios* and *homoiousios* were unscriptural, but also anathematised *anomoios*, instead proclaiming the Homoian doctrine of the 'likeness' (*to homoion*) of Son to Father: see Ath. *De synodis* 29.3–4. For the debate at Seleucia and the 'Homoian' doctrine of 'likeness' that resulted from it, see Introduction p. 17; Kelly (1972) 292; Barnes (1993) 146–7.

test me, what this could mean – a condemnation of 'unlikeness' by those who had condemned 'one substance' of Father and Son and had also denied 'of like substance'.[87] Then he told me that Christ is not like God, but is like the Father. This seemed to me still more obscure. When I asked him about this again, he replied with these words: 'I say that he is unlike God, but can be understood to be like the Father, because the Father willed to create a creature of this kind, who would have a will similar to his own, and would therefore be like the Father, because he would be the Son of his will, rather than of his divinity; but he is unlike God, because he is neither God nor was he born from God, i.e. from the substance of God.' Hearing these things I was dumbstruck and could not believe what was happening, until this most sacrilegious doctrine of 'likeness' was publicly proclaimed with the consensus of all of them.[88]

15   Those, however, who were preaching *homoiousios* condemned all of those who, entirely without any shame for their impiety, spoke these words most shamelessly. Having been condemned, they flew to their emperor, where they were received with honour, and strengthened their impieties with every intrigue they could concoct, denying that Christ is like God or born from God or that he is the Son by nature. These few dominated the many. Constantius extorted approval for his blasphemy through the threat of exile.[89] He boasted that he had now defeated the Easterners,

---

87 Hilary has moved from Greek theological terms to Latin translations here, and, as in the last part of chapter 12, is using *substantia* ('substance'), rather than *essentia* ('essence'), as a translation of *ousia*.

88 The general consensus referred to here is of the Homoians, rather than the council as a whole, as the next chapter makes clear. Hilary's account of the sacrilege of his unnamed opponent here does not represent the Homoian theology as presented at Seleucia in 359 or as ratified at Constantinople in 360. While it is true that these statements state only that the Son was 'like' the Father, not 'like' God, as well as rejecting the use of *ousia* terminology, at both Seleucia and Constantinople the Son was said to be 'God from God' (see Ath. *De synodis* 29.6, 30.3), although not 'true God from true God', as the Nicene Creed stated. The speech presented here bears some resemblance to the ideas of Eunomius, who was rehabilitated at Constantinople in 360 and made bishop of Cyzicus, although his ideas were not widely accepted. On his career and theology, see PCBE III 295–342 (Eunomios 1). Hilary is here claiming that Homoian theology is a front for the more radical subordinationism of Eunomian 'Anomoianism'. On these ideas, see Introduction pp. 13–18. See also n. 127 to chapter 23 below on Hilary's interpretation of the 'Blasphemy of Sirmium' in 357.

89 The 'Homoiousian' delegates from Seleucia eventually subscribed to the 'Homoian' formula on 31 December 359: see Introduction pp. 17–18; Soz. *HE* 4.23.8; Kelly (1972) 292; Barnes (1993) 148.

because he had subjected their ten delegates to his will;[90] through his prefect he threatened the people, and he also threatened the bishops who were confined within his palace; throughout the greatest cities of the East he substituted heretical bishops and gave them the protection of a heretical communion. In fact, all his actions were directed toward delivering up the whole world, for which Christ suffered, as a gift to the Devil.[91]

16 Even now he uses his customary trickery, as he did previously in other matters, to strengthen wickedness under a veneer of rectitude, and to establish insanity under the name of reason. 'I do not want', he says, 'expressions to be used that are not scriptural.'[92] But now I ask him who it is that gives orders to bishops and vetoes the form of the apostolic preaching.[93] Say this rather, if you think it right to say it: 'I do not want any new medical concoctions to combat new poisons; I do not want new wars to combat new enemies; I do not want new advice to combat new plots.' For if the Arian heretics shun *homoousios* today because they denied it previously, surely you reject it today so that they may still deny it now? The Apostle ordered us to avoid novelties of speech, but he specified the sacrilegious ones:[94] why do you, then, exclude the orthodox ones, when above all he said: *All Scripture is divinely inspired and useful.*[95] Nowhere in Scripture do you read 'incapable of being born': will it therefore have to be rejected because it is new? You declare that 'the Son is like the Father'. The Gospels do not preach this. Why do you not reject this statement? Novelty is desired in one matter, but banished in another. Where an opportunity for

90 These are the ten delegates sent by the majority at the Council of Seleucia to report their views to Constantius. Theod. *HE* 2.27 states that they included Eustathius of Sebasteia, Basil of Ancyra, Silvanus of Tarsus and Eleusius of Cyzicus.

91 See *Luke* 4.5–6.

92 The Nicene term *homoousios* was criticised during this period because of its absence from Scripture: see Ath. *De decretis* 1.1, as well as Introduction p. 5. It was condemned as unbiblical in the theological statement known as the 'Blasphemy of Sirmium' from 357, as preserved at Hilary, *De synodis* 11 and Ath. *De synodis* 28: see n. 127 to chapter 23 below. See also the 'Arian' letter from the Council of Ariminum in 359, preserved at Hilary, *Adu. Val. et Ursac.* A.VI, condemning both *homoousios* and all *ousia* language. In contrast, a defence of *substantia* (a Latin translation of *ousia*) as 'nothing new', since it 'was placed in our minds by many sacred Scriptures', was also written by the 'orthodox' bishops at the same council: see Hilary, *Adu. Val. et Ursac.* A.IX.1.2.

93 After the interlude on the Council of Seleucia, Hilary here returns to addressing Constantius directly in the second person.

94 See *1 Timothy* 6.20.

95 *2 Timothy* 3.16.

impiety lies open, novelty is admitted; but where it is the greatest, and the only, protection of religion, it is excluded.[96]

17   But I will not remain silent about the deceptive subtlety of your diabolical ingenuity. You decree that 'the Son is like the Father', which is not in Scripture, is to be preached, so that you can pass over 'Christ is equal with God', which is in Scripture. For this was the cause of the Lord's death: *Therefore the Jews sought even more to kill him, because he not only had broken the Sabbath, but also said that God was his Father, making himself equal with God.*[97] In saying this, John is proclaiming with a mighty voice that the Son by professing that God was his Father should be understood to have professed that he himself was equal to God. If you happen to say that Christ denied this equality between himself and God because he said: *The Son can do nothing of himself, except what he sees the Father doing,*[98] remember both that Christ made this reply when he was accused of having violated the Sabbath, in order to give priority in this matter to the authority of the Father working in him, and also that he attributed to himself an equality of power and honour: *All things that the Father does, the Son also does the same things likewise;*[99] and again: *That they should honour the Son, even as they honour the Father;*[100] and: *He that does not honour the Son does not honour the Father who has sent Him.*[101] If there is the same power, if there is the same honour, in what, I ask you, is equality lacking?

18   But 'likeness' pleases you, because it means that you do not have to hear: *I and the Father are one.*[102] This statement 'We are one' disregards neither union nor distinction.[103] Even though the Jews again maliciously

---

96 Hilary's complaint in this chapter is that his opponents are inconsistent in their attitude towards non-Scriptural definitions in theological statements. While they reject *homoousios* ('the greatest, and the only, protection of religion') and any other *ousia* terminology because it does not appear in the Bible, they are happy to accept *similis Patri Filius* ('the Son is like the Father'), which is not found in Scripture. On the term *innascibilis* ('incapable of being born'), see Hilary, *De synodis* 60, as well as chapter 22 below.

97 *John* 5.16.

98 *John* 5.19.

99 *John* 5.19.

100 *John* 5.23.

101 *John* 5.23.

102 *John* 10.30.

103 Here Hilary presents the combination of unity and diversity in this statement as representing an orthodox middle way between the 'Arian' tendency to draw too much of

accused him of making himself out to be God by this remark, surely the Lord himself did not deny it, when he said: *If I do not do the works of my Father, believe me not; but if I do, and you do not want to believe me, then believe my works, that the Father is in me and I in the Father?*[104] What, I ask you, is lacking from equality with God? Works? Nature? Declaration? For *the Father is in me and I in the Father* is equality, and expresses the reciprocity of equality, since both 'being' and 'being in' are shared by them. To do the works of his Father is nothing other than to employ the power of paternal divinity in himself. And indeed, to say that they are one is not to reject equality, but to furnish faith in their equality with an increased understanding.

19 So you forbid non-scriptural expressions to be used, and yet you yourself use non-scriptural expressions and also do not utter the expressions that are scriptural. You want it preached that the Son is like the Father, to avoid hearing from the Apostle: *Who, since he was in the form of God, did not think it robbery to be equal with God; but he emptied himself, taking upon him the form of a servant.*[105] Christ did not rob what he was, i.e. being in the form of God. Being in the form of God would not be equality with God, if being in the form of a servant were not equality with man. If Christ, in the form of a servant, is man, what is Christ, in the form of God, other than God? And so you want 'like' to be preached so that you do not have in your creed: *And let every tongue confess that Jesus is Lord in the glory of God the Father.*[106]

20 O this deceitful flattery of yours! For you cover water with straw, conceal pits under turf and bait snares with bits of food.[107] You think that you can satisfy the ignorant by saying 'like the Father according to the Scriptures.'[108] Hear even now the trickery of your impiety. Surely it is not unorthodox for us to say that man is like God according to the Scriptures,

a distinction between the Father and the Son and the 'Monarchian' heresy of Sabellianism, which failed to distinguish sufficiently between the Father, the Son and the Holy Spirit. Nicene Christians were sometimes accused of Sabellianism by their opponents. On this heresy and its use in the polemic of this period, see Introduction p. 2 and the Glossary.
104 *John* 10.37–8.
105 *Philippians* 2.6–7. This quotation is also used by Lucifer at *Moriundum* 10, 12.
106 *Philippians* 2.11.
107 Hilary is here comparing Constantius' theology to the setting of traps.
108 This was the definition which appeared in both the 'Dated Creed' written at Sirmium in 359 and the statement approved at the Council of Constantinople in 360, which followed

because it is said: *Let us make man in our image and likeness?*[109] Therefore man is made to the image and likeness of God the Father and God the Son. If asked, the orthodox will teach you what kind of image it is. But while man is created in the likeness and image of God, 'likeness' between the Father and Son is not being proclaimed. For the fact that the text says *'our'* is proof of equality, since no distinction is made in this mystery as to whose image and likeness it is.[110]

21   But nowhere will you find 'likeness' concerning the Son. The Apostle says that he is the image of God, but with an additional element of faith, lest you think of 'image' in terms of shaping.[111] For he says: *Who is the image of God invisible*, meaning that the image of God invisible, since he himself is invisible, is the invisible image of God.[112] For Scripture specifically assigned to man 'likeness to God' along with 'image', lest the proper possession of truth be ascribed to one for whom 'likeness' had been added to 'image'.[113] Finally, when it equalises in respect of power, and likeness in performing works is attributed to the Son, when an advancement of understanding is truly being taught, then it says this: *All things that the Father does, the Son also does the same things likewise.*[114] To do 'likewise' would appear to be too little, were it not for the fact that 'like things' are 'the same things'. Thus 'likeness of action' has been

on from the Councils of Seleucia and Ariminum. See Ath. *De synodis* 8.4, 30.3; Kelly (1972) 288–94, as well as Introduction p. 18.

109 *Genesis* 1.26. The Latin term for 'likeness' here, as elsewhere in this text, is *similtudo*.

110 Hilary's point here is that the verse from *Genesis* not only uses 'likeness' to define the relationship of man to God but also states that there is one 'image' and one 'likeness' of both the Father and the Son (hence the use of the plural 'our'), rather than distinguishing between them.

111 See *Romans* 8.29: *For those whom he did foreknow, he also did predestinate to be shaped to the image of his Son.*

112 *Colossians* 1.15. This verse appears in the Homoian creed at the Council of Seleucia in 359, where it was used to support the concept of 'likeness' between the Father and the Son: see Ath. *De synodis* 29.4, as well as Epiphanius, *Panarion* 73.25.5. In Hilary's Latin version of this verse, unlike the Greek original, the adjective *inuisibilis* could apply either to 'image' or 'God'.

113 Hilary's argument here is that while the term 'likeness', the basis of Homoian theology, implies the inferiority of the Son to the Father, and therefore actually makes them 'unlike' each other, being the 'image' of God is a reference to total equality when it is used to refer to the Son (*'who is the image of God invisible'*), although not when it refers to man in *Genesis*, since there it is qualified by the addition of the term 'likeness'.

114 *John* 5.19. The Latin for 'likewise' is *similiter*.

revealed, according to orthodoxy, to consist in the proper meaning of 'the same actions'. There is also in the Lord the *likeness of sinful flesh*;[115] but he does not possess merely the likeness of flesh, but the likeness of sinful flesh, in such a way that the one *in the form of God* is man, while the one *in the likeness of sinful flesh* is the likeness of man, since he is in the state of being man, but without the sin of man.[116] What clever statement of your belief is it to say 'the Son is like the Father according to the Scriptures', when only man was made in the image and likeness of God? Why, then, do you deceive with words? Why do you trick with artifice? Why do you not follow orthodoxy in saying *equal with God*, since that is what is according to the Scriptures?[117]

22   Are you afraid that in saying 'equal' you might mean 'incapable of being born'? But understand that in fact Christ has been recognised as being equal to God, because he proclaimed God to be his own Father, and that to testify that God was his own Father was a demonstration of his birth.[118] For me likeness is sacred, to exclude any possibility of 'oneness';[119] but I must not concede this to you, because in an orthodox manner I will explain that the same person is 'equal' and then that he is 'like'. I will proclaim religiously that he is 'like the Father', and also that he is 'like God', but I will proclaim 'like' in such as way that I always preface 'likeness' with the saying: *I and the Father are one*.[120] But you oppose all of these ideas, because you defend 'likeness' as an excuse: you deny that he is the Son by birth; you deny that he is God by nature; you deny that he is 'like' through equality; you deny that he is 'true' [God] through unity.[121] So now I ask

115 *Romans* 8.3.

116 *Philippians* 2.6; *Romans* 8.3. In analysing these quotations, Hilary is arguing that biblical passages that use the terms 'likeness' and 'likewise' to refer to the Son do not actually support the Homoian position, such that their statement that *the Son is like the Father according to the Scriptures* is not tenable.

117 *John* 5.18; *Philippians* 2.6.

118 See *John* 5.18.

119 'Oneness' here translates the term *unio*. Here Hilary seeks to avoid any accusation of falling into Sabellianism: see n. 103 to chapter 18 above. Similarly, he does not want his concept of 'equality' to be regarded as a sign that he accepted the idea that Christ was incapable of being born.

120 *John* 10.30. This passage is also used at Lucifer, *Moriundum* 10.34.

121 'Unity' here translates the term *unitas*, which Hilary defends as a quality of the Father and the Son, in opposition to both his 'Arian' opponents and the Sabellian concept of 'oneness'.

what 'likeness' you leave him, since you grant him nothing of the proper nature by which he is the Son.

23   And now, Constantius, I finally ask you what creed you believe in. Now I am carefully examining the history of your transformations, during which you ran down the sheer steps and descended all the way to the lowest abyss of your blasphemy.[122] For after the first creed at the Council of Nicaea, which was truly a creed, you convened another council at Antioch, where you made a new creed for yourself.[123] But it has happened to you, as tends to happen to inexperienced builders, who are always dissatisfied with their work, that you are always building and then always demolishing. And lest you accuse me of being an unjust judge of your intentions, I will explain what it is that displeases you in that same creed of the 'Dedication Council'. Unless I am mistaken, these are your words: 'Who was begotten from the Father, God from God, whole from whole, one from one, perfect from perfect, king from king, unalterable, the unchangeable image of his divinity, essence, power and glory.'[124] I myself am firmly grounded and still abide in the creed composed by the Fathers at Nicaea and so have no need of these words; but you, however, rescind them by amending them, and, without causing any harm to my faith, you seek out an opportunity for infidelity for yourself. Then, after the Council of Serdica, you directed all your concern for your catholic doctrine against Photinus at Sirmium.[125] But at once you recoiled in horror from what was contained in both creeds: 'As for those who say that the Son of God is from the non-existent, or from

---

122 The reference here to the 'lowest abyss' (*imum baratrum*) is reminiscent of Virgil's description of the whirlpool Charybdis at *Aeneid* 3.421.

123 The 'Dedication Council' of Antioch in 341, so called because it was held when the bishops were gathered for the dedication of a new church in the city: see Kelly (1972) 263–74; Barnes (1993) 57–9, as well as Introduction pp. 6–7.

124 This is taken from the section regarding Christ in the so-called 'Second Creed', officially ratified at the 'Dedication Council', albeit with some omissions: see Ath. *De synodis* 23; Kelly (1972) 268–70.

125 On the divided Council of Serdica in 343, where the 'eastern' and 'western' groups of bishops met separately and refused to come together in a single assembly, see Introduction p. 8, as well as Hanson (1988) 293–306; Barnes (1993) 71–86; Ayres (2004) 122–6; Parvis (2006) 210–45. On the long-running issue of whether the Council should be dated to 342 or 343, see Parvis (2006) 210–17, which argues coherently for 343. The Council of Sirmium, which condemned the city's bishop, Photinus, met in 351. Photinus, a pupil of Marcellus of Ancyra, was accused of being close to Sabellianism in his theology, as well as possibly espousing the 'Adoptionist' view that Christ did not exist until the Incarnation: see Soc. *HE* 2.29; Soz. *HE* 4.6; Kelly (1972) 281–2.

some other substance and not from God, or that there was ever a time or age when he was not, the holy and catholic Church regards them as alien.'[126] You quarrel with your friends and as an enemy you rebel against your own people. You subvert the old with the new, then rescind this innovation by amending it anew, and then condemn your amendments by further amendment. You even adopt condemnations of your own amendments to combat the nonsense of Ossius and the exaggerations of Ursacius and Valens.[127] But soon you decide that everything must be amended, or rather condemned; for you are even displeased with these few words, which are incredibly hateful to you: 'And if anyone says that the Father is older in time than his only-begotten Son, or that the Son is younger than the Father, let him be anathema.'[128]

24 We are not accusing you falsely about these annulments when we complain that they were carried out even more after the Council of Nicaea. For even if it was confirmed that no error underlies any of them, the influence of a devout will would not be present in them, because the alteration of good ideas is an exercise in evil, and unnecessary amendment is an opportunity for distortion. I remain silent about why you rescind our records of proceedings, produced by the fathers at Nicaea: for you do not agree with them. I only ask why you condemn your own. The Apostle

126 This statement is contained in the 'Fourth Creed' of the 'Dedication Council', which was sent to the western emperor Constans, in the 'Long Creed', which was adopted at Antioch in 344, and also in the creed promulgated by the Council of Sirmium in 351: see Ath. *De synodis* 25–7; Hilary, *De synodis* 34, 38; Kelly (1972) 271–3, 279–80, 281–2. The word which Hilary renders as *substantia* ('substance') in his quotation is not *ousia* in the original Greek creed, but is actually *hypostasis* (often translated into English as 'subsistence'). In fact, the 'Fourth Creed' avoids all mention of *ousia* terminology: see Introduction p. 7.
127 This is a specific reference to the so-called 'Blasphemy of Sirmium', drawn up in 357 by Hilary's great opponents Ursacius of Singidunum and Valens of Mursa, and which was signed by the aging Ossius of Cordoba. This document, preserved at Ath. *De synodis* 28 and Hilary, *De synodis* 11, condemns the use of *ousia* terminology and emphasises that the Father is greater than the Son. Hilary (at *De synodis* 10) also regards it as a specific attempt to deny that the Son is God. On these events, see Kelly (1972) 285–8; Simonetti (1975) 229–33; Brennecke (1984) 312–25, especially 323–4; Hanson (1988) 343–7; Barnes (1993) 138–9, as well as Introduction p. 12.
128 This is the eleventh anathema from the Council of Ancyra in 358, preserved at Hilary, *De synodis* 24. See also Epiphanius, *Panarion* 73.11.7. On this council, where a key role was played by Basil of Ancyra and a 'Homoiousian' theological formula was approved, see Introduction p. 14 and Barnes (1993) 139–40.

preaches *one faith and one baptism*;[129] and so whatever you have apart from the one faith is not faith but infidelity. For you who condemn the creed through amending it decree a condemnation of the creed, since you abolish it through another creed which will itself be abolished in turn through yet another.[130]

25   And so, since then, to what bishop have you left a clean hand? What tongue have you not forced to utter lies? What heart have you not turned to the condemnation of an earlier opinion? You ordain the condemnation of *homoousios*, the faith of antiquity and the pledge of piety. You have decreed that *homoiousios* be anathematised by the very same people who took it up: even though this has nothing to do with our faith, it is nevertheless a condemnation of their faith for those who are rescinding it.[131] You also condemn the term *substance*, by which you feigned piety to the Westerners at the Councils of Serdica and Sirmium.[132] That word, however, was received through the authority of the prophets and contains an understanding of the faith. And so you demand that everything previously approved must now be condemned; you force people to sanctify ideas that have always been repudiated. O you wicked man, making a mockery of the Church! Only dogs return to their own vomit;[133] you have forced Christ's priests to swallow what they have spat out. You command them in their

---

129 *Ephesians* 4.5.

130 Both 'faith' and 'creed' here are translations of *fides*. In the original Latin, Hilary's argument that the repeated writing of new creeds runs contrary to the Pauline statement of 'one faith' is clearer.

131 See chapters 14–15 above.

132 In his note on this passage (at 250), Rocher identifies Sirmium here as the gathering apparently organised by Basil of Ancyra in that city in 358, where the term *homoiousios* was used and briefly gained the assent of Constantius. It is more likely, however, that Hilary means the Council of Sirmium in 351, which he discussed at length in *De synodis* 38–62, as well as mentioning it alongside Serdica in chapter 23 above, where he states that it approved of the term *substantia*. On the Councils of Serdica and Sirmium and these theological issues, see n. 125 to chapter 23 above. On the highly confusing issue of the many councils attested as having been held at Sirmium during this period, see Barnes (1993) 231–2. In this section Hilary is keen to present Constantius as repeatedly changing his mind, as Lucifer also does at *Moriundum* 11. Certainly a lot of councils were held during this time with imperial approval, and a lot of theological statements were composed, but one could also characterise this as a process in which eastern Christians spent a long time seeking a compromise formula that would achieve widespread acceptance, rather than the result of the constantly shifting whims of an autocrat.

133 See *Proverbs* 26.11; *2 Peter* 2.22.

professions of faith to approve against themselves what they previously condemned: by denying they absolve those they held guilty and make themselves the guilty parties. You have driven everything to impiety and guilt, since everyone either stands guilty and impious because of their present position, or confesses themselves guilty and impious because of their previous position. Truth does not admit falsehood, nor does religion tolerate impiety.

26   You say that you are a Christian, but you yourself provide evidence that you are not and your deeds do not support your claim. For you have subjected the eastern bishops to your will; in fact, not only to your will, but also to your violence. You order that the subscriptions of the Africans, in which they had condemned the blasphemy of Ursacius and Valens, be returned.[134] You threaten those who resist and finally send people to seize it from them. Why? Do you believe that Christ does not judge except through a letter or that God needs a scrap of paper to prove a man's intentions?[135] Or that something which was written once and then violently snatched away by you can be banished from the consciousness of the divine power? These scraps of paper will follow you to ashes, but the condemnations of the guilty will live in God.[136] Your only achievement is that, through fear, posterity has been taught how it ought to judge them.

27   O by what great steps do you advance to impiety! Other men have always waged wars with the living, since a man has no cause against another man beyond death; but for you enmities never come to an end. For now you even attack our fathers, who have been received into eternal rest,

---

134 This is a reference to the gathering at Niké in Thrace in October 359, where a group of western delegates from the Council of Ariminum, led by Restitutus of Carthage, were compelled to abandon their defence of *homoousios* and their condemnation of a number of 'Arians', including Ursacius of Singidunum and Valens of Mursa: see Introduction p. 16 and Kelly (1972) 291. Hilary preserves a number of relevant documents in his fragmentary *Against Valens and Ursacius*, including the original condemnation of Ursacius and Valens (*Adu. Val. et Ursac.* A.IX.2–3), the bishops' letter to Constantius informing him of the decision (A.V.1 – also preserved in Greek at Ath. *De synodis* 10) and the letter from the western delegates at Niké in which they disavowed their earlier subscriptions against their opponents (A.V.3). Sulpicius Severus 2.43–4 describes the pressure placed on the remaining delegates at Ariminum to get them to rescind their previous statements and subscribe to the 'Homoian' creed.

135 See *Romans* 2.29; *2 Corinthians* 3.6.

136 See *Ezekiel* 28.18.

and you misguidedly violate their decrees. The Apostle taught us: *to share in the remembrances of the saints*;[137] you have compelled us to condemn them. Is there anyone today, living or dead, whose words you have not rescinded? The episcopates, which are seen now, have been completely destroyed by you, because there is no one who has not already condemned himself and also himself condemned the man from whom he received the priesthood. What remembrance of the saints will there now be to share in? The 318 bishops who convened at Nicaea are anathema to you.[138] Also, all of those who took part in the various declarations of faith since then are anathema to you. In addition, your father himself, dead now for a long time, is anathema to you, since he cared deeply for the Council of Nicaea, while you overthrow and defame it through your false ideas;[139] together with a few of your lackeys you sacrilegiously fight against human and divine judgement. Your powerful rule at this time does not give you licence to make judgements that will have force in the future. For there exist letters in which you ordered that ideas be accepted as orthodox which you now regard as criminal. Hear the holy meaning of words; hear the undisturbed constitution of the Church; hear the professed faith of your father; hear the confident pledge of human hope; hear the public consciousness of the heretics' condemnation; and understand that you are a foe of divine religion, an enemy of the remembrances of the saints and a rebel against your father's piety.

137 *Romans* 12.13.

138 While the actual number of bishops at Nicaea was probably around 300 (as stated at Ath. *Hist. Ar.* 66.3), the figure of 318 became popular in the middle of the fourth century, as it was the number of servants of Abraham who joined the patriarch in fighting the kings who had taken Lot captive: see *Genesis* 14.14.

139 Here Hilary is referring to Constantius' actual father, Constantine, who summoned the Council of Nicaea in 325. In contrast, see chapter 8, where Constantius' father is said to be the Devil.

LUCIFER OF CAGLIARI

The Necessity of Dying for the Son of God
(*Moriundum esse pro dei filio*)

1 It had certainly seemed right, Emperor Constantius, not to discuss the holy Scriptures again with you, with the very man whom we have found to be a corruptor of the truth, with you whom we have recognised from your actions actually to be one of those people who are called wise by themselves although they are actually following the path of foolishness. As we have said, it had seemed right after we brought such important matters to your attention to remain silent now, especially since we remember that it is written: *Answer not a fool according to his folly, lest you become like him,*[1] and again: *Speak not in the ears of a fool, lest, when he has heard, he mocks your intelligent words.*[2] But because I have found you still boasting of the power of your arms and the hollow authority of your rule, that you are able to destroy those whom you ought by reason to have established in the position that you had decided upon, I wanted by this book especially to make it known to your polluted and sacrilegious mind that, in all these matters where you think yourself mighty, you are actually wretched, and that all the fury of your torture is dismissed by the servants of God. For we want it clearly established in your mind that you will pass away together with your temporal, tottering, fragile and corruptible kingdom and you will come to eternal punishment, unless you look out for yourself while the opportunity exists, but Christians will assuredly reach eternal rest and will receive an incorruptible kingdom. Will you attempt to argue that you will attain the kingdom of heaven through this heresy of yours, you who, along with your equally pernicious Arians, being afraid lest one day you will be refuted by us Christians and will be forced to surrender by the exclaiming

---

1 *Proverbs* 26.4.

2 *Proverbs* 23.9. The opening of the text is quite similar to Cyprian's *Ad Demetrianum*, especially in its use of these two passages from *Proverbs* to justify not having written to a representative of imperial authority. See also the opening of Hilary's *In Constantium*, where there is also a statement of justification for now speaking out against the emperor.

truth itself, have abandoned discussion and resolved to take refuge in the power of your brittle arms?[3] As though you, an enemy of divine religion equipped with fragile weapons, could overcome men who will receive immortal rewards; as though you, the precursor of the Antichrist, could defeat devout servants of Christ, soldiers of God whom his only Son deemed worthy to invite to enjoy the everlasting bonds of friendship of his divinity, saying: *Blessed are you, when men shall revile you and, insulting you, will persecute and reproach you and speak all manner of evil against you. Rejoice and be exceeding glad, for great is your reward in heaven; for so persecuted they the prophets which were before you.*[4]

Impotent in every way, you thought that you could drive these men from their fixed position and overthrow those whom you see prepared to die for the only Son of God, since they have chosen not to be tortured in the underworld alongside you unbelievers, but to attain the heavenly kingdom; you had thought that through the worthless authority of your rule you could overcome men who shine forth as temples of God through the very confession of their faith.[5] For just as you Arians, by denying the Son of God, are marked out by the words of the prophets, apostles and sacred Gospels as the abodes of an unclean spirit, so we who confess the Son of God show ourselves to be temples of God.[6] Your cruel and sacrilegious mind was taken in by the advice of your fellow heretics and had expected that we, the soldiers of God, could have given in to your butchery, we

3 See Lact. *Diu. Inst.* 5.1.3: 'They fear lest one day they will be refuted by us and will be forced to surrender by the exclaiming truth itself.' As with many of the other passages from Lactantius reused by Lucifer, the objects of criticism here are persecuting pagans. The actions and punishments of 'tyrants', as well as the brave resistance of true Christians, are a common theme in Lactantius, and particularly in book 5 of the *Divine Institutes*. It can be seen throughout the passages from Lactantius employed by Lucifer in this work.

4 *Matthew* 5.11–12. The word 'only' here in the phrase 'only Son' translates the Latin term *unicus*, which was central to Lucifer's understanding of Christ and which he used widely throughout his works. The Old Latin version of the Bible, which Lucifer employed, used this term to render the Greek *monogenes* (as in the quotation from *John* 3.18 at Lucifer, *De Ath. II* 23), although Jerome later translated it as *unigenitus* in his Vulgate. See Pizzani (2001) 232–3, 244. See also Hilary, *In Const.* 4, where *unigenitus* is also employed for this purpose.

5 The concept of Christians as 'temples of God' comes from *2 Corinthians* 6.16.

6 The word 'confess' here translates the verb *confiteor*. For early Christians it was associated particularly with maintaining and proclaiming one's faith in opposition to persecution, and the term *confessor* came to be applied to those who had remained steadfast under torture. See, for example, Lact. *Mort. pers.* 35.2; Cyp. *Ep. passim.*

whom God describes as his temples thus: *I will dwell in them, and walk in them, and I will be their God and they shall be my people.*[7] You had decided that you could defeat these people, whom the apostle urges to exalt God and carry him in their bodies;[8] you had actually believed that you could subdue these people with the brittle weapons of your empire. But you know that, although I was standing in your palace within the curtain, the response you got from me was that your worthless authority had been trampled underfoot and all the servants of God agreed in mind, desire, purpose, strength and voice for the preservation of salvation.[9]

2 You see that, however much your tottering authority sees fit to rage against us, so much is it judged to be weak, despicable, hollow, feeble and base; for whenever your hand, roused by madness and villainy for our destruction, has prevailed, we recall that each time we have grown and emerged even more prominently as victors. You committed the greatest massacre in Alexandria, you ripped apart other individuals throughout the whole world, you destroyed those who were resisting you in many different locations; but, even though you are loath to hear it, they are all martyrs.[10] Believe me that we, who have faith that all these most blessed men, slain by your sword, are now in paradise, have resolved to be killed by you, because we have seen that it is better to have God as a devoted friend for all time than to be punished alongside you, who are the imitator of Judas Iscariot and the Jews. So it is in short, Constantius, that, fearless against the gnashings of the serpent that you have introduced, we have been prepared

---

7 *2 Corinthians* 6.16.

8 See *1 Corinthians* 6.20.

9 The phrase *intra uelum* ('within the curtain') appears in *Leviticus* 16.15 and 21.23, as well as *Numbers* 18.7, in prescriptions for Jewish Temple practice, although here it refers to approaching the inner sanctum of the imperial court, as the *uelum* (Greek: βῆλον) was the curtain that screened off the chamber in which visitors entered the emperor's presence: see Lampe s.v. βῆλον 1. The episode described here is probably either Lucifer's embassy to Constantius on behalf of Liberius of Rome in 354 to ask for the convening of a council or a meeting in the aftermath of that council, which took place at Milan in 355: see Barnes (1993) 116–17. The passage also employs the common trope within Christian martyr literature of the confrontation between confessor/martyr and persecuting official, which often harked back, in turn, to the paradigmatic account of Christ before Pilate in *Matthew* 27.11–14; *Mark* 15.1–5; *Luke* 23.1–7, 13–16; *John* 18.33–8.

10 This is probably a reference to the imperial action that caused Athanasius to flee from Alexandria in 356, thereby starting his third period of exile. On these events, see Introduction p. 24. A detailed account of this is given at Ath. *Hist. Ar.* 47–63, 81, as well as being mentioned in Hilary, *In Const.* 11 and chapter 8 below.

to face any death.[11] We can never repent of our decisions, even if we, who are seen to have resisted your cruel hands thus far, are slaughtered by you. For the death that you threaten to inflict on us has been prepared for all; but without doubt, as we see, no one else has ever achieved such great blessedness as the holy martyrs attained, except those who have conquered death by dying for the only Son of God.[12]

You torture, kill and eradicate men who have been consecrated to God, yet are unable to explain the causes of your hatred in performing these actions. Because you stray, you even grow angry with us, since we follow the true path, and although you could correct yourself through our salutary advice, you heap up your errors on top of cruel deeds, wrenching minds consecrated to God out from our eviscerated bodies because we have resolved to maintain our faith in God right up to the final laps of life.[13] You see that the situation is thus and this is certainly not without the greatest anguish for you when you realise that you cannot turn us from the only true religion, or from this course, which we steer to retrieve the prize of the heavenly calling;[14] not when you openly make yourself an enemy, nor when you pretend to be a friend (for you are seen to have in you he who deceived Eve),[15] nor when you concoct your words, by which you spread like a ulcer,[16] with a false and fabricated tumour of learning, by claiming

11 The serpent here is a reference to the Devil, who is frequently described in this way in early Christian literature.

12 Lucifer here makes the forthright claim that dying for the *unicus* Son of God (i.e. in the defence of 'Nicene' theology) is the only suffering that receives the same reward as those who were martyred under pagan persecutors. This forms part of his wider presentation of his contemporary circumstances as analogous to earlier attacks on the true faith.

13 See Lact. *Diu. Inst.* 5.1.6–7: 'They torture, kill and eradicate just men, yet are unable to explain the causes of their hatred because they have such vehement hatred. Because they stray they grow angry with those who follow the true path and although they could correct themselves, they heap up their errors on top of cruel deeds, staining themselves in the blood of the innocent and wrenching minds consecrated to God out from eviscerated bodies.'

14 See Novat. *De cibis iudaicis* 1.5: 'Aiming for the prize of the heavenly calling in Christ' and *Philippians* 3.14. The possible allusion to the third-century theologian Novatian here is not certain, especially as it would be the only one in the whole text. It is possible that Lucifer is merely making use of the same Latin translation of *Philippians* as Novatian. The word *brauium/brabium* ('prize') in this passage originally referred to the award given for victory in a competition. On athletic imagery in Christian persecution literature, see n. 297 to Ath. *Hist. Ar.* 79.4 on p. 110.

15 The Devil/serpent: see *Genesis* 3.1–6.

16 See *2 Timothy* 2.17. This comparison appears again at chapter 11.1–2 below.

that you, with all your infamies, are revoking every error with your defiled edict, even though you are the font of all error, announcing that you are the bearer of light, although you are actually besieged by every shadow.[17] Despite your complete lack of understanding, by realising that you are despised you can to some extent, however, finally comprehend that for this reason there is no way to deflect us from the way of truth, most brutal emperor Constantius.[18]

For we Christians know that the proper activity of faith is not to be dislodged from a position by either favourable or adverse circumstances, nor ever to be diverted from a resolved course. We see that every reproach is shut out by this one devout exclamation: 'I am a Christian and I refuse to be an apostate like you, Constantius';[19] by this one exclamation the defence of salvation and the bond of liberty and honour are bestowed;[20] we see that through this confession the shield of protection, a weapon against

17 It is unclear exactly which 'edict' is being referred to here, or even whether Lucifer is actually discussing an edict in the technical legal sense, as opposed to an imperial instruction conveyed via another medium, such as a letter to an official. Lucifer may here be alluding to the outcome of the Councils of Seleucia and Ariminum in 359, as well as the Council of Constantinople in January 360, which promoted the 'Homoian' creed. See Introduction pp. 16–18.

18 For the term 'way of truth', see *2 Peter* 2.2. The use of a negative superlative vocative (*immanissime* – 'most brutal') here is an inversion of the standard panegyrical practice of addressing emperors with exaggerated references to their virtues: see Introduction p. 36. On justice and clemency as important virtues in panegyrics (and the use of their corresponding vices of injustice and brutality in the invectives against Constantius), see Flower (2013) 101–2.

19 The phrase *Christianus sum* ('I am a Christian'), or the female equivalent, *Christiana sum*, appeared regularly in early Christian literature as a statement that was attributed to those who remained defiant in the face of persecution: see, for example, *Passion of Perpetua and Felicitas* 3.2, 6.4; *Acts of Cyprian* 1.2; *Acts of the Scillitan Martyrs* 9, 10, 13; *Acts of Maximilian* 1.2, 1.3, 2.6, 2.8, 2.9 (see Musurillo (1972) for editions and translations of these texts). Bremmer (1991) 16 n. 13 provides a list of examples of this phrase (and the Greek cognate Χριστιανός εἰμι) in martyr *acta*, commenting that it appears in all but two of the early texts that he examines. On the use of this phrase and the role of direct speech in martyr *acta* more generally, see Elliott (1987) 20–26.

20 See [Cypr.] *De laude martyrii* 2: 'By this the reward can be increased and reproach shut out. This is the foundation of life and faith, the defence of salvation, the bond of liberty and honour.' The pseudo-Cyprianic *De laude martyrii* is filled with statements about the salutary power of Christian martyrdom and the glory that comes with bravely opposing persecution, making it a very useful text for Lucifer's theme in this work. The word 'liberty' is here translating the term *libertas*, which also carries connotations of freedom of speech in the face of oppression: see n. 21 to Hilary, *In Const.* 3 at p. 118.

the Devil, who now rages against us through you, is bestowed on us; and in fact you say 'Deny that you are Christians.'[21] That knowledge, which recalls that the only Son of God provides the presence of his divinity to protect his own and make them victorious, ensures that we hold out firm against the looming danger, do not shudder at the savagery of your torturer and are revived rather than afflicted;[22] so it is ensured that we are restored to life by the very punishment by which you believe us to be obliterated. For we believe that he, for whom we suffer, is with us, and so the thing which you our punisher hoped would be useful for torture, we take upon ourselves to increase our strength.[23] So we are not broken by your buffeting evils and, however variedly we are tormented by your continual cruelty, so much more firmly are we strengthened.[24] For he is with us, he who protected the young Hebrews who believed in him in the fiery furnace;[25] he fortifies our minds, he directs our judgement, he inflames our hearts with his divine love and inspires them to tolerate the holy suffering; and so none of us believes that it is death which you threaten to impose, but rather immortality, not that a temporary punishment has been inflicted through you, but eternal glory.[26] For thus the sacred Scriptures reveal that martyrs of God are consecrated through torments and are crowned by the very trial

21 It was common in persecutions for Christians to be offered the opportunity to deny their faith and to be released if they did so: see Pliny, *Ep.* 10.96–7. Lucifer is here continuing to present his encounter with Constantius in terms reminiscent of confrontations with persecuting officials in martyr literature, just as he did with his statement 'I am a Christian.'

22 See [Cypr.] *De laude martyrii* 3: 'Consider what great glory it is … to oppose the looming danger and not shudder at the savagery of the torturer, so that a man can be believed to be revived rather than afflicted by suffering.'

23 See [Cypr.] *De laude martyrii* 3: 'The thing which the punisher thinks would be useful for torture, he [the confessor] takes upon himself to increase his strength.'

24 See Lact. *Diu. Inst.* 5.7.9: 'For, shaken by buffeting evils, [virtue] acquires stability and however often it is struck, so much more firmly is it strengthened.'

25 See *Daniel* 3.19–27, where king Nebuchadnezzar II of Babylon put three young men, Shadrach, Meshach and Abed-nego, into the fiery furnace as a punishment. Not only were they miraculously unharmed, but they were also joined in the furnace by a fourth figure, referred to as 'like the Son of God'. This figure has traditionally been interpreted by Christians as Christ. The same *exempla* appear at Hilary, *In Const.* 4.

26 See Cyprian, *Ep.* 6.2: 'Do not let anything be turned in your hearts and minds now other than the divine instructions and heavenly orders, through which the Holy Spirit has always roused us to tolerate suffering. Let no one believe that this is death, but rather that it is immortality, not a temporary punishment but eternal glory.' In this letter Cyprian is addressing a group of confessors who are being held in prison by the Roman authorities and is exhorting them to stand firm.

of suffering: *Precious in the sight of the Lord is the death of his saints*[27] and: *Though they have suffered torments in the sight of men, their hope is full of immortality. And having been a little chastised, they shall be greatly rewarded, for God proved them and found them to be worthy for himself. As gold in the furnace has he tried them, and received them like a burnt offering, and there will be regard for them in due time. They shall judge the nations, and have dominion over peoples, and their Lord shall reign for ever.*[28]

3   Therefore those who look forward to attaining such great bliss through the greatness of God must rejoice and trample your present evils underfoot, instead contemplating the joys that are to come.[29] For the divine words of the only Son of God are: *He that loves his life in this world shall lose it, but he that hates his life because of me shall keep it unto life eternal.*[30] We Christians hold fast to this divine instruction; we stand, and will stand firm, Constantius, even though your hook tears through our limbs and repeatedly furrows our wounds.[31] We are stronger than you, our torturer, and all your punishments, as our only thought is that this butchery of your cruelty will serve to bring us eternal glory.[32] Barbarians often spare the defeated and there is a place for mercy in war, even amongst those who live like wild animals.[33] But what you do to us is truly indescribable, for we have always wished you good fortune and are unfailing in our desires and constant prayers to God that this may come about.[34] You despoil,

27 *Psalms* 116.15 (115.6 LXX). This quotation also appears in Cyprian, *Ep.* 6.2.

28 *Wisdom* 3.4–6, 8. This quotation (also with the omission of verse 7) similarly appears in Cyprian, *Ep.* 6.2.

29 See Cyprian, *Ep.* 6.2: 'You must rejoice and trample present sufferings underfoot with joy for what is to come.'

30 *John* 12.25 (with minor alterations). This quotation also appears in Cyprian, *Ep.* 6.2.

31 The word *ungula* means a hoof, claw or talon, but here refers to an instrument of torture: see Lewis & Short s.v., as well as the quotation in the next footnote.

32 See [Cypr.] *De laude martyrii* 3: 'Even though the hook tears through the hardening ribs and repeatedly furrows the wounds ... he however stands firm, stronger than his punishments, as his only thought is that in this cruelty of the butchers Christ himself, for whom he endures, endures more.'

33 See Lact. *Diu. Inst.* 5.9.3: 'However the defeated are spared and there is a place for mercy in war.' In this passage, Lactantius is describing how the actions of persecutors are even worse than the treatment of enemies in wars.

34 See Lact. *Diu. Inst.* 5.9.4: 'But what they do to these people is indescribable, even though they do not know how to perform evil.' The phrase 'these people' refers to 'the just' (i.e. Christians).

proscribe, slaughter with the sword and punish in many ways; you deny burial to bodies that you decreed to be butchered; you ban almsgiving; you have filled the mines and all the places thought worthy of the name of exile with those of us who resist your cunning schemes; you never stop banishing the innocent and harassing them with hunger, thirst and nakedness.[35] You heap these evils upon us, who seek eternal blessedness.

But, most cruel emperor, you should realise that whatever your savagery has inflicted on us, or will inflict in the future, is mere illusion; for the death you imposed on the holy martyrs who preceded us was not real death or any loss or deprivation, but an investment in faith.[36] We Christians are always tortured with corrupt inquisitions by you tyrants during persecution.[37] For the methods used to force the guilty to confess are now also used to make us deny Christ, the only and most true Son of God. Just as those who are guilty confess and are deservedly condemned, so we, because we do not deny the Son of God, are crowned, because condemnation imposed by you is victory for us;[38] we are removed by you from public view because you do not dare blaspheme in our presence. For a single word from a soldier

35 The punishment of being sent to the mines could be regarded as tantamount to a death penalty. It is attested as having been used during the earlier persecutions under pagan emperors: see n. 221 to Ath. *Hist. Ar.* 60.1 at p. 91. The claim that Constantius used it against his theological opponents also appears at Hilary, *In Const.* 11 and Ath. *Hist. Ar.* 60.1–2, with the latter providing the specific example of a sub-deacon named Eutychius, who died on his way to the mines. The refusal of burial to the persecuted dead appears at Ath. *Hist. Ar.* 72.6, while Eusebius of Vercelli, in his *Ep.* 2, claims that Patrophilus, 'Arian' bishop of Scythopolis in Palestine, prevented him and his clergy from distributing alms while he was in exile in the city. At *Ep.* 2.4, Eusebius also claims that Patrophilus and his associates were trying to starve him to death.

36 The word 'investment' translates the Latin technical term *faeneratio*, which means 'money lent at interest', while 'loss' translates *damnum*, which is frequently used to refer to a financial loss. Lucifer here suggested that his death would operate in the same way as such a loan, by bringing him greater rewards in heaven. For the use of financial terms by Lucifer in discussing these issues, see also n. 113 to chapter 7 below.

37 Lucifer's use of 'you' here argues strongly for continuity between Constantius and earlier (pagan) emperors who persecuted Christians, thereby placing his own circumstances within a long-running struggle between good and evil: see Introduction p. 37. On the use of *tyrannus* ('tyrant') in polemical literature in this period, see n. 40 to Hilary, *In Const.* 7 on p. 122 above.

38 This statement continues the theme of inversion in the condemnation of Christians. Just as they are tortured to make them renounce their faith, while real criminals are being forced to confess their crimes, so the supposedly humiliating deaths of convicted Christians actually bring about their glorification.

of Christ can strike down the one who has possessed you and who speaks against our holy profession of faith, the one who, through you, thirsts for our blood, the one who lays siege to your mind.[39] He trembles at the presence of God's priests and cannot bear it when we oppose you who claim that the Son of God was created from nothing,[40] nor when we stand firm in opposition and, aided and protected by God's power, trample your threats and all the cruelty of your butchery underfoot. Undoubtedly, you know that you are chastised by the brave constancy and fortitude of the servants of him who says: *Fear not the one who is able to kill your body, but rather fear the one who is able to destroy both body and soul in hell.*[41]

We are also encouraged by the exhortations of his most blessed apostle Paul to trample you underfoot, tyrant of all tyrants: *We are sons of God; but if sons, then heirs of God, and joint-heirs with Christ; if it so be that we suffer with him, that we may be also glorified together.*[42] And again: *I reckon that the sufferings of this present time are not worthy to be compared with the future glory that shall be revealed in us.*[43] Contemplating the glory of this splendour, it is fitting that we servants of Christ endure all the acts of oppression and persecution that the Devil inflicts, not only through you but also through all his minions.[44] Since, although these troubles are many,

---

39 The image of the *miles Christi*, the 'soldier of Christ', was a common trope in early Christian literature and drew upon several passages in the New Testament, particularly *Ephesians* 6.10–18. For more on this topic, see von Harnack (1981) 27–64. Here Lucifer is claiming that Constantius is being controlled by the Devil.

40 Lucifer and other supporters of the Nicene theological position regularly claimed that their opponents thought Christ was a being created from nothing and thus not fully divine or eternal: see Introduction p. 3.

41 *Matthew* 10.28. Lucifer's text of this verse differs from both the Greek New Testament and the Old Latin Bible version of this passage, as preserved in Cyprian, *Ep.* 6.2, which states: *Fear not those who are able to kill the body, but are not able to kill the soul; rather fear the one who is able to destroy body and soul in hell.* Lucifer appears to have altered the text to make the killer of the body singular, in order to enhance his image of Constantius as the archetypal persecutor. See also Hilary, *In Const.* 1, where the same change has been made. 'Hell' here translates 'Gehenna', which is the Latin form of the Greek name γεέννα. This is the valley of Hinnom near Jerusalem, a place notable for the worship of the fire god Moloch (*2 Kings* 23.10) and so associated with fire and slaughter (*Jeremiah* 7.32, 19.6). It is also used to mean Hell in *Matthew* 5.22 and later Christian literature.

42 *Romans* 8.16–17. This quotation also appears in Cyprian, *Ep.* 6.2.

43 *Romans* 8.18. This quotation also appears in Cyprian, *Ep.* 6.2.

44 See Cyprian, *Ep.* 6.2: 'Contemplating the glory of this splendour, it is fitting that we endure all the acts of oppression and persecution.'

we are, however, freed from them all, we who believe that the Son of God is the true Son, and while we remember that the Father and the Son are two persons, we must nevertheless ascribe a single divinity to the Father and his only Son.[45] When the one who lays siege to your mind hears our just and irrefutable statements, because he cannot bear the truth, he rouses your bestial spirit so that you torment us as violently as possible and inflict agony with refined forms of torture, because we refuse to abandon the road to salvation.[46] Your excessive cruelty toys with our bodies, because we value the faith highly and do not deny that we are worshippers of God.[47] You oppress us with the whole might of your butchery and think that you will harm us, not realising that we relish the opportunity of being put to the test, since we believe that it would bring us the greatest bliss if in this contest of justice it should fall to us to be slain by your butchering hands for the Son of God. We stand firm with a devout mind against your insanity, for undoubtedly through us he, for whom we suffer, overcomes whatever you, profane one, with your empty rhetoric, worthless chatter and depraved desire, throw against our body to harm his divine majesty.[48] Your intransigent mind and stubborn cruelty of heart gives birth to all these things to destroy its salvation.

While you abandon the worship of God, led by your folly, seized by your rage and finally tormented by your whole savagery, which equally spurs you on and sweeps you away, we are protected against your savagery,

45 See Cyprian, *Ep.* 6.2: 'Although the troubles of the just are many, they are freed from them all because they believe in God.' Cyprian's simple criterion of faith was greatly extended by Lucifer to grant salvation only to those who assumed his particular theological stance. Lucifer sought here to stress that Christ was the 'true' Son of God, rather than simply being given the title of Son, as well as steering a middle course between both the Sabellian/'Monarchian' failure to distinguish adequately between the two persons of the Father and the Son and also the 'Arian'/'subordinationist' view that the Son did not possess fully the divinity of the Father. On these issues, see Introduction pp. 2–18 and the Glossary.

46 The one oppressing Constantius' mind here is the Devil.

47 See Lact. *Diu. Inst.* 5.9.10, 12: 'Therefore they torment and inflict agony with refined forms of torture and they regard it as insufficient simply to kill those whom they hate, unless cruelty toys with their bodies … But as for those who value the faith highly and do not deny that they are worshippers of God, they oppress them with the whole might of their butchery, as though they are thirsty for blood.'

48 See [Cypr.] *De laude martyrii* 4: 'We will be firm in our faith against these common insanities, undoubtedly overcoming and repelling whatever profane rhetoric throws against you to harm Christ.' and 5: 'For what is in them other than empty rhetoric, worthless chatter and the mind's depraved desire for words.'

you monster, by the very one whom you deny, and so we resist it, just as a breakwater withstands the ocean.[49] Although through you the diabolical waves crash upon us and the roving whirlpools of the world strike far and wide, our strength, firm as it is, will be ever firmer. Nor shall we succumb, overwhelmed by the waves of your attacks that boil around us,[50] but will always stand upright against all dangers, for the Christian spirit is not downcast when laid low and thrown to vice, but is high-minded and noble to such an extent that it remains firm and triumphant against all temptations. We Christians do not intend to savour the pleasures of this present, fragile life, but instead seek to attain the glory of eternal security and bliss, the possession of perpetual blessedness. This is the devout statement of the blessed apostle John, exhorting us to despise earthly things and to desire to pursue the heavenly: *The world passes away, and the lust thereof; but he that shall do the will of God abides for eternity, as God himself abides for eternity.*[51]

4   This being so, I want you to recognise that, with all your tricks and lies, and with the most enormous cruelty of your savagery, you lie beneath the feet of God's servants and we regard and consider all the glory of your hollow dominion as worthless; despite all the force and authority of your rule, we know that you are nothing but an insubstantial breeze. Perhaps one of your sycophants might say that we are only bragging. Do you not remember, Constantius, that I said to the judges, while you listened with the curtain drawn,[52] that even though you had ordered your whole army to direct all the weapons of your empire against us, who despise your blasphemy, so that your entire armament should strike against those who scorn your sacrilegious decree, yet we could never retreat from our resolved purpose? But on account of your prudent judgement, you decided that your soldiers

49 See [Cypr.] *De laude martyrii* 5: 'Their intransigent mind and stubborn cruelty of heart is always driven away from life-giving devotion and abandons it, led by their folly, seized by their rage and finally tormented by their whole savagery, which equally spurs them on and sweeps them away.'

50 See [Cypr.] *De laude martyrii* 4: 'Just as a breakwater withstands and resists the ocean; although the waves crash upon it and the rolling sea repeatedly strikes it; however its strength remains firm and does not succumb, overwhelmed by the waves that boil around it.'

51 *1 John* 2.17 (with minor amendments).

52 The phrase *uelo misso* ('with the curtain drawn') here appears to refer to an incident in which Lucifer was questioned, while the emperor listened from behind his curtain. On the curtain/veil, as well as the question of when this audience may have taken place, see n. 9 to chapter 1 above.

must die for you in every war, yet ordained that Christians must live as deniers of God.[53] Your men certainly feel the agony of their wounds, they feel anguish that they have perished, they feel anguish that they leave this light. But in fact we, first of all, cannot feel these tortures of punishments, in which Christ suffers, in which Christ toils for eternal salvation.[54] Secondly, since we regard present circumstances as inconsequential and will live always in that everlasting light, how can it be that we would not choose to die at your hands, which are polluted with sacrilege, for the sake of Christ, the Son of God, the giver of eternal life? For we understand that we cannot please God the Father unless, having been brought together by you to deny that God's only Son is his Son, we have proclaimed, even unto death itself, that he is the true Son of God.[55]

Your hateful mind resents our declaration that Christ the Son of God is the Word of God, the wisdom of God, the virtue of God, true God from true God, begotten from the Father, that is, from the substance of the Father, light from light, begotten not created, of one substance with the Father, which they call in Greek 'homoousios', through whom all things were made, without whom the Father never was.[56] You resent, worm

53 The reference to Constantius' 'prudent judgement' is a clear example of Lucifer's sarcastic employment of the terminology of imperial panegyric, as is also evident in his use of references to Constantius as 'most prudent' in phrases such as *prudentissime imperator* (*De Ath. I* 6.20–1; *De Ath. II* 29.1), *prudentissimus imperator* (*De Ath. I* 36.36; *De Ath. II* 6.39) and *rex prudentissime* (*De Ath. I* 42.41): see Laconi (2001b) 32–3. On commonly invoked imperial virtues, including *prudentia*, see Wallace-Hadrill (1981); Nixon and Rodgers (1994) 23–4.

54 See [Cypr.] *De laude martyrii* 6: 'In which Christ himself toils.' The original context also refers to the suffering of Christians during persecution.

55 As elsewhere, Lucifer is keen to defend the statement that Christ is the 'true' Son, as opposed to merely being having acquired the name. He is claiming that the subordinationist views of the 'Arians' deny the 'truth' of Christ's position as the Son, since they deprive him of other characteristics of God, as the following sentence make clear. The reference here to Christians being brought together to deny their faith could refer to a number of councils in Constantius' reign, including that at Milan in 355, after which Lucifer was exiled, or the gatherings at Seleucia and Ariminum in 359: see Introduction pp. 11, 16–18.

56 Here Lucifer is using the Latin word *substantia* ('substance') to translate the Greek term *ousia*, which can also be rendered into Latin as *essentia* ('essence'). On these terms, see also n. 83 to Hilary, *In Const.* 12 at p. 128. Lucifer's resolutely anti-Arian theological statement is based largely on the Nicene Creed, particularly in its use of the key term *homoousios* (ὁμοούσιος), meaning 'of the same *ousia*'. On these terms, see the Glossary below. On the Nicene Creed, see the Introduction p. 5 and Kelly (1972) 205–62; Ayres (2004) 92–8.

of Arius,[57] that we maintain that there is a single splendour, power, majesty, eternity and divinity of both the Father and his only Son, and that this, which we declared as legates in your palace and do not stop asserting, is not a novelty, but is rather that which has always been and is still believed by Christians, just as the sacred faith is seen to have been written at Nicaea against your Arian heresy and all other errors.[58] If you were to finally *open the eyes of your heart*,[59] which have been pierced by the fangs of the serpent, you would discover that the Church holds this faith, the Church defends this faith, knowing that it was passed down to it through the blessed apostles.[60] If you could travel through all the peoples of the world in an instant, you would discover, most ignorant emperor, that Christians everywhere hold the same faith as us, and, standing firm in this same defence of ours, they, like us, wish to die for the Son of God.[61]

But your novel preaching and upstart religion is a blasphemy ruinous to your salvation and introduced by you under the pretence of faith; not only is it too weak to reach the borders of the Roman empire, especially when you are hard pressed already, but also, wherever it had tried to fix roots, it withered and died, since naturally all the servants of God withdrew from both you and the few of your men who remained with you, whom the Lord had foretold as tares sown among the wheat.[62] The creator of deceit and

57 On the Alexandrian presbyter Arius, treated as the founder of the 'Arian heresy', which Constantius' opponents accused him of following, see Introduction pp. 2–4. While Lucifer uses a variety of negative images from the animal kingdom to describe Constantius, the term 'worm of Arius' is likely to be a specific reference to the circumstances of the heresiarch's demise, at least as described gleefully by Athanasius in *De morte Arii* 3, which includes a comparison with the death of Judas. Having entered a public convenience during a visit to Constantinople, Arius supposedly expired in a gruesome fashion apparently involving some kind of severe intestinal problem. Soc. *HE* 1.38 provided a particularly graphic account. See also Introduction p. 6.

58 If the reference to the confrontation in the palace is true, then it probably relates to either the preliminaries to the Council of Milan or the council itself and its aftermath, since Lucifer, the presbyter Pancratius and the deacon Hilarius acted as delegates for Liberius of Rome. Lucifer also defends the Nicene term *homoousios* against the charge of being novel and unscriptural, contrasting it with Constantius' faith later in this chapter. See n. 9 to chapter 1 above and Introduction p. 31 for more details.

59 *Ephesians* 1.18.

60 The serpent here is, of course, the Devil.

61 Here again, Constantius is being described as exemplifying the extreme opposite of an imperial virtue, in this case wisdom.

62 *Matthew* 13.25. The statement that Constantius is hard pressed may refer to Julian's

death has given, and still gives, all these things to you; through you he lures and deceives many with twisted charms; although he stands accused of every crime, he whispers to your most bitter heart that you should punish us, as though we were accused of some crime.[63] But look out at last, *open the eyes of your heart*,[64] where there is no light for you, but total darkness and great shadows move, and you will find that the death which you inflict through your flimsy power actually remakes life more complete, that it leads us away rather to glory, through fires, through swords, through chains and wild beasts, through whatever your madness, most pious emperor, will choose finally as the instrument of our murder.[65] With God watching over us, not only are we not destroyed but rather we are revived even more, for we remember that there is nothing above us except God; and so the mind dedicated and delivered up to God is ashamed to yield to you, who are dead already through your blasphemy, a dog barking against the truth, teeming with the worms of Arius.[66]

Whenever the souls of Christ's servants properly examine the real force of tortures, they observe that no torture is worse than a servant of Christ being defeated by you, a servant of our enemy. We recall that the Lord has said: *If any man wishes to come after me, let him deny himself to himself, and take up his cross and follow me. For whoever wants to save his life shall lose it; but whoever will lose his life for my sake shall find it. For what is a man profited, if he shall gain the whole world, and lose his own soul? Or what shall a man give in exchange for his soul?*[67] The dignity of martyrdom compels us Christians to spurn life through death, since through the Son of God a new form of salvation has been granted:

usurpation in Gaul in February 360, but is probably a description of events on the troublesome Persian frontier in the final years of Constantius' reign: see Dignas and Winter (2007) 88–90.

63 The 'creator of deceit and death' is another reference to the Devil acting as the emperor's nefarious puppeteer.

64 *Ephesians* 1.18.

65 See [Cypr.] *De laude martyrii* 7: 'For death makes life more complete, death leads away rather to glory.' Here is another example of Lucifer using panegyrical expressions in a sarcastic manner, addressing Constantius as 'most pious emperor'. On piety as a key virtue for both pagan and Christian emperors, and therefore a key theme in invective, see Flower (2013) 98–106.

66 For the dog barking against the truth, see Tert. *Adv. Marc.* 2.5.1, as well as *Revelation* 22.15. On the worms of Arius, see n. 57 above.

67 *Matthew* 16.24–6.

to be killed so that I do not perish.[68] We know that this instruction was handed down to us divinely, so that we preserve the strength of so great a name without any fear of soldiers; since for a long time now the desire for an everlasting monument has turned us from longing for this life, while the fellowship of Christ has separated us so that we trample underfoot all earthly concerns.[69] The assault of your cruelty increases, Constantius; but see that the glory of the soldiers of Christ increases also, and we are not in fact held back from the battle line by fear of tortures, but are rather called out to the battle line by your tortures themselves.[70] You will not be able to deny that it is so, when throughout the whole world you see Christians inspired to take up the conflict with an equal and similar ardour of virtue,[71] when you observe that your detestable flatteries cannot deceive the incorruptible stability of faith of the soldiers of Christ, nor can your insane threats terrify it, nor can the tortures of your butchery and the cruelty of your torments subdue it; for he clearly remains in us and is always stationed with us, he who said to the blessed apostles: *I am with you always, even unto the end of the world.*[72] He is present everywhere,

68 See [Cypr.] *De laude* martyrii 7: 'Such is the fall of martyrdom at first, while afterwards comes the fruit, which spurns life through death so that it can preserve life through death'; and Greg. Ilib. *Tract. Orig.* 18.23: 'For through Christ a new form <of salvation> has been discovered: to be killed so that you do not perish, to die so that you live.' This and the other four passages from the *Tractatus Origenis* that appear to be alluded to by Lucifer are all from the end of chapter 18 of that work, where the discussion of prophecies from *Daniel* and *Revelation* is concluded with praise of martyrdom.

69 See [Cypr.] *De laude martyrii* 9: 'You are not ignorant that this is the instruction handed down to us, so that we can preserve the strength of so great a name without any fear of soldiers; since for a long time now the desire for an everlasting monument has led us away from longing for this life, while our hopes for the future have divorced us from this and the fellowship of Christ has separated us from desiring any vices.'

70 See Cyprian, *Ep.* 10.1.1: 'The assault has increased, but the glory of the fighters has also increased. Nor have you been held back from the battle line by fear of tortures, but have rather been called out to the battle line by the tortures themselves.' This is another of Cyprian's letters addressed to 'martyrs and confessors', encouraging them to remain strong in the face of persecution, and it discusses the support that they receive from Christ in their trials.

71 'Virtue' here translates *uirtus*, which can also mean 'strength'. Lucifer uses this ambiguity for rhetorical effect at 11.66–7.

72 *Matthew* 28.20. See Cyprian, *Ep.* 10.1.2: 'They are roused to take up the conflict with a similar ardour of virtue, just as is proper for soldiers of Christ in the divine camp, so that flatteries cannot deceive their incorruptible stability of faith, nor can threats terrify it, nor can tortures and torments subdue it, since he who is in us is greater than he who is in this world.' It is interesting that Cyprian's 'similar ardour' has become 'equal and similar ardour'

for he is all-powerful, the Son of the omnipotent, and his eternity and divine power are one with the Father.

5 It is impossible to express how great a darkness of disbelief has enveloped you, how large a cloud of shadows and errors has engulfed your heart;[73] although you pretend to be a Christian, you strive to eradicate this name from the world.[74] In these circumstances you ought to realise that the readers will forgive me because my meagre capacity for eloquence has been insufficient to record the execration of you as much as your impiety deserves. For they have seen me give an example to all God-fearing people and provide material to those who will take up the cause, telling them how they can cut you down, since you are planted without the roots of eternal life. Do not say that we assail you with slanders if you happen to hear what you deserve, even though it is from uncultured Christians. We know that one should not insult one's enemies, but should pray for them instead;[75] for the Son of God, even though he is Lord of all things, did not utter insults when insulted.[76] But if the Lord of all things were to utter an insult, everything would surely be destroyed by the force of his great majesty. You undoubtedly respond to these things thus: 'In fact the Lord wanted you, as his bishop, to be soft, but you show yourself stubborn towards me.' The prophets, apostles and the chorus of evangelists teach that thou shalt not kill, but on the contrary you think it right to kill those consecrated to God. We Christians understand that, in order to please him whom we worship, there is a need for the things which we know that he delights and rejoices in.[77]

So if your actions were judged capable of pleasing God, we would all have to become murderers, profaners and blasphemers. O Constantius, it

in Lucifer's text. Hilary would probably be amused by this, since he argues at length (at *In Const.* 17–22) that 'similar' should be taken to mean 'equal' in the theological context of the Son's relationship with the Father.

73 See Lact. *Diu. Inst.* 5.10.11: 'How great a darkness, how large a cloud of shadows and errors has engulfed the hearts of men.' Lactantius is here referring to the ignorance of pagans, who mistake impiety for piety.

74 On Constantius falsely claiming the name of 'Christian', see Hilary, *In Const.* 9.

75 See *Romans* 12.14; *Matthew* 5.44.

76 See *1 Peter* 2.23.

77 See Lact. *Diu. Inst.* 5.10.17: 'In order to please God whom you worship, there is a need for those things which you know that he delights and rejoices in.'

is clear how deranged you are! Even though it is obvious that that subtle practitioner, the defrauder of innocents, has established himself in your mind, do you think that you have still not been exposed? You still shudder at a sheep, although you are a wolf,[78] you, who are called a wild beast by the most sacred prophets,[79] and a dog and a ravenous wolf by the most blessed apostles, you are dressed up like a minister of justice, although you are the instrument of injustice; do you really believe that you are a man, although you have nothing human except the outline and overall shape.[80] It pains you to be called an inhuman monster, to have nothing human except the outlines and overall shape. Tell me then, I implore you, whether you, the slaughterer of innocents, could deservedly be called a Christian and not rather insane, stupid and deranged, truly an enemy of the worship of God; for that is where piety, humanity and all justice dwell, where people learn not to return evil for evil,[81] where we are taught not to kill, but rather to be killed for the Son of God.

Seeing that your hollow authority has been spurned after your attempted sacrilege, you resort to torture; but the one whom you compel us to deny, the guardian of faith, the helmsman of salvation, the governor of souls, is always with us, is always present in our struggle, rousing the warriors and champions of his divine name.[82] So we stand firm, stronger than the slaves and ministers of your injustice, this is, stronger than your torturing, butchering thugs; we are inspired so that our beaten and torn limbs overcome your hook.[83] For how could the endless repetition of savage blows overcome the indestructible faith, since every soldier of Christ knows that he, for whom he suffers, is present with him, rejoicing in the

---

78 'Shudder' translates the Latin *perfrigescis*. On the imagery, see *Matthew* 7.15, as well as Hilary, *In Const.* 10–11.

79 See Lact. *Diu. Inst.* 5.11.1: 'Deservedly are they called wild beasts by the prophets.' Here and in the next passage used by Lucifer, Lactantius is referring to vicious and impious people.

80 See Lact. *Diu. Inst.* 5.11.3: 'So they are pleased that they were born humans, as they have nothing except the outlines and overall shape.'

81 See *Romans* 12.17.

82 See Cyprian, *Ep.* 10.3: 'How willingly the guardian of faith fought and won in these his servants ... He was present in their struggle, rousing the warriors and champions of his name.' This is a reference to the support given by Christ to tortured Christians. Note that 'his name' in Cyprian has become 'his divine name' in Lucifer's version, thereby underscoring the divinity of the Son.

83 On the hook, or *ungula*, see n. 31 to chapter 3 above.

fortitude of his servants?[84] Without doubt we, the servants of Christ, stand firm, strengthened by his majesty, with a free voice and a pure mind; yes, we are naked before your brittle weapons, but we are clothed in those arms which the blessed apostle exhorted us to put on, saying: *Finally, be strong in the Lord, and in the power of his might. And put on the arms of God, that you may be able to stand firm against the wiles of the Devil; for you wrestle not against flesh and blood, but against powers, against the rulers of the darkness of this world, against the spirits of wickedness in the heavens. Wherefore accept the arms of God, that you may be able to withstand on the evil day, and having done all, to stand firm, having your loins girt about with truth, clothed in the breastplate of justice and having shod your feet with the preparation of the gospel of peace; above all, taking the shield of faith, wherewith you shall be able to quench all the fiery darts of the most wicked one, and the helmet of salvation and the sword of the Spirit, which is the Word of God, praying always with all prayer and supplication in the Spirit and watching thereunto.*[85]

So because your cruelty, and that of your father,[86] cannot possibly overcome those who have been armed in this way, those who are defended by so great a power, as has often been said, we have stood firm, do stand firm and, until you devour our bodies, will stand firm, defended by the salutary shield of Christ, girt with the breastplate of his piety, guided by the Holy Spirit, steadfast and, above all, speaking out more and more, repelling any suggestion of servitude.[87] For we are secure and have faith that we

---

84 See Cyprian, *Ep.* 10.2.2: 'The tortured have stood stronger than the torturers and the beaten and torn limbs have defeated the beating and tearing hooks. The endless repetition of savage blows could not overcome the indestructible faith.'

85 *Ephesians* 6.10–18. See Cyprian, *Ep.* 10.2.2: 'His servants stood firm with a free voice, a pure mind and divine strength; certainly they were naked before earthly weapons, but, as believers, they were armed with the arms of the faith.'

86 This may be a reference to Constantine as a cruel and persecuting emperor, or possibly a description of the Devil, as Lucifer uses *pater* ('father') to refer to both in his descriptions of Constantius. Certainly, elsewhere in his writings he gives a negative portrayal of Constantine, which is highly unusual in orthodox literature and forms a marked difference from Hilary and Athanasius, both of whom treat Constantine highly favourably, contrasting him with his heretical son. See also 7.4–5 below, as well as *De non parc.* 13.19–20; *De non conu.* 9.60–5. Diercks (1978) 475 regards all uses of *pater* that are not obviously about Constantius to be references to the Devil. On this issue, see also Tietze (1976) 187–8; Humphries (1997) 457–8; Flower (2013) 93–4.

87 In reading *auctores* (translated as 'speaking out') here, I am following Laconi (1998) and the manuscript tradition, rather than Diercks, who reads *auctiores* ('more intensified').

cannot be drawn from our resolved course by any of your traps, or your cunning, sophistry or tricks, since we know that death is the end of sins, and next follows the life which is forever; let us embrace the instructions of his blessed apostle and seek to be recognised as imitators and allies of him, who stated that, *though our old humanity perish, the inward is renewed* and *if the earthly house of our body were dissolved, a heavenly one would be built* and that *having been placed in the body, we are absent from the Lord.*[88] We will not be able to bring abundant praises to God with the apostle in the heavenly kingdoms unless first, having purged death, we come to claim the immortal prizes.[89]

6   Therefore when our bodies have been shattered and utterly destroyed by you, let us accept that we are more whole; when death has been inflicted by you, then let us believe rather that we can live. Why do you Constantius, an emperor temporarily but an egregious idiot forever, still presume to inflict torments that annihilate you and, in contrast, resurrect us? An evil and depraved policy drives you to extinguish us, and you are swift to spill the blood of the servants of God's only Son, not knowing that heaven is laid open by our blood and the fires of Gehenna are extinguished by our blood.[90] You are guided by earthly ambition, we by heavenly majesty, for we shudder at the thought of losing eternal salvation.[91] We know that we must die for God; for while the fires of Tartarus will hold you for eternity, unless you make the journey from the camp of the Devil to the army drawn up in the heavenly camp, so we will rejoice in heaven if we disregard your threats and tortures and choose to be sacrificed for the Son of God by you, most savage beast and inhuman monster.[92] For *blessed are they who suffer persecution for righteousness' sake, for theirs is the*

---

88   *2 Corinthians* 4.16, 5.1, 5.6.

89   The apostle referred to here is Paul, author of the preceding biblical quotations. Lucifer's image is of the destruction of the earthly body through martyrdom, and the attainment of the 'prize' or 'reward' of eternal life through victory in this conflict.

90   See [Cypr.] *De laude martyrii* 9: 'Heaven is opened by our blood and the dwelling-place of Gehenna gives way to our blood.' On Gehenna, which is often translated as 'Hell', see above n. 41 to chapter 3 above.

91   See [Cypr.] *De laude martyrii* 10–11: 'On one side you are guided by earthly ambition, on the other by heavenly majesty. If you fear to lose salvation, know that you can die.' The original passage refers to the choice faced by the potential martyr.

92   Tartarus was the name given to the lowest regions of the underworld in classical mythology.

kingdom of heaven.[93] But he did not say, 'blessed are those who inflict persecution'.

We Christians know that we have been made soldiers of Christ so that, having confessed our commander in this theatre of war that you have proclaimed, we might attain victorious triumphs and die in arms.[94] So the more you rage against us, the more merciful you are seen to be when you deign to kill one who confesses himself to be a Christian.[95] But you are judged to be most accursed when under the pretence of affection and a desire for discussion you flatter us in order to destroy us, as though it could be to our advantage to be driven from our position and preserved by you, but condemned by God.[96] We know that you are afraid lest, despite all the punishments devised by your abominable ingenuity, we die still steadfast in our faith; but nonetheless you inflict various pitiless tortures. At every moment you persecute us so violently and desire to butcher us in every different way, but you have resolved that we must not be killed,[97] as though it is only death that makes the soldiers of Christ blessed and not rather the case that as the tortures become more grievous, so they bestow a greater glory for virtue.[98] For we who know that the life of justice is richer and longer do not turn our backs on this field of battle, nor do we cross over to your camp of God's enemy;[99] but placed instead among these executions

---

93 *Matthew* 5.10.

94 See Greg. Ilib. *Tract. Orig.* 18.21: 'Without fear we follow our commander in this theatre of war.'

95 See Lact. *Diu. Inst.* 5.11.11: 'The more savage he is, the more merciful is he found to be.' Lactantius, like Lucifer, is here contrasting obvious persecutors with the more deceptive kind who pretend to be merciful and do not actually kill Christians, but rather try to make them deny their faith. See above n. 19 to chapter 2 on the importance of the exclamation *Christianus sum* ('I am a Christian') in martyr literature.

96 On this theme of Constantius as a flattering and, therefore, more destructive persecutor, see Hilary, *In Const.* 5.

97 See Lact. *Diu. Inst.* 5.11.11: 'He is the more savage butcher who has resolved to kill no one.'

98 See Lact. *Diu. Inst.* 5.11.16: 'As though it is only death that makes them blessed and not rather the case that as the tortures become more grievous, so they bestow a greater glory for virtue.'

99 See Greg. Ilib. *Tract. Orig.* 18.22: 'Backs must not be turned on this field of battle … and the camp of the enemy must not be sought.' In the *Tractatus Origenis*, this passage is followed by the declaration *sed magis pro deo, pro sacris legibus moriendum est* ('but rather it is necessary to die for God, for the sacred laws'), which may have influenced Lucifer's choice of title for this work.

inflicted by you, we seek to be brought back to God's sheepfold, whence the Devil snatched you and made you his minion.

But I do not say this so that you will spare us. For just as you have discovered with the people you have already killed, you will discover that we Christians are firm in our faith, enduring in pain, victors in the interrogation,[100] through him who certainly does not abandon his confessors; acknowledging that we are his soldiers, as you see, we struggle bravely and fight resolutely.[101] For we know that great is the glory, immense the exaltation and unique the sanctity that adorn the life of eternal salvation through the honour of suffering; greatest is the nobility to disregard, rather than dread, the torments inflicted by your power, to trample underfoot, rather than be terrified by, your madness;[102] for you rage so savagely against innocents and, although you are the teacher of blasphemy, injustice and all cruelty, you actually believe that you can pass for a pious, prudent and just Christian, when you are blind, stupid and ignorant of the truth.[103] Realise, devourer of innocents, that he whom Christ watches over can never be defeated by your tortures: he defeats hunger, he has no regard for thirst; he conquers the squalor of the cell and the horror of the prison's punishments through the force of his inner strength; he tramples every punishment underfoot, crushes all tortures and does not fear any death that you, with such great effort, threaten to impose.[104] You think that you can overcome one who remembers that it is written: *What shall I render unto the Lord for all his benefits towards me? I will take the cup of salvation, and call upon the name of the Lord. Precious in the sight of the Lord is the death of his saints:*[105]

---

100 See Cyprian, *Ep.* 10.4.4: 'They were firm in their faith, enduring in pain, victors in the interrogation.'

101 See Cyprian, *Ep.* 10.4.4: 'Struggle bravely, fight resolutely.'

102 See [Cypr.] *De laude martyrii* 12: 'For great is the glory, most beloved brothers, that adorns the life of eternal salvation through the honour of suffering; great before the face of the Lord and in the sight of Christ is the grandeur to disregard, rather than dread, torments inflicted by the greatest power.'

103 See Lact. *Diu. Inst.* 5.12.1: 'What should you say to those who deem as lawful the butchery of old tyrants raging savagely against innocents.'

104 See Cyprian, *Ep.* 37.3.1–2: 'You defeat hunger, you have no regard for thirst, you trample underfoot the squalor of the cell and the horror or the punishing prison through the force of inner strength; here punishment is conquered, torture is crushed and death is not feared.' This letter of Cyprian is addressed to a group of imprisoned confessors, including the presbyters Moyses and Maximus.

105 *Psalms* 116.12–13, 15 (115.3–4, 6 LXX).

and: *Who shall separate us from the love of Christ? Shall tribulation, or distress, or persecution, or famine, or nakedness, or peril, or sword? As it is written: for your sake we are killed all the day long; we are accounted as sheep for the slaughter; but in all these things we overcome through him that loved us.*[106]

7 In fact I cannot see how you could lure us away from these salutary teachings. For although you never stop raising up those who agree with your heresy with all your impious favours in order to entice us, just as you turned Epictetus and the others from servants of God into lackeys for you and your father, nevertheless let that madness be absent from us, lest we prefer lies to truth, or the prosperity of your kingdom, offered by you, entices us.[107] Keep your worthless glory for yourself and preserve all the prudent judgement of your most ignorant heart for yourself and your comrades, to whom you have been bound by a likeness of manners. Leave us our folly when we confess that Christ the Son of God is the true Son, when we defend him as being of one substance with the Father and when we proclaim that we wish to be killed for his sake, rather than deny his divinity; leave us this sort of folly.[108] Why do you devote effort to making us abandon this? Why do you think you can dislodge the truth, ignoring the fact that it is strong by its own power?[109] Why do you see God's people resisting your terrible growls and pitiless tortures with an unbroken spirit, if not because it is the faith of the apostles and Gospels that we are defending?[110] They resist your cruelty, they trample your frenzy underfoot, for in them there is the hope of everlasting immortality and the heavenly life, and in them is kindled the

106 *Romans* 8.35–7.
107 See Lact. *Diu. Inst.* 5.12.10: 'Let that madness be absent from us, lest we prefer lies to truth … Will any prosperity ever entice us?' For Epictetus, bishop of Centumcellae, see PCBE II.1 634–6 (Epictetus 2) and Ath. *Hist. Ar.* 75.2 with n. 278 at p. 105. On Lucifer's references to Constantius' 'father', see n. 86 to chapter 5.
108 See Lact. *Diu. Inst.* 5.12.11: 'Let them leave us our folly.' The description of orthodoxy as 'folly' here is, of course, deeply sarcastic. Here Lucifer explains key aspects of his theological disagreement with the 'Arians': that Christ is the true Son of God, rather than merely receiving this as a title; that he is *homoousios* (*unius substantiae*) with the Father, as stated in the Nicene Creed; and therefore that he really has full, true divinity. On these theological issues, see Introduction pp. 2–18 and the Glossary. On the use of *substantia* as a Latin translation of the Greek term *ousia*, see n. 56 to chapter 4.
109 See Lact. *Diu. Inst.* 5.13.1: 'For the truth is strong by its own power.'
110 See [Cypr.] *De laude martyrii* 15: 'We must resist with spirit all the terrible and pitiless growls of the attackers of this world.'

fire of longing for eternal light and in them the security of the promised blessedness rejoices.[111] For as we are completely secure, knowing that we will come to enjoy eternal life, we tolerate everything gladly, since we declare that we do not think these tortures to be our own, but rather the punishments of you, our torturer.[112] We Christians weigh the losses of the body against the profits of the soul;[113] we calculate a crown in wounds and from the tortures and pains inflicted by you we triumph most joyful in Christ.[114]

8 Call to mind from the recent record of your crimes, Constantius, how you put your brand on the city of Alexandria, how many people a single mark of your signature suddenly struck down, how many it caused to be mown down with the sword, how many to be consumed by hunger and thirst or slaughtered in prison, how many it caused to be throttled with their breath cut off.[115] Even though you have raged against the blessed martyrs, whom your gladiatorial spirit has killed, with all these cruelties, you rage even more cruelly against us, for you hold your sword back and you strive so that the release of death does not come to relieve us too quickly. We suffer our whole body being shredded and burned, thereby proving that nothing so befits the dignity and constancy of the wise as not being driven from their opinion and purpose by any terrors, and that being tortured and dying for the sake of God is extremely beneficial and those dedicated to God cannot be defeated by your tortures, and that it is you instead who are laid low and reduced to nothing.[116] Hear what is

111 See [Cypr.] *De laude martyrii* 15: 'For in us there is the hope of eternity and the heavenly life, and in us is kindled the fire of longing for light and in us the security of the promised immortality rejoices.'

112 See Cypr. *Ad Fortunatum* 11: 'How great a solace it is in his torments not to think the tortures to be his own, but to look forward to the punishments due to his torturer.' In the original passage Cyprian is discussing a comment made to the persecuting second-century BC king Antiochus IV by one of the martyrs in *2 Maccabees* 7.16–17. This biblical passage is one of the ones quoted by Hilary at *In Const.* 6 as part of his own presentation of Constantius as behaving like a number of earlier villains from Scripture.

113 Lucifer again uses financial terms – *damna* ('losses') and *lucra* ('profits') – to describe his situation: see n. 36 to chapter 3 above.

114 For a crown of triumph as the achievement of the martyr: see n. 297 to Ath. *Hist. Ar.* 79.4 at p. 110.

115 On the events in Alexandria when Athanasius was expelled in 356, see n. 10 to chapter 2 above.

116 See Lact. *Div. Inst.* 5.13.14–15: 'Tender age endures the whole body being shredded and burned ... nothing so befits the dignity and constancy of the wise man as not being able

written in the twenty-sixth psalm: *The Lord is my light and my salvation; whom shall I fear? The Lord is the defender of my life; of whom shall I be afraid? When evildoers come upon me to eat up my flesh, my persecutors and my enemies, they were weakened and fell. Though a host should encamp against me, my heart shall not fear. Though war should rise up against me, in this will I be confident. One thing have I desired of the Lord, that will I seek; that I may dwell in the house of God all the days of my life.*[117]

Therefore, since the strength of justice is perfected in these sufferings, since we do not feel the punishment, because Christ suffers in us, and because where there is no blame, there is no penalty, how did you think that you could defeat by these actions those who are dedicated and devoted to God, in whom the unconquered faith provides an increase of strength?[118] I believe (and of course the truth does not deceive me) that, even though you still bear down on us with all your forces of butchery so that you rip apart our limbs and plough up our lacerated joints, a torturer raging continually against our blood, you can never defeat the household of God or be able to overpower the army of Christ; you will never be able to conquer us with pains or bend us with agonising punishments.[119] We Christians do not refuse any punishments or any death; we cannot tremble at your tyrannical orders or the swords of your judges, because we stand against you, armed with the sword of God.[120] The blessed apostle says to the Ephesians: *Finally you are strengthened in the Lord, and in the power of his might, clothed in the arms of God, that you may be able to*

to be driven from his opinion and purpose by any terrors, but rather to be tortured and die.' The first part of this passage from Lactantius describes the constancy of young Christians during persecution, while the second refers to the notion of virtue shared by both pagan philosophers and Christian. In the final third of this sentence I have followed the readings in Laconi (1998) in both changing the punctuation and amending *perpetua* ('perpetual') to *per tua* ('by your').

117 *Psalms* 27.1–4 (26.1–4 LXX).

118 Both uses of 'strength' in this sentence are translations of *uirtus*. On this term, see n. 71 to chapter 4 above.

119 See [Cypr.] *De laude martyrii* 15: 'I have seen it happen (and the truth does not deceive me) that, even though the savage hands of the attackers ripped apart his limbs and the raging torturer ploughed up his lacerated joints, he did not defeat the martyr ... he [the martyr] is not conquered by pains or broken by agonising punishments.'

120 See Lact. *Diu. Inst.* 5.13.17: 'They do not refuse any punishments or any death, lest they turn away from faith and justice; they do not tremble at tyrannical orders or the swords of officials.'

*stand firm against the wiles of the Devil; for you wrestle not against flesh
and blood, but against powers, against the rulers of the darkness of this
world, against the spirits of wickedness.*[121] Since you, through whom all
the demons rage for our death, cannot overcome men clothed in the arms
of God, we encourage you to give yourself over to us finally, lest you be
tortured for all eternity together with those whom the apostle describes.

So even amongst the shadows of your prison, the sons of light could not
be defeated by the son of shadows;[122] as if those in whom the originator of
light thought fit to reside could even feel the shadows! Virtue must endure
what mortal nature has taught must be endured; for, if you try to consume
our limbs with fire, we will perceive that it is you rather than us who will
be incinerated in our bodies; for since we hurry willingly and eagerly to
die for the faith, we take it for granted that we cannot lose life, but that
instead we actually seek out the eternal life after the fragile. Undoubtedly
the edge of your sword always stands drawn ready to murder Christians;
however, the point of your sword appears to us blunter than all lead, just
like the sharpness of your spirit. We endure everything, secure in our
suffering, as though we were inflicting the punishments that we suffer,
because the one who rages against us through you is laid low by our faith.
For we know that we cannot be destroyed by the death inflicted through
your malice,[123] since we have believed in Christ the giver of eternal life,
the one true Son of God, and we believe and know well that the bodies
which you now burn, wrench and lacerate will also be resurrected to
eternal light and life. For if we knew that we would become nothing after
being killed by you, we would certainly be incredibly stupid if we did
not take care of this life so that it might be as long as possible and filled
with all benefits; this action could be appropriate for us, if we had decided
to be ruled by you rather than by the commands of God.[124] But in the
current situation, since, if our current life were to be taken away by you,

121 *Ephesians* 6.10–12.
122 For the expression 'sons of light', see *1 Thessalonians* 5.5.
123 The translation follows the text in Laconi (1998) here, reading *non enim morte per
tuam malignitatem inlata deleri nos posse nouimus*, as opposed to Diercks' *non enim mortem
<in> perpetuam malignitate inlata deleri nos posse nouimus* ('for we know that we cannot
be destroyed into eternal death, with malice having been inflicted').
124 See Lact. *Diu. Inst.* 5.18.2: 'For if we become nothing after death, it is certainly the
action of an incredibly stupid man not to take care of this life so that it might be as long as
possible and filled with all benefits.' This is, obviously, a position that Lactantius does not
support.

an immortal one would be taken up, so, for the sake of the Son of God, his servants must spurn this present life with all its good things, since all loss of this sort is outweighed by immortality.[125]

9   See, Constantius, what great courage,[126] what great strength of mind, what certainty of faith was present in those whom you killed and is still present in those who continue to resist your sacrilege; see that those blessed martyrs, who we see already established in the heavenly kingdom through God's power, and these others, whom you have not yet been able to kill, have all stood firm against you, inhuman beast, who never stops threatening us with acts speakable and unspeakable, because you have always preferred and still do prefer to hear with greater tolerance that rival emperors are rising up against you than that victors stand firm, confessing that Christ is the Son of God.[127] For your heart, besieged by the shadows of every error, and your mind, blinded by a thick gloom, had decided to turn us all away from God through your heresy, and to make us first your clients and then your fellow lackeys.[128] But the truth has defeated you, along with the one who is in you, the one who strove to devise these things;[129] for the truth possesses its own power.[130] In fact, on top of those tortures you

125 See Lact. *Diu. Inst.* 5.18.3: 'The wise man must spurn this present life with all its good things, as all of its loss is outweighed by immortality.'
126 'Courage' here translates *uirtus*, which has been rendered as 'strength' and 'virtue' elsewhere: see nn. 71 and 118 to chapters 4 and 8 above. This term can represent a range of positive, 'masculine' qualities.
127 See Cyprian, *Ep.* 55.9.1: 'What great courage there is in his assumption of the episcopate, what great strength of mind, what certainty of faith … He sat fearless on the priestly throne at Rome while a hostile tyrant threatened the priests of God with acts speakable and unspeakable, because he would be able to hear with greater patience and tolerance that a rival emperor was being raised up against him than that a priest of God was established at Rome.' This and the following passage from the same letter form part of Cyprian's description of the bravery of Cornelius, bishop of Rome, and the response to it by the third-century emperor Decius. On Lucifer's use of this letter, see Flower (2013) 171–3. On the use of the word *tyrannus* ('tyrant') by Cyprian in this passage, see Barnes (1996) 58.
128 The word *conuerte* in this sentence, found in manuscript *V*, is clearly corrupt, although the overall sense of the passage is clear, and some form of the verb *conuertere* ('turn') is needed here. Laconi (1998) (along with Ugenti (1980) and Ferreres (1982)) prints *conuertens*, which is found in manuscript *G*, and argues (at 335–6) for a form of 'nominative absolute' clause here, to explain the fact that the present participle does not agree with *cordi* and *animo*. Hartel (1886) suggests *conuertere* (although the passage would be clearer if *et* were also added after this infinitive). Another possible emendation would be *conuertenti*.
129 This is, of course, the Devil.
130 See Lact. *Diu. Inst.* 5.13.1: 'For the truth possesses its own power.'

have already inflicted, at every moment we wait for you still to add to them by appointing more savage butchers, more ferocious punishers, who can slaughter with the sword or crucify or scorch with fire or hack at our bowels and limbs through some form of punishment as yet unknown, inflicting these on the soldiers who are devoted to God and who resist your monstrous edicts, so that we trample your threats and tortures and torments through the power of faith and the compassion of God.[131] We will always stand firm through the Lord, as we stand now, since it is not us who defeat the gnashing of your teeth, but rather him in us, him by whose help we are guided, by whose strength we are preserved.[132]

For how mighty are you, and what kind of man, that you can strip us of the good things that have been divinely granted to us?[133] You seize us, you torment us, you make us destitute, you condemn, bind, burn and even kill us in pitiful ways, but, nevertheless, you cannot conquer the unconquered faith of the Christians.[134] Because of this you ought to have realised that you will pay the price for your heresy and cruelty, and, in contrast, since the narrowest track leads sublimely through this difficult obstruction to the prize of immortality, we cannot give in to your cruelty, for we know that martyrdom is an individual imitation of the Lord's courage.[135] The road of the martyrs is so arduous and packed with trials and difficulties that no one can complete it through human strength; but we, who are aided by the assistance of divine favour, must always trample you underfoot, just as we trample you now. So it is our pleasure not only not to fear you,

131 See Cyprian, *Ep.* 55.9.2: 'For he [Cornelius] sat at that time waiting for the butchers of his own body and the executioners of the ferocious tyrant to slaughter with the sword or crucify or scorch with fire or hack at his bowels and limbs through some form of punishment as yet unknown, inflicting these on Cornelius who was resisting monstrous edicts and trampling threats and tortures and torments through the power of faith.'

132 'Strength' here translates another occurrence of the term *uirtus*. For the gnashing of teeth as a characteristic of villains, see n. 264 to Ath. *Hist. Ar.* 72.5 at p. 103.

133 See Lact. *Diu. Inst.* 5.18.7: 'Who can be so ungrateful, so envious, so powerful that they can strip virtue of the good things that have been divinely granted to it?'

134 See Lact. *Diu. Inst.* 5.18.9: 'It [virtue] is seized, tormented, destroyed, made destitute, it is deprived of its hands, its eyes are removed, it is condemned, bound, burned and even killed in pitiful ways.' The original passage in Lactantius is itself a slight adaptation of a quotation from Cicero that he had already introduced at *Diu. Inst.* 5.12.5–6.

135 See Lact. *Diu. Inst.* 5.18.11: 'With a difficult obstruction, the narrowest track leads sublimely to the prize of immortality.' For the image of the narrow track to salvation, see *Matthew* 7.14.

enemy of the worship of God, but to deliberately provoke you as well.[136] You are provoked, even though you are always expected not to show pity, pitiless as you are, but to kill. And so our good fortune cannot be divided, because, even when we are killed for the Son of God, he lives in us with love, he who raises us up in adversity and is our strength in the battles of persecution. For you could set forth against the worshippers of God by whatever methods you like, but you would never be able to purge their imprinted virtue, since worldly matters cannot lure them, nor tortures terrify them.

10 Since this is the case, what can I call you, persecutor of God's house, other than wretched, since you obey the behests of your plundering demons, whose goads have driven you to plot to perpetrate these actions, and through whom you gladly err in your sacrilege with this false conviction fixed in your heart. Indulge your congenital stupidity.[137] If only you were willing simply to be ignorant and stray from the truth with only your fellow blasphemers the Arians! You also try to drag us in as partners in your crimes and you proscribe and you despoil;[138] but we know that poverty acquired for Christ's sake is a form of the utmost happiness. You inflict death, you butcher; but not only do we not pull our neck away, we even hold out our hands so that we can be sacrificed for the only Son of God.[139] Why have I recounted these details? So you know that your punishments have

---

136 See Cyprian, *Ep.* 31.5.1: 'Not only do we not fear the enemies of truth, we provoke them as well.' This passage is taken from a letter sent to Cyprian by Moyses, Maximus and other confessors, responding to a message that they had received from him. On these figures, see n. 104 to chapter 6 above.

137 See Lact. *Diu. Inst.* 5.19.2: 'What can I call them other than wretched, since they obey the behests of their plunderers … and, with a false conviction fixed, they gladly err and indulge their stupidity?' Lactantius is describing persecuting pagans in this and the following passage from the *Divine Institutes*. 'Congenital' here translates *tibi insitae* (an emendation suggested by Diercks) as a description of Constantius' stupidity. The manuscripts read *tibi ignit(a)e* ('kindled for you'). Laconi (1998) suggests amending the text to *<e>t ibi ignorantiae* ('and ignorance here').

138 See Lact. *Diu. Inst.* 5.19.4: 'If only they were willing simply to be ignorant and stray from the truth alone! They also try to drag others in as partners in their crime.'

139 The translation here follows Laconi's text, which prints *manus protendimus* ('hold out our hands'), which is transmitted in manuscript *G*. Diercks gives the emendation *damus* ('we offer [our neck]'). The statement would have more force and make better sense if *manus* were omitted, so that it read 'but not only do we not pull our neck away, we even hold it out so that we can be sacrificed for the only Son of God'.

no force against the servants of Christ and that we cannot take fright at that which we always expect to come.

You resent being called a heretic, but, however, you dare to say that the Son cannot be compared or made equal with the Father; we, who defend the single divinity of the Father and the Son, say that the Son is equal to the Father.[140] We believe what the blessed apostle Paul believed, who says about the Son: *Who, since he was in the form of God, did not think it robbery to be equal with God.*[141] What is *Who, since he was in the form of God* except that the Son, like God the Father, is changeless, immutable, inestimable, indescribable, eternal and perfect? What is *Who, since he was in the form of God* except that the Son dwells in the same unattainable light as the Father, except that there is a single divine exaltation of the Father and the Son? The Holy Spirit, abiding in the blessed apostle and already then seeing the hearts of all you heretics, added the explanation that the Son is *in the form of God*: *Who, since he was in the form of God, did not think it robbery to be equal with God.* The blessed apostle says that the Son is equal to the Father, making it clear that there is a single divinity of the Father and the Son; but you, together with the lackeys of your blasphemous audacity and the comrades of your blasphemy, dare to say: 'We cannot equate or compare the Son with the Father.' But why do you think the Lord said, *he that has seen me has also seen the Father* and *the Father and I are one*, unless because there is a single power of the Father and the Son?[142]

You say that the Son has a beginning; however, we say that he is without beginning, since everything that has a beginning must also be able to have an end.[143] Therefore, since we believe that the only Son of God is eternal,

---

140 Lucifer here defends the doctrine of the equality of Father and Son, in opposition to 'subordinationist' views and the 'Homoian' view that the Son is 'like' the Father: see Introduction pp. 3, 15, as well as Hilary, *In Const.* 17–22.

141 *Philippians* 2.6. This passage is also used by Hilary at *In Const.* 19.

142 *John* 14.9, 10.30. The latter passage is also used at Hilary, *In Const.* 22.

143 See Lact. *Diu. Inst.* 7.1.6: 'Since whatever has a solid and weighty body and had a beginning at some point must also have an end.' In the original passage Lactantius is describing the creation of the world. The resemblance between Lucifer's text and this line in the *Divine Institutes* is relatively minor in comparison to the others noted here, and this particular borrowing from Lactantius is also something of an outlier, since almost all the rest are drawn from book 5 or the first four chapters of book 6. It should, therefore, be regarded as doubtful, but I have included it here for the sake of completeness. The

that is coeternal with the Father, and you enemies of God deny this, do we not absolutely rightly label you sons of pestilence, deranged and stuffed with all insanity? The blessed apostle proclaims this about you, just as he did then about the Jews: *As they did not choose to retain God in their knowledge, God gave them over to a reprobate mind, to do those things which are not proper;*[144] and to the Philippians: *Brethren, be imitators together of me, and mark them which walk in this way, as you have our model. For many walk, of whom I have told you often, and now tell you even weeping, that they are the enemies of the cross of Christ, men whose end is destruction, whose God is their belly, and whose glory lies in their shame; who mind earthly things;*[145] and also to Timothy about you, Constantius, and your most beloved fraternity of the damned: *Now the Spirit speaks expressly that in the latter times some shall depart from the faith, giving heed to seducing spirits, and doctrines of devils, speaking lies in hypocrisy, having their conscience seared with a hot iron.*[146]

The Holy Spirit further strikes and destroys you through the voice of the same blessed apostle Paul: *In the last days perilous times shall come. For there will be men who will be lovers of their own selves, covetous, proud, haughty, blasphemous, disobedient to parents, unthankful, wicked, without natural affection, without faith, false accusers, intemperate, fierce, without kindness, traitors, reckless, conceited, lovers of pleasures more than of God, having the appearance of piety, but denying the power thereof: from such turn away;*[147] and below: *Now as Jannes and Mambres withstood Moses,*[148] *so will these also resist the truth in the same way,*[149]

'Homoian' creed put forward at Seleucia in 359 stated that the Son was begotten from the Father 'before all ages' (Ath. *De synodis* 29.6), but for Lucifer such a statement still implied a lack of eternity on the part of the Son. The creed agreed at Constantinople in January 360 also incorporated the phrase 'before every beginning' to describe the begetting of the Son: see Ath. *De synodis* 30.2.

144 *Romans* 1.28.

145 *Philippians* 3.17–19.

146 *1 Timothy* 4.1–2.

147 *2 Timothy* 3.1–5.

148 *2 Timothy* 3.8–9. Jannes and Mambres (usually called Jambres) are the names traditionally given to the Egyptian sorcerers who advised Pharaoh when the plagues struck and were defeated by Moses: see *Exodus* 7.11, 8.19, 9.11.

149 The biblical text has the present tense of the verb 'resist', but Lucifer's use of the future tense ('will resist') in his quotation better suits his treatment of it as a prophecy about Constantius.

men of corrupt minds and reprobates concerning the faith; but they shall proceed no further, for their folly shall be manifest unto all men, as theirs also was; and below: *For there will be a time when they will not endure sound doctrine, but after their own lusts shall they heap up to themselves teachers, having itching ears; and they shall turn away their ears from the truth, and shall be turned unto fables.*[150]

11 Abandoning the apostolic faith and having been turned unto fables, since the Holy Spirit foretold through the voice of the apostle that your speech is able to spread like an ulcer,[151] you call the orthodox heretics and a little later you denounce as blasphemy the faith which you called orthodox and which you compelled us to adopt. In the same way a little later still you now again confirm as orthodox the faith that you had deemed blasphemous when acting against Adoxius at Antioch.[152] After that you ordered Adoxius to be established at Constantinople, because you approved him as orthodox.[153] So may you know from this example how great a gulf separates truth and falsehood, since although you are yourself an expert, or so you think, and you have an appointed number of functionaries,[154] nevertheless we know that you have been unable to persuade anyone except those who have been terrified by your butchery. So we, for whom nature

150 *2 Timothy* 4.3–4. In this chapter, Lucifer has moved from theological argument, based mostly on discussion of *Philippians* 2.6, and is now quoting a sequence of biblical statements about the coming of people who would oppose the true faith, identified here as prophecies specifically concerning Constantius and his theological allies.

151 See *2 Timothy* 2.17. See also n. 16 to chapter 2 above.

152 Lucifer here makes a (punning) reference to Eudoxius, bishop (successively) of Germanicia, Antioch and Constantinople. Eudoxius means 'of good faith', while Lucifer calls him Adoxius, meaning 'faithless'. Lucifer here presents Constantius as repeatedly changing his mind, as Hilary also does at *In Const.* 25. The action against Eudoxius at Antioch is probably a reference to the letter that Constantius sent to the Antiochene church denouncing Eudoxius, in response to the views presented by the Council of Ancyra in 358: see Soz. *HE* 4.14; Barnes (1993) 140. In this letter, Constantius also supported the view that the Son is *homoiousios* ('of like substance') with the Father, which was then rejected, along with all use of *ousia* in theological statements, at Seleucia and Ariminum in 359 and Constantinople in 360: see Ath. *De synodis* 29–30. On all these events, see Introduction pp. 14–18.

153 Eudoxius was installed as bishop of Constantinople at the council held in that city in January 360: see Barnes (1993) 148–9.

154 The word 'functionaries' here translates Lucifer's term *dictatores*. These would seem to be imperial officials of some sort, put in place to espouse Constantius' theological beliefs: see the note at Laconi (1998) 361. Lucifer may here be referring pejoratively to those bishops with whom he disagrees.

suffices for eloquence and who are strangers to all knowledge of pagan literature, have the power to destroy every heresy, because the truth and the matter itself speak.[155] You and your henchmen have swallowed the whole art of pagan letters; we know only sacred Scripture. Our speech is common, while yours is polished, embellished, even deserving to be called eloquent;[156] but your studied speech, sweet through artifice, cannot persuade any Christian, except one is not really a Christian, but is merely called it, like you, since, although you are a wolf, you are judged to be one of the sheep by the ignorant.[157]

Who is that stupid except those who, like you, have drunk every folly? Who of God's servants does not desire to be honoured by death in the service of devotion?[158] Who does not long to pour out his own blood for Christ when a death of this sort makes life more whole and acquires everlasting glory?[159] As you see, we stand firm protected by the strength of God, shod in the teachings of the Gospel,[160] in a fixed and immovable position, so that our feet cannot be carried off in a headlong fall by you. We stand firm holding the shield of faith, so that the fiery darts of the enemy, thrown by you, are utterly unable to find their mark, since they always rebound against you.[161] Our heads are protected by the helmet of salvation, and the word of the Lord is on our lips, so that the enemy who is established in you is dispatched by the spiritual sword and is equally laid low and scattered.[162] You will see that the holy faith, which you have been compelling us to abandon, is the shield

---

155 See Lact. *Diu. Inst.* 5.19.16: 'And so let them know from this how great a gulf separates truth and falsehood; since although they are eloquent, they are unable to persuade. The unskilled and the inelegant can persuade, because the truth and the matter itself speaks.' The figures being criticised here are learned pagans. The phrase *res ipsa et ueritas* echoes Cicero, *Pro Roscio* 15.44. The claim to be employing a simple *sermo piscatorius* (fisherman's speech), in contrast to 'cunning' pagan learning, was a common trope in early Christian literature, as well as drawing on earlier classical criticism of 'sophistry'. On Lucifer's education, see Introduction p. 31.

156 See Lact. *Diu. Inst.* 5.1.15–16: 'The prophets spoke with common and simple speech as to ordinary people. They are therefore rejected by those who wish to hear and read nothing except what is polished and eloquent.'

157 See *Matthew* 7.15, as well as the use of this imagery in Hilary, *In Const.* 10–11.

158 See [Cypr.] *De laude martyrii* 23: 'So that death honours the service of devotion.'

159 See [Cypr.] *De laude martyrii* 23: 'Undoubtedly death make life more whole and acquires lost glory.'

160 See *Ephesians* 6.15.

161 See *Ephesians* 6.16.

162 See *Ephesians* 6.17; *1 Thessalonians* 5.8.

of our soul and a strong, impenetrable and unbroken breastplate, which no weapons of the Devil, brought in by you, can pierce.[163]

Seeing such great resolution by the Christians, you say, 'The dogma of the Arians, once adopted by me, must be defended'. You say such things while wandering from the truth with good intentions.[164] For you recognise that there is nothing more important in human affairs than religion and that it must be defended with the greatest force.[165] You defend it with the sword, but we know that religion must be defended not by killing, but by dying for God and by enduring all these evils that you inflict.[166] What cruelty of yours will be able to defeat those who defend religion in such a way? For if any of your soldiers in the flimsy army of your dominion keeps his pledge to you, a mortal to a mortal king, in some outstanding deed, he becomes dearer and more beloved; if he dies he achieves the greatest glory in your eyes, worthless man, because he met his death for the sake of you, his commander. How much more important then must it be for the pledge to God, the eternal emperor, to be preserved by us, the soldiers of his clemency.[167] Although the duty of devotion that we have undertaken compels us to perform these tasks, because you are blind, not believing that Christ is true God, the son of true God, and because you are ignorantly wretched, as you have not escaped the shadows of everlasting death, you had wanted to return us also to that ancient blindness, so that we would seem to have abandoned prudence along with sight, not ignorantly, but

163 See *1 Thessalonians* 5.8; *Ephesians* 6.14. The *sancta fides* ('holy faith') here could also be a specific reference to the Nicene Creed, since *fides* can mean a written statement of faith.

164 This comment is bitterly sarcastic.

165 See Lact. *Diu. Inst.* 5.19.20–1: 'They say, "The sacred rites, adopted publicly, must be defended". With what good intentions the wretched wander from the truth! For they recognise that there is nothing more important in human affairs than religion and that it must be defended with the greatest force, but they are just as wrong in the manner of their defence as in their religion.' Here Lucifer has reworked a passage from Lactantius concerning the religious activities and persecutions by pagan rulers, adapting it to refer to 'the dogma of the Arians'.

166 See Lact. *Diu. Inst.* 5.19.22: 'Religion must be defended not by killing, but by dying.'

167 See Lact. *Diu. Inst.* 5.19.25: 'For if anyone in the army of an earthly king keeps his pledge in some outstanding deed, if he lives afterwards he becomes dearer and more beloved; if he dies he would achieve the greatest glory, because he met his death for the sake of his commander. How much more important then must it be for the pledge to God, the emperor of all, to be preserved?' This passage makes use of the dual meaning of *fides* as both the pledge of loyalty made by a soldier and also the Christian faith or a creed.

abominably.[168] For since we know well that there is only a single damnation of death for you, since you refuse to believe, but our sufferings would be doubled if we rejected our faith and preferred to return to destruction, how did you think that we could be separated from the love of God either by your false flatteries, which actually kill while they entice, or by every type of cruel torture? Who would reject such great joy that has been offered to him, except someone even more wretched than you, when he realises that through the confession of that one phrase 'I am a Christian', troubles recede, joys arise, kingdoms are laid open and eternal empires are prepared?[169]

You say, 'Deny the Son of God, or the power of my rule will destroy you.'[170] How much better it is to be destroyed by Christ's enemy than by Christ! How brilliant is it to be slain by you, the friend of the Antichrist, and so resurrected by Christ! Who does not wish to be revealed to be a comrade and ally of the patriarchs, prophets, apostles, martyrs and all just men, rather than of Judas, whose imitator you have clearly been? John the Baptist was executed in prison by your pestilential companion Herod:[171] the savagery of Herod killed James;[172] the apostle John was exiled to an island;[173] the blessed Peter was crucified;[174] the blessed apostle Paul was bound, shut away in prisons, scourged, repeatedly stoned and finally killed.[175] We, who see that they all became friends of God by enduring these things most joyfully, ourselves prefer to be slaughtered by your cruel hand than to yield to your butchery. Why do you regard us with hatred; why do you persecute us with such savagery? Surely it is because we profess ourselves Christians. The blessed men whom we just mentioned

---

168 'Ancient blindness' in this passage is a reference to traditional Greco-Roman religion. Lucifer here stresses the concept of the Son as 'true God from true God', which appears in the Nicene Creed, but not in the Homoian statements supported by Constantius: see chapter 4 above.

169 See [Cypr.] *De laude martyrii* 24: 'Through the confession of one voice troubles recede, joys arise, kingdoms are opened, empires are prepared.' For the phrase *Christianus sum*, which is particularly associated with martyrs, see n. 19 to chapter 2 above.

170 'Power' here translates *uirtus*, which, as mentioned above, can also mean 'virtue'. As such, the statement that Lucifer places in Constantius' mouth is also a snide remark about the emperor's inversion of the qualities and actions expected of a ruler.

171 *Matthew* 14.3–10; *Mark* 6.17–27.

172 *Acts* 12.1–2.

173 *Revelation* 1.9.

174 Eus. *HE* 3.25.5.

175 *Acts* 21.33, 22.24–5; Eus. *HE* 3.25.5.

were also killed for the only Son of God by your fellow tyrants, because they said that they were his servants. The Holy Spirit, speaking through the mouth of the devout David, says this on behalf of our people: *If we have forgotten the name of our God and if we have stretched out our hands to a strange God, does not God search this out? For he knows the secrets of the heart; since for your sake are we killed all the day long, we have been counted as sheep for the slaughter.*[176] But you Constantius, temporary emperor, have been enslaved by Arian idolatry and say, 'I gnash my teeth in my resurgent madness and desire your death; be afraid and become apostates with me.'[177]

12 Hearing these words, you do not wish to heal your wounds, but instead continue in a blind and irrational rage through the instigation of those who work themselves into your mind and rouse ignorant you to fury.[178] These are spirits, to which you are known to sacrifice, because you deny the only Son of God,[179] and, because they cannot do us any harm themselves – for we are protected by God's majesty – through you, their lackey, they persecute us, whom they perceive to be their most hostile foes, and through you, their lover, they practise their savagery as violently as they can, believing that they will violate our faith through your butchering intervention.[180] The doctrine of all the sacred Scriptures is that the principal and perfect form of justice is to believe in the Son of God. So it is that with you, our interrogator,[181] having been defeated, these demons within you are also defeated, because it is not the strength of our fragile bodies that gives us victory, but rather his [Christ's] clemency. He gives us strength to remain steadfast among every instrument of your butchery, so that rather than being broken by the agonies of our wounds or the blows of interrogation, we

176 *Psalms* 44.20–2 (43.20–2 LXX).
177 On the gnashing of teeth, see n. 132 to chapter 9 above.
178 See Lact. *Diu. Inst.* 5.21.2–3: 'It is led by a blind and irrational rage ... Those spirits ... work themselves into their minds and rouse these ignorant men to fury.' Lactantius is here discussing what is behind the persecution of Christians.
179 The pagan gods were often described by Christian authors as demons or spirits that had tricked men into worshipping them. Here Lucifer continues to equate Constantius' rejection of Nicene Christology with acceptance of paganism.
180 See Lact. *Diu. Inst.* 5.21.6: 'Since they [the spirits] cannot do any harm to those men [Christians] themselves, through public hatred they persecute them, whom they perceive to be their opponents, and they practise they savagery as violently as they can.'
181 The term 'interrogator' translates *quaestionarius*, which refers to the person who questions people within a *quaestio* ('judicial inquiry'), often through torture.

are exalted instead.[182] This is the true worship of God, in which the minds of the worshippers offer themselves as immaculate victims for God.[183]

But do you really think that any worshipper of God is so slow and stupid that the fire of such great desire does not rouse and arm him, that it does not urge him, incite him and finally inflame him with those torches of love, by which the holy prophets, apostles and martyrs were inflamed? Which of us, I ask you, would our mind not drive to die for Christ at your cruel hands? Which of us would it not rouse to persevere to the heights and glory of martyrdom not only through the things that you inflict but also through even crueller ones? For undoubtedly these punishments are easily overcome if the glory of the punishments themselves is placed before the eyes. For the instruments of torture are disregarded when so great a reward is provided for suffering.[184] Your torments are defeated by indestructible rewards, Constantius, and torture is crushed, and death, which actually restores life when it is imposed, is subjugated.[185] The wounds inflicted by you would have caused us pain, emperor, if they had not immediately made us friends of God; for since we are confident that we will be truly victorious, that we will lose nothing of salvation, if we are punished by you for the sake of the Son of God, how could we yield to your impotent gnashing of teeth?[186]

You believed, and I think you still vainly believe, that we could and can be subjugated by your force. How long will you abuse God's patience, Constantius?[187] In fact I urge you instead to drive these matters from your

182 See [Cypr.] *De laude martyrii* 25: 'Not by the agonies of wounds or the blows of interrogation.' The original passage also refers to how martyrs are not broken by these torments.

183 See Lact. *Diu. Inst.* 6.2.13: 'This is the true worship, in which the mind of the worshipper offers itself as an immaculate victim for God.' Lactantius' original passage is not referring specifically to martyrdom, but rather to virtuous Christian piety more generally.

184 See Greg. Ilib. *Tract Orig.* 18.23: 'So it is that all torments are easily overcome if the glory of the punishments themselves is placed before the eyes, and the instruments of torture are disregarded when a great reward is provided for suffering'.

185 See [Cypr.] *De laude martyrii* 24: 'Punishments are defeated, death is subjugated, life is brought in' (referring to the power of the martyr's confession) and Greg. Ilib. *Tract Orig.* 18.24: 'Let us give up a brief life, so that an eternal one is restored to us when we die.'

186 On the gnashing of teeth, see n. 132 to chapter 9 above.

187 A modification of the opening of Cicero, *In Catilinam* 1.1: 'How long will you abuse our patience, Catiline?' This is one of only a few allusions to 'classical' literature in the works of Lucifer.

shadowy faculties and let your thick skull accept these ideas, since they can set you on the road that leads to the kingdom of God. Take up at last the route that leads you to the feast of Abraham, Isaac and Jacob, the friends of God. For you, a man of utter injustice,[188] dared to think yourself just, placing yourself above all the bishops appointed to the holy Church by the judgement of God and condemning the holy faith which the Church holds and has always held; and you strove to preach the blasphemy brought forth from the mouth of your fellow heretic Arius, now through your lackeys, now by your edict, now by your own mouth stuffed with unclean spirits.[189] Yet you want to call yourself an unblemished worshipper of God, performing every action piously, but not one can be found, out of all those kings who are called tyrants, who was ever crueller, most detestable or a greater blasphemer than you. Because I have already made clear to your ignorance, in the book entitled 'On Apostate Kings',[190] that this is the situation, I now want you to know that unless you change your course quickly, unless you believe, as we do, that the only Son of God has reigned with the Father always and that the Father never existed without the Son, and also that there is one kingdom of the Father and his only Son and that the Father and the Son possess one divinity, you will perish for eternity, because your master Arius said that the Son of God is a creature and you have raised his blasphemy to heaven with your praises.[191]

We urge you, we beg you, we implore you to become most dear to God, but you complain that you suffer injury at our hands. So you look to the worthless judgement of your rank, as though this could rescue you from eternal tortures. You hold your haughty head above the priests of the Lord, not heeding what is written: *Whosoever exalts himself shall be humbled,*

---

188 On this inversion of imperial virtues, see n. 18 to chapter 2 above.

189 On the Alexandrian presbyter Arius, after whom 'Arianism' is named, see Introduction pp. 2–6. On the identification of this 'edict', see n. 17 to chapter 2 above.

190 This is Lucifer's extant work *De regibus apostaticis*, which surveys the Old Testament to find examples of rulers who abandoned the true faith so that he could compare them with Constantius. For the *exempla* used in this text, see Tietze (1976) 95–7, as well as Laconi (2002) 243–6; (2004) 129–32, 140–42. The Latin text can be found in Diercks (1978) 135–61, while there is an Italian translation in Ugenti (1980) 83 113.

191 On the co-eternity of the Father and the Son, see n. 143 to chapter 10 above. Lucifer's complaint here also incorporates the common criticism that 'Arian' theology made the Son into part of the created order, rather than acknowledging his full divinity. On these issues, see Introduction p. 3.

and he that humbles himself shall be exalted.[192] The apostle says about the only Son of God, whom you persecute in us: *Who, since he was in the form of God, did not think it robbery to be equal with God; but he emptied himself, taking upon him the form of a servant, and was found in fashion as a man; he humbled himself unto death, even the death of the cross.*[193] He always was and is and will be in the form of the Father, being the true Son, changeless and immutable, because the Son of the omnipotent is all-powerful God, yet he deigned to humble himself for the sake of our salvation, to transform us from abject and base to upright and exalted.[194] This holy humility of his has caused you, a rabid dog, to bark against his divine majesty, seeing only what is written in the Holy Scriptures about the humility that he took up and ignoring that which describes his eternal divinity.[195]

13   How do you respond to these points, Constantius, you whom the bishops of your Arian dogma frequently acclaim as bishop of bishops: do you believe or don't you believe that those who die for the sake of the only Son of God will possess the kingdom of heaven?[196] If you believe it, why do you compel us to deny his eternity? Why do you not stop persecuting his believers? Why do you not leave them in peace? Why are you always restless and always hostile towards us, showing yourself to be a violent persecutor, a treacherous enemy, but under the name of peace? It pains me that you have stocked up such great evils for yourself; I lament that you have put yourself completely outside any hope of eternal life. But although you not only hack at us with swords but are also grinding us with your teeth, be sure, however, that we, protected by God, will overcome your madness, and so do not think to look down on us because you see that our bodies are fragile; for what is most powerful is that we remain strong, uplifted and fortified by wisdom and carrying equipment and defences in our hearts and minds. How do we now see ourselves equipped? How do we perceive ourselves to be safe and fortified? How do we know that we are wise unless because we both shun your blasphemy and gladly give

192 *Luke* 14.11, 18.14.
193 *Philippians* 2.6–8 (with minor omissions).
194 For the theological statements made here from exegesis of *Philippians* 2.6, see chapter 10 above.
195 On the 'barking dog' metaphor, see n. 66 to chapter 4 above.
196 Some modern scholars have taken at face value Lucifer's claim that the 'Arians' addressed Constantius as 'bishop of bishops'. On this issue, see Flower (2013) 21 n. 70.

our mortal bodies over to your sword for the sake of the only Son of God, knowing that, although you have the strength to destroy our earthly domicile, you cannot destroy the heavenly abode that we have? For we know, therefore, that benefits and evils have been offered to us, so that our entire capacity for prudence is directed to distinguishing between benefits and evils.[197]

What is stupider than to fear you and to deny God? What is wiser than to trample your heinous head underfoot and, through this act, to please God? Thus you see that we stand firm prepared with all our strength in the contest of justice, with inviolate faith, devoted strength and an uncorrupted mind, prepared to stand firm against the battle-line that has been assembled by you, as fearless soldiers of the living God.[198] For we bravely carry the shield of faith by which, protected also by God, whatever the Devil throws by your hands is extinguished.[199] Since our feet are shod and protected by the teaching of the Gospel, you are trampled underfoot, even though you are the emperor,[200] and the serpent in you, which roars for the slaughter of us innocents, is crushed, since through you, its butcher, it is not strong enough to bite and trip.[201] For God wants us to be oppressed by you, not so that we desert the faith and the road of the patriarchs, apostles and martyrs but so that, pressured by you to deny the only Son of God, we do not even refuse to undergo death. Unlike you, we are not so stupid and misguided that we would choose to cast off that which leads to salvation, but take up what is mortal. We do not flee from the remedy of heavenly medicine. For we perceive that, even though a doctor cuts with a knife, cauterises with an

197 See Lact. *Diu. Inst.* 7.4.15: 'Therefore benefits and evils have been offered to him [man], because he has received wisdom and his whole capacity is directed to distinguishing between benefits and evils.' See also *1 Kings* 3.9.

198 See Cyprian, *Ep.* 58.8.2: 'Let us arm ourselves, most beloved brothers, with all strength and let us prepare for the contest with an uncorrupted mind, inviolate faith and devoted strength. Let the camp of God proceed against the battle-line that is assembled against us.' This letter was written by Cyprian to the Christian laity at Thibaris and contains the advice that they should resist persecution by the Roman authorities.

199 See Cyprian, *Ep.* 58.9.1: 'Let us bravely carry the shield of faith, so that, protected by it, whatever the enemy throws can be extinguished.' See also *Ephesians* 6.16.

200 The term 'emperor' here translates *augustus*, which means the senior emperor (as opposed to the lesser title of *caesar*, which was held by Julian in the last years of Constantius' reign).

201 See Cyprian, *Ep.* 58.9.1: 'Let our feet be shod and protected by the teaching of the Gospel, so that when the serpent begins to be trampled underfoot and crushed by us, it will not be able to bite and trip.'

hot iron and leads the sick man to every pain through the fire of mustard, it is not, however, harmful to be cut, burned, consumed and sliced, but rather it is beneficial, since it removes detrimental pains through pains administered for the sake of healing.[202]

God wants us to destroy death through death, to dispel eternal tortures through temporary torments, to abolish the everlasting punishments to come through your punishments. Although you might take life from us, we certainly believe that it can be granted instead, and in fact an eternal life in place of the temporary, an everlasting and incorruptible life in place of the fragile and crumbling.[203] You deem it insufficient for those confessing themselves Christians to simply be executed with the sword, unless you have inflicted all manner of punishments on their bodies. It makes no difference with what kind of death you decide to punish us, since through this we are admitted to enjoy eternal life, through this your madness is extinguished, while we, in contrast, are brought to life. For even if you think me wretched because I would rather be killed by absolutely any cruel punishment for the sake of the Son of God than lose the eternal glory of the blessed martyrs, I know that I must die in some way or other. In fact I will give you examples of many who perish more agonisingly in their beds, distended by some internal abscess and contorted by the pain of their writhing sinews.[204] It matters for what cause, not from what tree, I hang.

14   What do you say, most idiotic king?[205] Is it just or unjust that I am sent by you to these punishments, to a penalty of this sort? If unjust, the

---

202 See Tert. *Scorpiace* 5.5–6: 'This is the great perversity of men, to cast off that which leads to salvation, to take up pernicious matters, seek out dangers and shun cures ... For there are many who flee from the remedy of heavenly medicine ... This is clearly because of the savagery of medicine with its scalpel, hot iron and fire of mustard; it is not, however, detrimental to be cut, burned, consumed and sliced, since it inflicts beneficial pains.' In this and the following passage used by Lucifer Tertullian is discussing martyrdom and explaining how it might seem destructive, but is actually salutary. For an example of the use of mustard in Roman medicine, see Celsus, *De medicina* 4.2.9.

203 See Tert. *Scorpiace* 5.9: 'If he [God] wanted ... to destroy death through death, dissolve killing through killing, dispel tortures through tortures, obliterate punishments through punishments and grant life by taking it away.'

204 For a graphic description of a painful death through illness, see, for example, Lact. *Mort. Pers.* 33 on the grisly demise of the emperor Galerius.

205 On Lucifer's inversion of the conventionally exaggerated imperial virtues, including prudence and wisdom, see n. 18 to chapter 2 above.

cross will be for you, the crucifier, not me, whom you will have crucified; if just, the guilt of my crime will begin to torture me, not your penalties. But it makes absolutely no difference how I meet my end, whether you kill me with a nail or a lance, with my hands tied back behind my back or spread and stretched out, whether I am bent over or upright and raised high; it does not matter whether you kill me sleeping in my bed, whether you cut my neck with a sword while I am standing or shear my head off with an axe, whether you fix me to a stake or a cross, whether you roast me with fire or bury me alive, whether you cast me from a rock or submerge me in the sea, whether, having endeavoured with a *labandago* and great forces, you propel my head far from my body with one enormous blow, or whether you trifle with my body, piercing it for a long time with an arrow sharper than all sharpness; even though your cruelty devises a hundred thousand different forms of execution, the death that you inflict from any of them will bring me nothing except immortality.[206] I can do nothing but rejoice when you inflict such things, since I know that through these punishments, all punishment can be ended. For I am aware that these things, which are external, can happen through your savagery, but I judge it wholly unimportant to me if birds and dogs rip apart my body, if they cling to my body, if wild beasts leap on me, while you stand watching with those cruel eyes, and lying on the ground I am reduced to nothing but bones by their teeth and claws, since after all these things I will be intact to God. For when you have devoured my body with these kinds of immense forces of your bestial inhumanity, the creator of all things will repair and remake it, and in fact it will be eternal and incorruptible, rather than destroyed.

But you ought to know that punishment without end will come to you, our most unjust persecutor, and nor should you think that you will escape unpunished, when you believed that the name of the only Son of God ought

---

206 Lucifer's extensive list incorporates many different forms of execution attested from the Roman world. There is no mention of being thrown to wild beasts, but Lucifer deals with that a couple of sentences later. Lucifer, like some other ancient authors of martyr literature, displays a rather disturbing glee for the details of judicial violence, in a phenomenon that has been described as 'a sacred pornography of cruelty': see Hopkins (1999) 114. *Labandago* is a *hapax legomenon* and so the identity of this instrument of torture is a mystery. Souter, in his *Glossary of Later Latin*, speculates that it is a guillotine: Souter s.v. *labandago*. It is certainly clear from the context that it is some kind of device for facilitating violent and even explosive decapitation.

to be placed beneath your feet and impiously and wickedly trampled.²⁰⁷ This is the statement of the blessed apostle: *The sufferings of this present time are not worthy to be compared with the glory that is to come*,²⁰⁸ which we will certainly attain, if we choose to be killed by you rather than to deny the Son of God. Since this revelation and splendour has shone upon all of us believers, his servants will be forever blessed and assembled in his kingdom; you, on the other hand, if you decide to remain in your unbelief, will remain in the shadows outside, being a deserter from the ranks and an enemy of the truth, because you have carried out the will of the Devil.²⁰⁹ So, unless you extricate yourself from his traps, you must be tormented by unquenchable fire alongside him, as it is written.²¹⁰ We are not saying these things from ourselves at all; for we read it stated in the most holy prophet about you transgressors, about you blasphemers who deny that the only Son of God is the true Son and about all those who refuse to believe in him: *Their worm shall not die, neither shall their fire be quenched.*²¹¹ If you persist in this madness, you will be forever in inescapable shadows. Just as we who confess the Son of God will achieve the prize of immortality and obtain eternal light, so you, who deny him, must be given over to destruction and eternal shadows.²¹² The road you follow will not lead you to heaven, as the Arians falsely tell you, but to the very citadel of the earth, to the left path of evil and impious Tartarus: this is the way of that apostate whose every whim you, his lackey, are found to fulfil;²¹³ this is the way,

207 See Lact. *Diu. Inst.* 5.23.1: 'The most unjust persecutors ... should not think that they will escape unpunished' and 5.23.2: 'They place his [God's] eternal name beneath their feet, to be impiously and wickedly trampled.'

208 *Romans* 8.18.

209 On the 'shadows outside', see *Matthew* 8.12.

210 See Cyprian, *Ep.* 58.10.2: 'When this revelation has come, when the splendour of God has shone upon us, we will be as blessed and happy, honoured by the Lord's esteem, as they who will be left behind will be wretched, who as deserters from God and rebels against him have carried out the will of the Devil and must be tormented by unquenchable fire along with him.' For the 'unquenchable fire', see the following quotation from *Isaiah*.

211 *Isaiah* 66.24. This statement comes from the end of the prophecy of Isaiah. As in chapter 10 above, Lucifer is here identifying a biblical prophecy as a specific prediction about Constantius. On the importance of the Son as true Son, see n. 108 to chapter 7 above.

212 See Lact. *Diu. Inst.* 6.3.17: 'He will achieve the prize of immortality and obtain eternal light' and 'He must be given over to destruction and eternal shadows.' In this and the following passages, Lactantius is discussing the paths of virtue and vice, which lead, respectively, to Heaven and Hell. He is here describing the contrasting fates of the men who walk on these two paths.

213 The apostate (*refuga*) here is the Devil.

I tell you, of that serpent who turns you from the heavenly route to hold to the road of injustice.[214] This is the wide and broad road that the Lord describes in the Gospel, saying: *How wide and broad is the road that leads to destruction.*[215]

So if you refuse to look after yourself then it cannot be doubted that you are among those whom the blessed John strikes, saying: *But now the axe is laid unto the root of the trees; if any does not bring forth good fruit it will be cut down and cast into the fire.*[216] Therefore since you are exceedingly bitter trees bearing the fruit of death, namely sinning against God,[217] unless you make the transition to the heavenly road, you and your comrades will be cut down so that you go headlong swifter than speech into a deep abyss, from where you will certainly see those whom you now persecute unjustly, just as then the rich man saw Lazarus in the lap of Abraham, Isaac and Jacob, the friends of God, and of all the prophets, apostles and martyrs.[218] You will not avoid these punishments, Constantius, unless you first believe that the only Son of God is the true Son of God and then confess, as has often been said, that he has always reigned and reigns now with the Father, that is without beginning or end, and you also transfer yourself from the wicked assembly of the Arians to the orthodox Church, that is from death to life, and confess, as we orthodox confess, that the Father, Son and Holy Spirit are a perfect trinity and possess a single divinity.[219]

---

214 See Lact. *Diu. Inst.* 6.4.1–2: 'But to the very citadel of the earth, and the left path inflicts punishments for evil and leads to impious Tartarus. This is the way of that accuser who with depraved religions turns men from the heavenly route and leads them onto the road of destruction.' The phrase *at laeua malorum|exercet poenas, et ad impia Tartara mittit* ('the left path inflicts punishments for evil and leads to impious Tartarus') is from Vergil, *Aeneid* 6.542–3. On Tartarus, see n. 92 to chapter 6 above.

215 *Matthew* 7.13.

216 *Luke* 3.9. These words are spoken by John the Baptist.

217 See *Wisdom* 4.5.

218 See Lact. *Diu. Inst.* 6.4.4: 'It [the left path] breaks off so suddenly that no one can see the trap before he falls headlong into a deep abyss.' See *Luke* 16.19–31 for the parable of the rich man and the beggar Lazarus; see also *Luke* 13.28.

219 On the importance of the Son as true Son and the doctrine of the co-eternity of the Father and the Son, see nn. 108 and 143 to chapters 7 and 10 above. The single divine *ousia* of the Father and the Son is important to Nicene opposition to 'Arianism', although the Holy Spirit was not discussed as much in the 350s, since the main arguments revolved around Christology. See Introduction pp. 2–18 and the Glossary.

15   Thus you hate Christians and persecute them in every way, as though your malevolence could defeat those who have embarked on that hard and difficult road, although they are held in contempt, derision and hatred by you;[220] however, through the whole of this present life they want to be poor, humble, ignoble and subjected to your injustices, believing that by enduring all those things that are known to be bitter for the sake of God they will achieve those exceptional rewards which the apostle says must come, rewards which *the eye has not seen, nor the ear heard; nor has it entered into the heart of man, the things which the Lord has prepared for them that love him.*[221] So, because God will reveal these things to those who love him, loving him we know that when we offend you, when we are punished by you, we are pleasing to God. And so your murderous judgement cannot possess any authority to punish us for eternity, since you who condemn must be condemned, in fact, to pay an eternal penalty. But eternal joys will sustain us, whom you torture, tear, slaughter, and a great and immense happiness will hold us and perpetual blessedness will receive us.[222] Understand therefore that power has been given to us divinely to condemn you instead, while you think that you condemn us, and to punish you, sacrilegious Constantius, while you believe that you can punish us, since he whom you deny saw fit to give authority to us, his bishops, so that whatever we bind on earth is also bound in heaven.[223] For the sake of God we endure temporal evils so that we may attain eternal benefits;[224] we flee the temporal things that you offer to us as benefits, since eternal evils follow these benefits of yours. Therefore we have chosen to endure these present troubles, which you think are injurious to us, in order that, because an illustrious confession persists in us, we may deserve to receive eternal and immortal benefits, just as you will incur immortal evils together with those who, fearing you, are discovered to have submitted to your will and to have forsaken the instructions of God because they saw fit

---

220 See Lact. *Diu. Inst.* 6.4.10: 'Therefore the just man, because he has embarked on that hard and difficult road, must be held in contempt, derision and hatred.' Lactantius is here describing the attitude of foolish people towards a man who is walking on the path of virtue.
221 *1 Corinthians* 2.9. See Lact. *Diu. Inst.* 6.4.11: 'So he [the just man] will be poor, humble, ignoble, subject to injustice and yet enduring all those things that are bitter.'
222 The juxtaposition of terms in the phrase *felicitas perpetuaque* ('happiness and perpetual') may be an allusion to the famous North African martyrs Perpetua and Felicitas.
223 See *Matthew* 16.19, 18.18.
224 See Lact. *Diu. Inst.* 6.4.12: 'So that whoever chooses present evils with justice will achieve greater and more certain benefits.'

to choose present benefits and spurn future ones.[225] For *more to be desired than gold are they, and many precious stones, sweeter also than honey and the honeycomb. For your servant keeps to them and in the keeping of them there is great reward.*[226]

We know that this life, which you strive so hard to destroy, is extremely brief; we know that the benefits and evils of this life are fleeting, but that the benefits of that eternal life, which we desire to attain, are everlasting; for we know that, in place of those fleeting benefits, by which you are enticed and delighted, eternal evils will come to you, and that in place of these fleeting evils, eternal benefits will come to us Christians, whom you despise and whom you never stop lacerating with all the powers of your dominion.[227] You have read that it is so in the 125th Psalm: *The Lord has done great things among them*;[228] and below: *They that sow in tears shall reap in joy. Going out they went out and wept, casting their seeds; but returning they shall return in exultation bringing their sheaves*;[229] and in the 128th: *Blessed is everyone that fears the Lord, that walks in his ways. You shall eat the labours of your fruit; you are blessed and it shall be well with you.*[230] Undoubtedly it shall be well unto eternity with those who have not denied the Son of God, those who will obtain the labours of his holy confession; in contrast, if you decide that you must always persist in this madness in which you now live, it shall be ill with you forever, receiving those rewards that Judas Iscariot now receives.[231] Then we will see you as a suppliant, but, however, all the future lamentation of your penitence will be futile, since it is here, in fact, that either eternal life or eternal death is acquired.[232]

---

225 See Lact. *Diu. Inst.* 6.4.12: 'But whoever prefers present benefits to justice will fall into greater and longer lasting evils.'

226 *Psalms* 19.10–11 (18.10–11 LXX).

227 See Lact. *Diu. Inst.* 6.4.13–14: 'Because this physical life is fleeting, so its evils and benefits must also be fleeting; because the spiritual life, which contrasts with the earthly, is everlasting, so its benefits and evils are everlasting. Thus it is that in place of fleeting benefits, eternal evils will come, and in place of fleeting evils, eternal benefits will come.'

228 *Psalms* 126.3 (125.3 LXX).

229 *Psalms* 126.5–6 (125.5–6 LXX). The superfluous participles in this passage provide a good illustration of the literal translations of the Greek that appear frequently in the early Latin translations of the Bible.

230 *Psalms* 128.1–2 (127.1–2 LXX).

231 This sentence echoes the language of the biblical quotation that precedes it.

232 Lucifer's point here is that it will do Constantius no good to repent in Hell. He needs to do so in this life, as that determines what happens it eternity.

We want you to know that we are always turning these following matters over in our heart and contemplating them day and night: your perpetual punishments and the eternal prizes and rewards of the servants of God; what he threatens as a punishment for you, who deny and are a persecutor of his name; and, in contrast, what he promises as everlasting glory to those who confess it.[233]

---

233 See Cyprian, *Ep.* 58.11: 'Let this consideration be daily and nightly, always holding before our eyes and turning over in our minds and thoughts what are the punishments of the unjust and the prizes and rewards of the just, what the Lord threatens as a punishment for those who deny and, in contrast, what he promises as everlasting glory to those who confess.' This passage is taken from very close to the end of Cyprian's letter.

EDITIONS AND TRANSLATIONS
OF ANCIENT TEXTS

The standard Latin titles for works, together with details of modern critical editions, are provided here. English versions of the titles are given in brackets, as are details of translations of the texts, where available.

Altercatio Heracliani	*Altercatio Heracliani laici cum Germinio, episcopo Sirmiensi* (*The Dispute between Heraclianus the layman and Germinius, bishop of Sirmium*) A. Hamman (ed.) (1958) *Patrologiae Cursus Completus Series Latina, Supplementum* I, Paris, 345–50. (Translated in R. Flower (2013) *Emperors and Bishops in Late Roman Invective,* Cambridge, 230–7.)
Ambr. *Ep.* 77	Ambrose of Milan, *Epistula* 77 (*Letter* 77) M. Zelzer (ed.) (1982) *Sancti Ambrosi Opera Pars X, Epistulae et Acta Tom. III: Epistularum Liber Decimus, Epistulae extra Collectionem, Gesta Concili Aquileiensis,* CSEL 82.3, Vienna, 126–40. (Translated in J. H. W. G. Liebeschuetz (2005) *Ambrose of Milan: Political Letters and Speeches,* Translated Texts for Historians vol. 43, Liverpool, 204–12.)
Ath. *Ad Ep. Aeg.*	Athanasius of Alexandria, *Epistula ad Episcopos Aegypti et Libyae* (*Letter to the Bishops of Egypt and Libya*) K. Metzler (ed.) (1996–2000) *Athanasius: Werke* I.1, Berlin, 39–64. (Translated in A. Robertson (ed.) (1892)

	St. Athanasius: Select Works and Letters, Select Library of Nicene and Post-Nicene Fathers, Second Series, vol. 4, Oxford, 222–35.)
Ath. *Apol. c. Ar.*	Athanasius of Alexandria, *Apologia contra Arianos* / *Apologia Secunda* (*Defence against the Arians*, or *Second Defence*) H. G. Opitz (ed.) (1935–41) *Athanasius: Werke* II.1, Berlin, 87–168. (Translated in A. Robertson (ed.) (1892) *St. Athanasius: Select Works and Letters,* Select Library of Nicene and Post-Nicene Fathers, Second Series, vol. 4, Oxford, 100–147.)
Ath. *Apol. Const.*	Athanasius of Alexandria, *Apologia ad Constantium* (*Defence to Constantius*) H. C. Brennecke, U. Heil and A. von Stockhausen (edd.) (2006) *Athanasius: Werke* II.1, Berlin, 279–309. (Translated in A. Robertson (ed.) (1892) *St. Athanasius: Select Works and Letters,* Select Library of Nicene and Post-Nicene Fathers, Second Series, vol. 4, Oxford, 238–53.)
Ath. *De decretis*	Athanasius of Alexandria, *De decretis Nicaenae synodi* (*On the Decisions of the Nicene Council*) H. G. Opitz (ed.) (1935–41) *Athanasius: Werke* II.1, Berlin, 1–45. (Translated in A. Robertson (ed.) (1892) *St. Athanasius: Select Works and Letters,* Select Library of Nicene and Post-Nicene Fathers, Second Series, vol. 4, Oxford, 150–72.)
Ath. *De fuga*	Athanasius of Alexandria, *Apologia de fuga sua* (*Defence for his Flight*) H. G. Opitz (ed.) (1935–41) *Athanasius: Werke* II.1, Berlin, 68–86.

(Translated in A. Robertson (ed.) (1892)
St. Athanasius: Select Works and Letters,
Select Library of Nicene and Post-Nicene
Fathers, Second Series, vol. 4, Oxford,
255–65.)

Ath. *De morte Arii*   Athanasius of Alexandria, *Ad
Serapionem de morte Arii* (*Letter to
Serapion on the Death of Arius*)
H. G. Opitz (ed.) (1935–41) *Athanasius
Werke:* II.1, Berlin, 178–80.
(Translated in A. Robertson (ed.) (1892)
St. Athanasius: Select Works and Letters,
Select Library of Nicene and Post-Nicene
Fathers, Second Series, vol. 4, Oxford,
564–6.)

Ath. *De synodis*   Athanasius of Alexandria, *De synodis
Arimini et Seleuciae* (*On the Councils of
Ariminum and Seleucia*)
H. G. Opitz (ed.) (1935–41) *Athanasius:
Werke* II.1, Berlin, 231–78.
(Translated in A. Robertson (ed.) (1892)
St. Athanasius: Select Works and Letters,
Select Library of Nicene and Post-Nicene
Fathers, Second Series, vol. 4, Oxford,
451–80.)

Ath. *Ep. Enc.*   Athanasius of Alexandria, *Epistula
Encyclica* (*Encyclical Epistle*)
H. G. Opitz (ed.) (1935–41) *Athanasius:
Werke* II.1, Berlin, 169–77.
(Translated in A. Robertson (ed.) (1892)
St. Athanasius: Select Works and Letters,
Select Library of Nicene and Post-Nicene
Fathers, Second Series, vol. 4, Oxford,
92–6.)

Ath. *Hist. Ar.*   Athanasius of Alexandria, *Historia
Arianorum* (*History of the Arians*)
H. G. Opitz (ed.) (1935–41) *Athanasius:
Werke* II.1, Berlin, 183–230.
(Translated in this volume.)

Ath. *V. Ant.*

Athanasius of Alexandria, *Vita Antonii* (*Life of Antony*)
G. J. M. Bartelink (ed.) (1994) *Athanase d'Alexandrie: Vie d'Antoine,* Sources chrétiennes 400, Paris.
(Translated in A. Robertson (ed.) (1892) *St. Athanasius: Select Works and Letters,* Select Library of Nicene and Post-Nicene Fathers, Second Series, vol. 4, Oxford, 195–221.)

Augustine, *De haeresibus*

Augustine of Hippo, *De haeresibus ad Quodvultdeus liber unus* (*On Heresies, to Quodvultdeus*)
R. vander Plaetse and C. Beukers (edd.) (1969) *De haeresibus,* CCSL 46, Turnhout, 283–345.
(Translated in L. G. Müller (1956) *The De Haeresibus of Saint Augustine,* Washington D.C.)

Collatio

Collatio Legum Mosaicarum et Romanarum (*Comparison of Mosaic and Roman Laws*)
R. M. Frakes (ed.) (2011) *Compiling the Collatio Legum Mosaicarum et Romanarum in Late Antiquity,* Oxford (with translation).

Cyprian, *Ep.*

Cyprian of Carthage, *Epistulae* (*Letters*)
G. F. Diercks (ed.) (1994–96) *Sancti Cypriani Episcopi Epistularium,* 2 vols, CCSL 3B and 3C.
(Translated in G. W. Clarke (1984–9) *The Letters of St. Cyprian of Carthage,* 4 vols, New York.)

[Cypr.], *De laude martyrii*

[Cyprian of Carthage], *De laude martyrii* (*On the Glory of Martyrdom*)
G. Hartel (ed.) (1871) *S. Thasci Caecili Cypriani Opera Omnia,* CSEL 3.3, 26–52.
(Translated in R. E. Wallis (1869) *The Writings of Cyprian, Bishop of Carthage,*

	Vol. II, Containing the Remainder of the Treatises, together with the Writings of Novatian, Minucius Felix, etc., Ante-Nicene Christian Library, vol. XIII, Edinburgh, 231–52.)
Epiphanius, *Panarion*	Epiphanius of Salamis, *Panarion* (*Medicine Chest*) K. Holl (ed.) (2013, 1980, 1985) *Epiphanius*, GCS, 3 vols, rev. by J. Dummer, C.-F. Collatz and M. Bergermann. (Translated in F. Williams (2009–13) *The Panarion of Epiphanius of Salamis*, 2nd edn, 2 vols, Leiden.)
Eus. *HE*	Eusebius of Caesarea, *Historia ecclesiastica* (*Ecclesiastical History*) T. Mommsen and E. Schwartz (edd.) (1999) *Eusebius Werke. Band 2: Kirchengeschichte*, GCS n.f. 6.1–3, 2nd edn, rev. by F. Winkelmann. (Translated in H. J. Lawlor and J. E. L. Oulton (1927–28) *Eusebius, Bishop of Caesarea: The Ecclesiastical History and the Martyrs of Palestine*, 2 vols, London. See also *Eusebius: The History of the Church from Christ to Constantine*, tr. G. A. Williamson, rev. A. Louth, London, 1989.)
Eus. *Mart. Pal.*	Eusebius of Caesarea, *Liber de martyribus Palaestinae* (*On the Martyrs of Palestine*) G. Bardy (ed.) (1958) *Eusèbe de Césarée: Histoire ecclésiastique Livres VIII–X et les martyrs en Palestine*, Sources chrétiennes 55, Paris, 121–74. (Translated in H. J. Lawlor and J. E. L. Oulton (1927–28) *Eusebius, Bishop of Caesarea: The Ecclesiastical History and the Martyrs of Palestine*,

	2 vols, London, I 327–400. See also P. Schaff and H. Wace (edd.) (1890) *Eusebius: Church History, Life of Constantine the Great, and Oration in Praise of Constantine,* Select Library of Nicene and Post-Nicene Fathers, Second Series, vol. 1, Oxford, 342–56.)
Eus. *VC*	Eusebius of Caesarea, *De Vita Constantini* (*Life of Constantine*) F. Winkelmann (ed.) (1975 [1991]) *Eusebius Werke. Band 1, Teil 1: Über das Leben des Kaisers Konstantin,* GCS, Berlin, rev. edn. (Translated in Averil Cameron and S. G. Hall (1999) *Eusebius: Life of Constantine,* Oxford.)
Eus. Verc. *Ep.*	Eusebius of Vercelli, *Epistulae* (*Letters*) V. Bulhart (ed.) (1957) *Eusebii Vercellensis episcopi quae supersunt,* CCSL 9, 103–10. (Translated in R. Flower (2013) *Emperors and Bishops in Late Roman Invective,* Cambridge, 242–51.)
Greg. Ilib. *Tract. Orig.*	Gregory of Elvira, *Tractatus Origenis de libris Sanctarum Scripturarum* (*Origen's Discussion of the Books of Holy Scripture*) V. Bulhart (ed.) (1967) *Gregorii Iliberritani episcopi quae supersunt,* CCSL 69, 5–146.
Greg. Naz. *Or.* 4	Gregory of Nazianzus, *Oratio* 4 (*Speech* 4) J. Bernardi (ed.) (1983) *Grégoire de Nazianze: Discours 4–5, Contre Julien,* Sources chrétiennes 309, Paris, 86–292. (Translated in C. W. King (1888) *Julian the Emperor,* London, 1–85.)
Hilary, *Ad Const.*	Hilary of Poitiers, *Liber II ad Constantium* (*Address to Constantius*)

	A. Feder (ed.) (1916) *S. Hilarii Episcopi Pictaviensis Opera. Pars Quarta*, CSEL 65, 197–205. (Translated in L. R. Wickham (1997) *Hilary of Poitiers: Conflicts of Conscience and Law in the Fourth-Century Church*, Translated Texts for Historians, vol. 25, Liverpool, 104–109.)
Hilary, *Adu. Val. et Ursac.*	Hilary of Poitiers, *Aduersus Valentem et Ursacium/Collectanea Antiariana Parisina* (*Against Valens and Ursacius*) A. Feder (ed.) (1916) *S. Hilarii Episcopi Pictaviensis Opera. Pars Quarta*, CSEL 65, 43–193. (Translated in L. R. Wickham (1997) *Hilary of Poitiers: Conflicts of Conscience and Law in the Fourth-Century Church*, Translated Texts for Historians, vol. 25, Liverpool, 15–103.)
Hilary, *Contra Auxentium*	Hilary of Poitiers, *Contra Arianos uel Auxentium Mediolanensem* (*Against Auxentius*) (sections 1–12) J.-P. Migne (ed.) (1845) *Sancti Hilarii Pictaviensis Episcopi Opera Omnia*, vol. 2, PL 10, 610–18. (sections 13–15) M. Durst (1998) 'Das Glaubensbekenntnis des Auxentius von Mailand: historischer Hintergrund – Textüberlieferung – Theologie – Edition', *JbAC* 41, 118–68, at 161–3. (Translated in R. Flower (2013) *Emperors and Bishops in Late Roman Invective*, Cambridge, 252–60.)
Hilary, *De Synodis*	Hilary of Poitiers, *De Synodis* (*On the Councils*) J.-P. Migne (ed.) (1845) *Sancti Hilarii Pictaviensis Episcopi Opera Omnia: Tomus II*, Patrologia Latina 10, Paris, 479–546.

	(Translated in W. Sanday (ed.) (1899) *St. Hilary of Poitiers: Select Works,* Select Library of Nicene and Post-Nicene Fathers, Second Series, vol. 9, Oxford, 342–56.)
Hilary, *In Const.*	Hilary of Poitiers, *Liber In Constantium* (*Against Constantius*)
	A. Rocher (ed.) (1987) *Hilaire de Poitiers: Contre Constance,* Sources chrétiennes 334, Paris.
	(Translated in this volume.)
Hilary, *Liber I ad Constantium*	Hilary of Poitiers, '*Liber I ad Constantium*'/*Appendix ad Collectanea Antiariana Parisina* ('*Book I to Constantius*' – this is actually part of Hilary's *Against Valens and Ursacius*)
	A. Feder (ed.) (1916) *S. Hilarii Episcopi Pictaviensis Opera. Pars Quarta,* CSEL 65, 181–7.
	(Translated in L. R. Wickham (1997) *Hilary of Poitiers: Conflicts of Conscience and Law in the Fourth-Century Church,* Translated Texts for Historians, vol. 25, Liverpool, 65–9.)
Hippol. *Haer.*	Hippolytus of Rome, *Refutatio omnium haeresium* (*Refutation of All Heresies*)
	M. D. Litwa (ed.) (2016) *Refutation of All Heresies,* Atlanta, GA (with translation).
Historia acephala	*Historia acephala*
	A. Martin (ed.) (1985) *Histoire 'acephale' et index syriaque des lettres festales d'Athanase d'Alexandrie,* Sources chrétiennes 317, Paris, 138–68.
	(Translated in A. Robertson (ed.) (1892) *St. Athanasius: Select Works and Letters,* Select Library of Nicene and Post-Nicene Fathers, Second Series, vol. 4, Oxford, 496–9.)

Iren. *Haer.* Irenaeus of Lyon, *Adversus Haereses* (*Against the Heresies*) Book 1: A Rousseau and L. Doutreleau (edd.) (1979) *Irénée de Lyon: Contre les hérésies, Livre I,* Sources chrétiennes 263–4, Paris. (Book 1 translated in D. J. Unger (1992) *St. Irenaeus of Lyons: Against the Heresies, Volume 1,* rev. J. J. Dillon, Ancient Christian Writers 55, New York.)

Jerome, *De uiris illustr.* Jerome, *Liber de uiris illustribus* (*On Illustrious Men*) W. Herding (ed.) (1879) *Hieronymi De viris inlustribus liber. Accedit Gennadii Catalogus virorum inlustrium,* Leipzig. (Translated in P. Schaff and H. Wace (edd.) (1892) *Theodoret, Jerome, Gennadius, Rufinus: Historical Writings, etc.,* Select Library of Nicene and Post-Nicene Fathers, Second Series, vol. 3, Oxford, 359–84.)

Jerome, *Vita Hilarionis* Jerome, *Vita Hilarionis* (*Life of Hilarion*) E. M. Morales (ed.) (2007) *Jérôme: Trois vies de moines (Paul, Malchus, Hilarion),* Sources chrétiennes 508, Paris, 212–98. (Translated in C. White (1998) *Early Christian Lives,* London, 89–115.)

Lact. *Diu. Inst.* Lactantius, *Diuinae Institutiones* (*Divine Institutes*) Book 3: S. Brandt (ed.) (1890) *L. Caeli Firmiani Lactanti opera omnia, Pars I: Divinae Institutiones et Epitome divinarum institutionum,* CSEL 19. Book 5: P. Monat (ed.) (1973) *Lactance: Institutions divines, Livre V,* Sources chrétiennes 204–5, Paris. Book 6: C. Ingremeau (ed.) (2007) *Lactance: Institutions divines, Livre VI,* Sources chrétiennes 509, Paris.

	(Translated in A. Bowen and P. Garnsey (2003) *Lactantius: Divine Institutes,* Translated Texts for Historians, vol. 40, Liverpool.)
Lact. *Mort. pers.*	Lactantius, *De Mortibus Persecutorum* (*On the Deaths of the Persecutors*) J. L. Creed (ed.) (1984) *Lactantius: De Mortibus Persecutorum,* Oxford Early Christian Texts, Oxford (with translation).
Lucifer, *De Ath. I*	Lucifer of Cagliari, *Quia absentem nemo debet iudicare nec damnare sive De Athanasio Liber I* (*That No One Ought to Be Judged or Condemned While Absent, or Concerning Athanasius, Book I*) G. F. Diercks (ed.) (1978) *Luciferi Calaritani opera quae supersunt,* CCSL 8, 3–75.
Lucifer, *De Ath. II*	Lucifer of Cagliari, *Quia absentem nemo debet iudicare nec damnare sive De Athanasio Liber II* (*That No One Ought to Be Judged or Condemned While Absent, or Concerning Athanasius, Book II*) G. F. Diercks (ed.) (1978) *Luciferi Calaritani opera quae supersunt,* CCSL 8, 77–132.
Lucifer, *De non conu.*	Lucifer of Cagliari, *De non conueniendo cum haereticis* (*On Not Coming Together with Heretics*) G. F. Diercks (ed.) (1978) *Luciferi Calaritani opera quae supersunt,* CCSL 8, 165–92.
Lucifer, *De non parc.*	Lucifer of Cagliari, *De non parcendo in Deum delinquentibus* (*On Not Sparing Those Who Commit Offences Against God*) G. F. Diercks (ed.) (1978) *Luciferi Calaritani opera quae supersunt,* CCSL 8, 195–261.

Lucifer, *De regibus*

Lucifer of Cagliari, *De regibus apostaticis* (*On Apostate Kings*)
G. F. Diercks (ed.) (1978) *Luciferi Calaritani opera quae supersunt,* CCSL 8, 135–61.
(Translated into Italian in V. Ugenti (ed.) (1980) *Luciferi Calaritani: De regibus apostaticis et Moriundum esse pro dei filio,* Lecce, 83–113.)

Lucifer, *Moriundum*

Lucifer of Cagliari, *Moriundum esse pro dei filio* (*The Necessity of Dying for the Son of God*)
G. F. Diercks (ed.) (1978) *Luciferi Calaritani opera quae supersunt,* CCSL 8, 265–300.
(Translated in this volume.)

Novat. *De cibis iudaicis*

Novatian, *De cibis iudaicis* (*On Jewish Foods*)
G. F. Diercks (ed.) (1972) *Novatiani opera quae supersunt,* CCSL 4, 89–101.
(Translated in R. E. Wallis (1869) *The Writings of Cyprian, Bishop of Carthage, Vol. II, Containing the Remainder of the Treatises, together with the Writings of Novatian, Minucius Felix, etc.,* Ante-Nicene Christian Library vol. XIII, Edinburgh, 382–95.)

Philostorgius, *HE*

Philostorgius, *Historia Ecclesiastica* (*Ecclesiastical History*)
J. Bidez (ed.) (1981) *Philostorgius: Kirchengeschichte,* GCS, 3rd edn, rev. by F. Winkelmann.
(Translated in P. R. Amidon (2007) *Philostorgius: Church History,* Atlanta, Georgia.)

Rufinus, *HE*

Rufinus, *Historia Ecclesiastica* (*Ecclesiastical History*)
(Books 10-11) E. Schwartz, T. Mommsen and F. Winkelmann (edd.)

(1999), *Eusebius Werke, Band 2: Die
Kirchengeschichte*, 2nd edn, GCS n.f. 6,
Berlin, 2.957–1040.
(Translated in P. R. Amidon (1997) *The
Church History of Rufinus of Aquileia,
Books 10 and 11*, Oxford.)

Soc. *HE*   Socrates, *Historia Ecclesiastica*
(*Ecclesiastical History*)
G. C. Hansen (ed.) (1995) *Sokrates:
Kirchengeschichte*, GCS n.f. 1.
(Translated in P. Schaff and H. Wace
(edd.) (1891) *Socrates, Sozomenus:
Church Histories*, Select Library of
Nicene and Post-Nicene Fathers, Second
Series, vol. 2, Oxford, 1–178.)

Soz. *HE*   Sozomen, *Historia Ecclesiastica*
(*Ecclesiastical History*)
G. C. Hansen (ed.) *Sozomenos:
Kirchengeschichte*, Fontes christiani 73,
4 vols, Turnhout, 2004.
(Translated in P. Schaff and H. Wace
(edd.) (1891) *Socrates, Sozomenus:
Church Histories*, Select Library of
Nicene and Post-Nicene Fathers, Second
Series, vol. 2, Oxford, 239–427.)

Sulpicius Severus, *Chronicle*   Sulpicius Severus, *Chronica* (*Chronicle*)
G. de Senneville-Grave (ed.) (1999)
Sulpice Sévère: Chroniques, Sources
chrétiennes 441, Paris.
(Translated in P. Schaff and H. Wace
(edd.) (1894) *Sulpitius Severus, Vincent
of Lerins, John Cassian*, Select Library
of Nicene and Post-Nicene Fathers,
Second Series, vol. 11, Oxford, 71–122.)

Sulpicius Severus, *Vita Martini*   Sulpicius Severus, *Vita Martini* (*Life of
Martin*)
J. Fontaine (ed.) (1967–9) *Sulpice Sévère:
Vie de Saint Martin,* 3 vols, Sources
chrétiennes 133–5, Paris.

(Translated in C. White (1998) *Early Christian Lives,* London, 134–59. See also F. R. Hoare (1954) *The Western Fathers, being the Lives of SS. Martin of Tours, Ambrose, Augustine of Hippo, Honoratus of Arles and Germanus of Auxerre,* London, 10–44.)

Theod. *HE*
Theodoret, *Historia Ecclesiastica (Ecclesiastical History)* L. Parmentier and G. C. Hansen (edd.) (1998) *Theodoret: Kirchengeschichte,* GCS n.f. 5, 3rd edn, Berlin. (Translated in P. Schaff and H. Wace (edd.) (1892) *Theodoret, Jerome, Gennadius, Rufinus: Historical Writings, etc.,* Select Library of Nicene and Post-Nicene Fathers, Second Series, vol. 3, Oxford, 33–159.)

Tomus ad Antiochenos
Tomus ad Antiochenos (Synodal Statement to the Antiochenes) H. C. Brennecke, U. Heil and A. von Stockhausen (edd.) (2006) *Athanasius: Werke* II.1, Berlin, 340–51. (Translated in A. Robertson (ed.) (1892) *St. Athanasius: Select Works and Letters,* Select Library of Nicene and Post-Nicene Fathers, Second Series, vol. 4, Oxford, 483–6.)

Urk.
Urkunden zur Geschichte des arianischen Streites, 318–328 (Documents concerning the History of the Arian Conflict, 318–328) Lfrg. 1–2: H. G. Opitz (ed.) (1934) *Athanasius: Werke* III.1, Berlin.

BIBLIOGRAPHY

Adams, J. N. (2003) *Bilingualism and the Latin Language*, Cambridge.

Ayres, L. (2004) *Nicaea and its Legacy: An Approach to Fourth-Century Trinitarian Theology*, Oxford.

Barnes, T. D. (1988) 'Review of Rocher (1987)', *JThS* (n.s.) 39: 609–11.

— (1992) 'Hilary of Poitiers on his exile', *Vigiliae Christianae* 46: 129–40 (repr. in id. [1994], no. XVII).

— (1993) *Athanasius and Constantius: Theology and Politics in the Constantinian Empire*, Cambridge, MA.

— (1994) *From Eusebius to Augustine: Selected Papers 1982–1993*, Aldershot.

— (1996) 'Oppressor, persecutor, usurper: the meaning of "tyrannus" in the fourth century', in G. Bonamente and M. Mayer (edd.) *Historiae Augustae Colloquium Barcinonense*, Atti dei Convegni sulla Historia Augusta IV, Bari, 55–65.

— (2009) 'The exile and recalls of Arius', *JThS* 60: 109–29.

Barry, J. (2016) 'Heroic bishops: Hilary of Poitiers's exilic discourse', *Vigiliae Christianae* 70: 155–74.

Beckwith, C. L. (2005) 'The condemnation and exile of Hilary of Poitiers at the Synod of Béziers (356 C.E.)', *JECS* 13: 21–38.

Bienert, W. A. (1993) 'Sabellius und Sabellianismus als historisches Problem', in H. C. Brennecke, E. L. Grasmück and C. Markschies (edd.) *Logos: Festschrift für Luise Abramowski zum 8. Juli 1993*, Beihefte zur Zeitschrift für die neutestamentliche Wissenschaft und die Kunde der älteren Kirche 67, Berlin, 124–39.

Borchardt, C. F. A. (1966) *Hilary of Poitiers' Role in the Arian Struggle*, Kerkhistorische Studiën 12, The Hague.

Brakke, D. (2001) 'Jewish flesh and Christian spirit in Athanasius of Alexandria', *JECS* 9: 453–81.

— (2010) *The Gnostics: Myth, Ritual, and Diversity in Early Christianity*, Cambridge, MA.

Bremmer, J. N. (1991) '"Christianus sum": the early Christian martyrs and Christ', in G. J. M. Bartelink, A. Hilhorst and C. H. Kneepkens (edd.) *Eulogia: Mélanges offerts à Antoon A.R. Bastiaensen à l'occasion de son soixante-cinquième anniversaire*, Instrumenta Patristica 24, Steenbrugge, 11–20.

Brennecke, H. C. (1984) *Hilarius von Poitiers und die Bischofsopposition gegen*

Konstantius II.: Untersuchungen zur dritten Phase des arianischen Streites (337–361), Patristische Texte und Studien 26, Berlin.

— (1988) *Studien zur Geschichte der Homöer. Der Osten bis zum Ende der homöischen Reichskirche*, Beiträge zur historischen Theologie 73, Tübingen.

— (2010) 'Die letzten Jahre des Arius', in A. von Stockhausen and H. C. Brennecke (edd.) *Von Arius zum Athanasianum. Studien zur Edition der 'Athanasius Werke'*, Texte und Untersuchungen zur Geschichte der altchristlichen Literatur 164, Berlin, 63–83.

Brennecke, H. C., Heil, U., von Stockhausen, A. and Wintjes, A. (2007) *Athanasius: Werke III.1: Dokumente zur Geschichte des Arianischen Streites. 3. Lieferung: Bis zur Ekthesis makrostichos*, Berlin.

Brown, P. R. L. (1992) *Power and Persuasion in Late Antiquity: Towards a Christian Empire*, Madison, WI.

Burgess, R. W. (2008) 'The summer of blood: the "great massacre" of 337 and the promotion of the sons of Constantine', *Dumbarton Oaks Papers* 62: 5–51 (repr. in id. *Chronicles, Consuls, and Coins: Historiography and History in the Later Roman Empire*, Farnham, 2011, no. X).

Burns, P. C. (1994) 'Hilary of Poitiers' road to Béziers: politics or religion?', *JECS* 2: 273–89.

Burrus, V. (1989) 'Rhetorical stereotypes in the portrait of Paul of Samosata', *Vigiliae Christianae* 43: 215–25.

Castelli, E. A. (2004) *Martyrdom and Memory: Early Christian Culture Making*, New York.

Chadwick, H. (1972) 'The origin of the title "oecumenical council"', *JThS* (n.s.) 23: 132–5 (repr. in id. *History and Thought of the Early Church*, London, 1982, no. XI).

Charlesworth, J. H. (ed.) (1983–5) *The Old Testament Pseudepigrapha*, 2 vols, London.

Corti, G. (2004) *Lucifero di Cagliari: Una voce nel conflitto tra chiesa e impero alla metà del IV secolo*, Studia Patristica Mediolanensia 24, Milan.

Diercks, G. F. (1978) *Luciferi Calaritani opera quae supersunt*, CCSL 8, Turnhout.

Dignas, B. and Winter, E. (2007) *Rome and Persia in Late Antiquity: Neighbours and Rivals*, Cambridge.

Doignon, J. (1971) *Hilaire de Poitiers avant l'exil: recherches sur la naissance, l'enseignement et l'épreuve d'une foi épiscopale en Gaule au milieu du IVᵉ siècle*, Paris.

Durst, M. (1998) 'Das Glaubensbekenntnis des Auxentius von Mailand: historischer Hintergrund – Textüberlieferung – Theologie – Edition', *JbAC* 41: 118–68.

Duval, Y.-M. (1970) 'Vrais et faux problèmes concernant le retour d'exil d'Hilaire de Poitiers et son action en Italie en 360–363', *Athenaeum* 48: 251–75 (repr. in id. *L'extirpation de l'Arianisme en Italie du Nord et en Occident*, Aldershot, 1998, no. III).

Elliott, A. G. (1987) *Roads to Paradise: Reading the Lives of the Early Saints*, Hanover, NH.

Elton, H. (2006) 'Warfare and the military', in N. Lenski (ed.) *The Cambridge Companion to the Age of Constantine*, Cambridge, 325–46.

Ernest, J. D. (2004) *The Bible in Athanasius of Alexandria*, The Bible in Ancient Christianity 2, Leiden.

Ferreres, L. (1977) 'Las fuentes de Lucifer de Cálaris en su *Moriundum esse pro dei filio*', *Anuario de Filología* 3: 101–15.

— (ed.) (1982) *El tratado "Moriundum ese pro Dei Filio" de Lucifer de Cagliari*, Studia Latina Barcinonensia 5, Barcelona.

Flower, R. (2013) *Emperors and Bishops in Late Roman Invective*, Cambridge.

Galvão-Sobrinho, C. R. (2013) *Doctrine and Power: Theological Controversy and Christian Leadership in the Later Roman Empire*, The Transformation of the Classical Heritage 51, Berkeley, CA.

Gardner, I. and Lieu, S. N. C. (edd.) (2004) *Manichaean Texts from the Roman Empire*, Cambridge.

Glare, P. G. W. (ed.) (1982) *Oxford Latin Dictionary*, Oxford.

Gwynn, D. M. (2007) *The Eusebians: The Polemic of Athanasius of Alexandria and the Construction of the 'Arian Controversy'*, Oxford.

— (2012) *Athanasius of Alexandria: Bishop, Theologian, Ascetic, Father*, Oxford.

Haas, C. (1997) *Alexandria in Late Antiquity: Topography and Social Conflict*, Baltimore, MD.

Hanson, R. P. C. (1988) *The Search for the Christian Doctrine of God: The Arian Controversy, 318–381*, Edinburgh.

Hartel, G. (1886) *Luciferi Calaritani opuscula*, CCSL 14, Vienna.

Honigmann, E. (1953) *Patristic Studies*, Studi e testi 173, Vatican City.

Hopkins, K. (1963) 'Eunuchs in politics in the later Roman empire', *Proceedings of the Cambridge Philological Society* n.s. 9: 62–80.

— (1999) *A World Full of Gods: Pagans, Jews and Christians in the Roman Empire*, London.

Humphries, M. (1997) 'In Nomine Patris: Constantine the Great and Constantius II in Christological polemic', *Historia* 46: 448–64.

— (1998) 'Savage humour: Christian anti-panegyric in Hilary of Poitiers' *Against Constantius*', in M. Whitby (ed.) *The Propaganda of Power: The Role of Panegyric in Late Antiquity*, Mnemosyne Supplementum 183, Leiden, 201–23.

Hunt, D. (1998) 'The successors of Constantine', in Averil Cameron and P. D. A. Garnsey (edd.) *The Cambridge Ancient History Volume XIII: The Late Empire, A.D. 337–425*, Cambridge, 1–43.

Johnson, A. (2012) 'Hellenism and its discontents', in S. Johnson (ed.) *The Oxford Handbook of Late Antiquity*, Oxford, 437–66.

Johnson, M. J. (2009) *The Roman Imperial Mausoleum in Late Antiquity*, Cambridge.

Jones, A. H. M. (1964) *The Later Roman Empire 284–602: A Social, Economic and Administrative Survey*, 3 vols, Oxford.

Kannengiesser, C. (ed.) (1974) *Politique et théologie chez Athanase d'Alexandrie: actes du colloque de Chantilly, 23–25 septembre 1973*, Théologie historique 27, Paris.

— (1982) 'Athanasius of Alexandria, *Three Orations Against the Arians*: A Reappraisal', *Studia Patristica* 17.3: 981–95.

— (2001) 'L'*Histoire des Ariens* d'Athanase d'Alexandrie: une historiographie de combat au IVᵉ siècle', in B. Pouderon and Y.-M. Duval (edd.) *L'historiographie de l'Église des premiers siècles*, Théologie historique 114, Paris, 127–38.

Kaufman, P. I. (1997) 'Diehard Homoians and the election of Ambrose', *JECS* 5: 421–40.

Kelly, C. M. (1998) 'Emperors, government and bureaucracy', in Averil Cameron and P. D. A. Garnsey (edd.) *The Cambridge Ancient History Volume XIII: The Late Empire, A.D. 337–425*, Cambridge, 138–83.

— (2004) *Ruling the Later Roman Empire*, Cambridge, MA.

Kelly, J. N. D. (1972) *Early Christian Creeds*, 3rd edn, London.

— (1977) *Early Christian Doctrines*, 5th edn, London.

Kopecek, T. A. (1979) *A History of Neo-Arianism*, 2 vols, Patristic Monograph Series 8, Cambridge, MA.

Laconi, S. (ed.) (1998) *Luciferi Calaritani: Moriundum esse pro Dei Filio*, Rome.

— (ed.) (2001a) *La figura e l'opera di Lucifero di Cagliari: una rivisitazione. Atti del I Convegno Internazionale, Cagliari, 5–7 dicembre 1996*, Studia Ephemeridis Augustinianum 75, Rome.

— (2001b) 'Il ritratto di Costanzo II nelle pagine di Lucifero di Cagliari', in Laconi (2001a), 29–62.

— (2002) 'Figure retoriche e argomentazione nell'opera di Lucifero di Cagliari', *Annali della Facoltà di Lettere e Filosofia dell'Università di Cagliari* n.s. 20: 223–99.

— (2004) *Costanzo II: ritratto di un imperatore eretico*, Rome.

Lang, U. M. (2000) 'The Christological controversy at the Synod of Antioch in 268/9', *JThS* (n.s.) 51: 54–80.

Lenski, N. (2002) *Failure of Empire: Valens and the Roman State in the Fourth Century A.D.*, The Transformation of the Classical Heritage 34, Berkeley, CA.

Lewis, C. T. and Short, C. (1879) *A Latin Dictionary, founded on Andrews' Edition of Freund's Latin Dictionary*, Oxford.

Leyerle, B. (2009) 'Mobility and the traces of empire', in P. Rousseau (ed.) *A Companion to Late Antiquity*, Chichester, 110–23.

Lienhard, J. T. (1999) *Contra Marcellum: Marcellus of Ancyra and Fourth-Century Theology*, Washington D.C.

Long, J. (1996) *Claudian's In Eutropium: Or, How, When, and Why to Slander a Eunuch*, Chapel Hill, NC.

Louth, A. (2004) 'The fourth-century Alexandrians: Athanasius and Didymus', in F. M. Young, L. Ayres and A. Louth (edd.) *The Cambridge History of Early Christian Literature*, Cambridge, 275–82.

Lyman, R. (1993) 'A topography of heresy: mapping the rhetorical creation of Arianism', in M. R. Barnes and D. H. Williams (edd.) *Arianism after Arius: Essays on the Development of the Fourth Century Trinitarian Conflicts*, Edinburgh, 45–62.

Maraval, P. (2013) *Les fils de Constantin: Constantin II (337–340), Constance II (337–361), Constant (337–350)*, Paris.

Markschies, C. (1992) *Valentinus Gnosticus? Untersuchungen zur valentinianischen Gnosis mit einem Kommentar zu den Fragmenten Valentins*, Wissenschaftliche Untersuchungen zum Neuen Testament 65, Tübingen.

Martin, A. (1974) 'Athanase et les Mélitiens (325–335)', in Kannengiesser (1974), 31–61.

— (1985) (ed. and trans.) *Histoire 'acephale' et index syriaque des lettres festales d'Athanase d'Alexandrie*, Sources chrétiennes 317, Paris.

— (1996) *Athanase d'Alexandrie et l'église d'Égypte au IVe siècle (328–373)*, Collection de l'École française de Rome 216, Rome.

McLynn, N. B. (1994) *Ambrose of Milan: Church and Court in a Christian Capital*, The Transformation of the Classical Heritage 22, Berkeley, CA.

— (1997) 'Diehards: a response', *JECS* 5: 446–50.

Meloni, P. (2001) '"Quousque tandem abuteris Dei patientia, Constanti?". L'aspro linguaggio del vescovo Lucifero e le peregrinazioni del suo esilio', in Laconi (2001a), 73–86.

Merk, A. (1912) 'Lucifer von Calaris und seine Vorlagen in der Schrift "Moriendum esse pro Dei filio"', *Theologische Quartalschrift* 94: 1–32.

Millar, F. (1984) 'Condemnation to hard labour in the Roman empire, from the Julio-Claudians to Constantine', *PBSR* 52: 124–47 (repr. in id., *Rome, the Greek World, and the East, Volume 2: Government, Society, and Culture in the Roman Empire*, ed. H. M. Cotton and G. M. Rogers, Chapel Hill, NC, 2004, 120–50).

Muehlberger, E. (2015) 'The legend of Arius' death: imagination, space and filth in late ancient historiography', *Past and Present* 227: 3–29.

Musurillo, H. (1972) (ed.) *The Acts of the Christian Martyrs*, Oxford.

Nixon, C. E. V. and Rodgers, B. S. (edd.) (1994) *In Praise of Later Roman Emperors: The Panegyrici Latini*, The Transformation of the Classical Heritage 21, Berkeley, CA.

Opitz, H. G. (ed.) (1935–41) *Athanasius: Werke* II.1, Berlin.

Parvis, S. (2006) *Marcellus of Ancyra and the Lost Years of the Arian Controversy 325–345*, Oxford.

Pelland, G. (1997) 'Eusebio e Ilario di Poitiers', in E. dal Covolo, R. Uglione and G. M. Vian (edd.) *Eusebio di Vercelli e il suo tempo*, Biblioteca di scienze religiose 133, Rome, 247–54.

Piras, A. (2001) 'Bibbia e *sermo biblicus* negli scritti luciferiani', in Laconi (2001a), 131–44.
Pizzani, U. (2001) 'Presenze lattanziane nel *Moriundum esse pro Dei filio* di Lucifero di Cagliari', in Laconi (2001a), 223–52.
Potter, D. S. (2014) *The Roman Empire at Bay, AD 180–395*, 2nd edn, Abingdon.
Rapp, C. (2005) *Holy Bishops in Late Antiquity: The Nature of Christian Leadership in an Age of Transition*, The Transformation of the Classical Heritage 37, Berkeley, CA.
Rees, R. (2012) 'The modern history of Latin panegyric', in R. Rees (ed.) *Latin Panegyric*, Oxford, 3–48.
Robertson, A. (ed.) (1892) *St. Athanasius: Select Works and Letters*, Select Library of Nicene and Post-Nicene Fathers, Second Series, vol. 4, Oxford.
Rocher, A. (ed.) (1987) *Hilaire de Poitiers: Contre Constance*, Sources chrétiennes 334, Paris.
Simonetti, M. (1967) 'Osservazioni sull "Altercatio Heracliani cum Germinio"', *Vigiliae Christianae* 21: 39–58.
— (1975) *La crisi ariana nel IV secolo*, Studia Ephemeridis Augustinianum 11, Rome.
— (1980) 'Sabellio e il Sabellianismo', *Studi storico-religiosi* 4: 7–28 (repr. in id. *Studi sulla cristologia del II e III secolo*, Studia Ephemeridis Augustinianum 44, Rome, 1993, 217–38).
Smulders, P. (1995) *Hilary of Poitiers' Preface to his* Opus Historicum: *translation and commentary*, Vigiliae Christianae Supplement 29, Leiden.
Sotinel, C. (2009) 'Information and political power', in P. Rousseau (ed.) *A Companion to Late Antiquity*, Chichester, 125–38.
Souter, A. (1949) *A Glossary of Later Latin to 600 A.D.*, Oxford.
Stead, G. C. (1976) 'Rhetorical method in Athanasius', *Vigiliae Christianae* 30: 121–37.
Talbert, R. J. A. (ed.) (2000) *Barrington Atlas of the Greek and Roman World*, Princeton.
Tietze, W. (1976) *Lucifer von Calaris und die Kirchenpolitik des Constantius II.: Zum Konflikt zwischen dem Kaiser Constantius II. und der nikänisch-orthodoxen Opposition (Lucifer von Calaris, Athanasius von Alexandria, Hilarius von Poitiers, Ossius von Córdoba, Liberius von Rom und Eusebius von Vercelli)*, PhD diss., Tübingen.
Trevett, C. (1996) *Montanism: Gender, Authority and the New Prophecy*, Cambridge.
Ugenti, V. (ed.) (1980) *Luciferi Calaritani: De regibus apostaticis et Moriundum esse pro dei filio*, Lecce.
Vaggione, R. P. (1987) *Eunomius: The Extant Works*, Oxford.
— (2000) *Eunomius of Cyzicus and the Nicene Revolution*, Oxford.
Vinson, M. (1994) 'Gregory Nazianzen's Homily 15 and the genesis of the Christian cult of the Maccabean martyrs', *Byzantion* 64: 166–92.

von Harnack, A. (1981) *Militia Christi: The Christian Religion and the Military in the First Three Centuries*, trans. by D. McInnes Gracie, Philadelphia, PA (originally published as *Militia Christi: Die christliche Religion und der Soldatenstand in den ersten drei Jahrhunderten*, Tübingen, 1905).

Wallace-Hadrill, A. (1981) 'The emperor and his virtues', *Historia* 30: 298–323.

Wickham, L. R. (1997) *Hilary of Poitiers: Conflicts of Conscience and Law in the Fourth-century Church*, Translated Texts for Historians 25, Liverpool.

Williams, D. H. (1991) 'A reassessment of the early career and exile of Hilary of Poitiers', *Journal of Ecclesiastical History* 42: 202–17.

— (1992) 'The anti-Arian campaigns of Hilary of Poitiers and the "Liber Contra Auxentium"', *Church History* 61: 7–22.

— (1995) *Ambrose of Milan and the End of the Arian-Nicene Conflicts*, Oxford.

— (1996) 'Another exception to later fourth-century "Arian" typologies: the case of Germinius of Sirmium', *JECS* 4: 335–57.

— (1997) 'Politically correct in Milan: a reply to "Diehard Homoians and the election of Ambrose"', *JECS* 5: 441–6.

Williams, R. (2001) *Arius: Heresy and Tradition*, 2nd edn, London.

GLOSSARY

IMPERIAL RANKS AND TITLES

comes (pl: *comites*) – the rank of *comes*, or 'companion', was created by Constantine I and reflected the holder's connections with the imperial centre. Although the title was bestowed on some members of the bureaucracy *ex officio*, it was also granted to other individuals who attracted the personal attention and favour of the emperor. The *comites* were divided into three grades, although the rationale and operation of this division remain obscure. See Kelly (2004) 196–9.

curiosus (pl: *curiosi*) – the *curiosi* were officials drawn from the *agentes in rebus* (a sub-division of the *palatini* – see below) and carried out inspection duties for the *cursus publicus* (the imperial post and messenger service) and at ports, although provincial appeals to them (here and elsewhere) suggest that they soon came to be seen as important official figures. See Jones (1964) I 103–4, II 578–80.

dux (pl: *duces*) – the *dux* was the military commander of the frontier regions of a province or a group of provinces. The title developed during the separation of military and civil powers that was begun by the Tetrarchy at the end of the third century and continued during the reign of Constantine I. See Elton (2006) 330–31.

notarius (pl: *notarii*) – the *notarii* were clerks and bureaucratic officials in the imperial secretariat, but were also regularly employed as representatives of the emperor on official business throughout the empire, including investigating the behaviour of other officials. See Jones (1964) II 572–4; Kelly (1998) 159–60.

palatinus (pl: *palatini*) – *palatini* was a general title for the civil and administrative functionaries who constituted the central imperial bureaucracy. As well as the *notarii*, this group also included the *agentes in rebus* (messengers who also performed some similar tasks as the *notarii*) and the members of the various *scrinia* (clerks who dealt with correspondence, judicial matters and records). See Jones (1964) II 572–86; Kelly (1998) 162–9.

vicarius (pl: *vicarii*) – the *vicarius* was a late Roman civilian official who oversaw the governors of a group of provinces, known as a diocese, and reported to the Praetorian Prefect of the region. See Jones (1964) I 373–5; Kelly (2004) 72.

THEOLOGICAL TERMS

More information on all these terms and their use in the theological disputes of this period can be found in the Introduction, as well as in footnotes to relevant parts of the translations.

Anomoian – this title has often been given to the theologians Aetius and Eunomius, as well as their followers, because they supposedly stated that the Son was *anomoios* ('unlike') the Father. This is a misrepresentation that was employed by their enemies, leading to the 'Anomoians' being presented as a heretical sect in chapter 76 of the *Panarion* of Epiphanius of Salamis. Modern scholarship has sought other terms for them, including 'Neo-Arians' and the more neutral 'Heterousians', which reflects their view that the Son is 'of different essence' from the Father.

Arian – in a narrow sense, this title could refer to those who agreed with the theological beliefs of the Alexandrian presbyter Arius, which probably included the notion that the Son is inferior to the Father and is not co-eternal with him. The term did, however, quickly come to be used in a tendentious manner by 'Nicene' authors such as Athanasius as a way of creating a unified, negative identity for their opponents in the theological disputes of this period, even though many of the figures they criticised openly disavowed Arius' beliefs. It is this polemical sense of the word that is to be found throughout the texts translated in this volume. Modern scholarship has sought to provide more neutral and accurate titles for the different theological positions that were deemed 'Arian', leading to the creation of terms such as 'Homoiousian', 'Heterousian' and 'Homoian'. The 'Arians' or 'Ariomaniacs' were to have a long afterlife in heresiological literature and were presented as both the heirs and progenitors of other heretical groups.

homoios – this Greek term, meaning 'like', came to prominence in 359 and 360 as a simple description of the resemblance that the Son has to the Father, accompanied by the phrase 'as the Holy Scriptures say and teach'. In the 'Dated Creed' of 359 *homoios* is followed by the words *kata panta* ('in all respects'), but these were dropped in the final agreements after the Councils of Seleucia and Ariminum and at the Council of Constantinople in 360. This theological settlement, which is often referred to as 'Homoian', was called 'Arian' by its opponents, but nonetheless had a long afterlife, especially among the 'barbarian' successor kingdoms of the early medieval West.

homoiousios – this term, meaning 'of like essence', appears to have been coined in the late 350s as an attempt to define the relationship between the Father and the Son, and briefly enjoyed the support of Constantius II. It is particularly associated with Basil, bishop of Ancyra, and was acceptable to some 'Nicene' figures, including Hilary of Poitiers, although Epiphanius of Salamis went on to describe the advocates of *homoiousios* as 'Semi-Arians' at *Panarion* 73.

homoousios – this term for the relationship between the Father and the Son was adopted at the Council of Nicaea in 325 and means 'of the same essence'. It was criticised as unscriptural, but was fiercely defended by the three authors in this volume and eventually succeeded in being widely, although not universally, accepted as orthodox after the Council of Constantinople in 381.

hypostasis – this Greek term is frequently translated into English as 'subsistence', although 'substance' is also used. It was sometimes rendered into Latin as *substantia*, which could cause confusion since this word was also employed by some authors as the equivalent of the Greek theological term *ousia* – see, for example, p. 128 n. 83 and p. 137 n. 126 on Hilary, *In Const.* It did not feature particularly prominently in the theological debates covered by the texts in this volume, although it does appear in the 'Fourth Creed' of Antioch and in the statement produced by the Council of Sirmium in 351. It played a significant role in the theological settlement adopted at the Council of Constantinople in 381, whereby the Trinity was described as consisting of three *hypostaseis* in a single *ousia*.

ousia – this Greek term, often translated into English as 'essence' or 'substance', was widely discussed in fourth-century theological definitions of the relationship between the Father and the Son in the Trinity. It is fundamental to the description of the Son as *homoousios* ('of the same essence'), which was adopted at the Council of Nicaea in 325 and which was defended by the three authors in this volume, as well as to the formulation of *homoiousios* ('of like essence'), which was briefly prominent in the later 350s, and the 'Heterousian' ('of different essence') position taken by Aetius and Eunomius. Some theologians avoided *ousia* altogether on the grounds that it was not scriptural, and its use was explicitly rejected in the 'Blasphemy of Sirmium' and the 'Homoian' creeds of 359/360. Hilary uses the terms *essentia* and *substantia* to render it into Latin, which sometimes caused confusion, since *substantia* was also employed as a translation of the Greek term *hypostasis* – see p. 128 n. 83 and p. 137 n. 126 on Hilary, *In Const.*

Sabellius/Sabellianism – Sabellius is believed to have been a presbyter at Rome, probably in the third century, who advocated a 'Monarchian' theology (in which God was regarded as a single 'person' or 'principle'), stressing the oneness of the Trinity, with the Father, Son and Holy Spirit being merely 'modes' of the Godhead. This involved differentiating between the three persons to a much lesser extent than many other theologians did. For this reason, the accusation of 'Sabellianism' was sometimes used by fourth-century Christians as a way of attacking positions, including the Nicene *homoousios*, which they regarded as not articulating the relationship between the Father and the Son (or of the Trinity as a whole) with sufficient distinction. See Epiphanius, *Panarion* 62; Simonetti (1980); Bienert (1993).

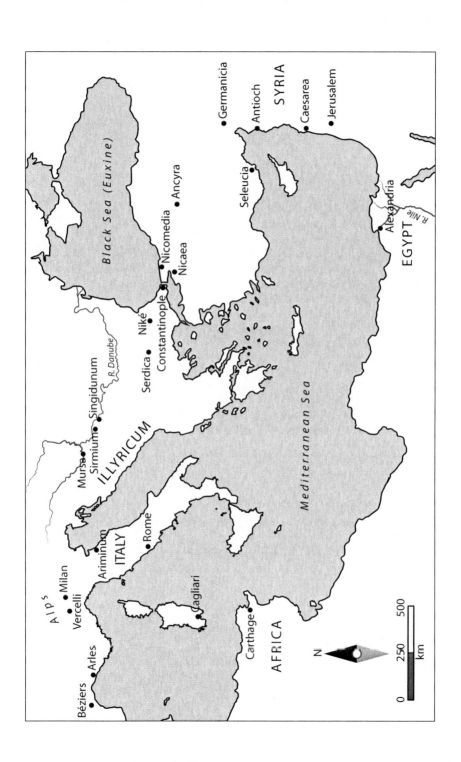

GENERAL INDEX

Abed-nego (Old Testament character) 119, 146

Ablabius, Flavius (praetorian prefect) 99 n. 253

Abraham (Old Testament patriarch) 78, 140 n. 138, 177, 183

Acacius (bishop of Caesarea) 17–18, 53, 62, 106 n. 279, 128 n. 80, 129 n. 86

Achaea 62

Achillas (bishop of Alexandria) 108

Adelphius (bishop of Onuphis in Lychni) 101

Adoxius (punning name for a bishop) 171

see also Eudoxius (bishop of Germanicia, Antioch and Constantinople)

Adrianople 54, 90 n. 218

Aetius (theologian) 13–14, 208–9

Africa 62

Agathodaimon (bishop of Schedia) 102

Agathus (bishop of Phragonis and part of Helearchia in Egypt) 102

Ahab (king of Israel) 25, 36, 40 n. 9, 79, 81 n. 181, 86, 97

Alexander (bishop of Alexandria) 2, 4, 5, 21, 100–101, 108

Alexander (bishop of Constantinople) 6, 44 n. 26, 109 n. 293

Alexandria 21–3, 58, 105, 153 n. 57
violence in 12, 22, 24–5, 47–51, 54–7, 64–5, 72, 81–94, 99–100, 111–4, 126, 143, 163

see also Caesareum (Alexandria)

Altercatio Heracliani cum Germinio 28–9, 105 n. 275

Amalekites 70 n. 137

Ambrose (bishop of Milan) 123 n. 45

Ammianus Marcellinus (historian) 1

Ammon ('Arian' heretic) 101

Ammoniaca/Ammon (city at the Siwa Oasis) 101

Ammonius (bishop, probably of Pachnamunis) 101–102

Ammonius (exiled bishop) 102

Ammonius (layman) 61

Anagamphus (exiled bishop) 101

anomoios/Anomoian see Heterousian

anomoiousios 14 n. 59, 128–30

Antichrist, the 3, 25, 30, 33, 80, 97, 100, 104, 106–111, 115, 117–20, 122, 127, 142, 174

Antioch 32, 56, 77, 121 n. 36, 171
see also councils; creeds

Antiochus IV (Seleucid monarch) 120, 163 n. 112

Antony (monk) 50

Apollo (exiled bishop) 102

Apollonius (exiled bishop) 102

Apulia 62

Arbitio (consul in 355) 114

Arian/Arianism 1, 3–6, 9–10, 18–20, 25, 28 n. 135, 29 n. 141, 33 n. 161, 34, 36–7, 39, 42, 44 n. 27, 48, 53, 55–6, 61–3, 65–9, 71–2, 74–80, 83, 85–9, 91–7, 100, 103–104, 107–111, 116 n. 16, 120 n. 33, 124 n. 52, 131, 132 n. 103, 135 n. 121,

INDEX OF PASSAGES FROM NON-BIBLICAL
TEXTS EMPLOYED BY LUCIFER OF CAGLIARI